A HUNDRED YEARS OF PROGRESS

AUTHOR'S PREFACE

This centenary history has been compiled mainly from the official records of the Association, and I wish here to acknowledge a debt of gratitude to the officials and staff of the Head Office for their co-operation and assistance throughout. My thanks are also due to the Edinburgh Branch for kindly making available material which helped me to bridge a number of gaps in the official records pertaining to the early period.

I am also indebted to Professor A. L. Macfie, Mr J. D. M. Bell, and Mr D. J. Robertson, my colleagues in the Political Economy Department of Glasgow University, for their patient reading of the script and helpful criticism.

Finally, I wish to record my appreciation of the fact that the Association, while giving me every assistance so far as making available the necessary material was concerned, in no way interfered with the use to which I put it. In consequence, I accept full responsibility for the form of this history and for the conclusions drawn.

S. C. G.

A HUNDRED YEARS
OF PROGRESS

THE RECORD OF
THE SCOTTISH TYPOGRAPHICAL
ASSOCIATION
1853 TO 1952

BY

SARAH C. GILLESPIE
M.A.

Printed for the Association by
ROBERT MACLEHOSE AND CO LTD
GLASGOW
1953

Printed in Great Britain

SCOTTISH TYPOGRAPHICAL ASSOCIATION

This is to Certify that

Mr.

Association on

Signed

CONTENTS

APPENDIXES

FOREWORD

BY THE RT. HON. THOMAS JOHNSTON, P.C., LL.D.

If suddenly we were bereaved of our printed heritage:
if there should swiftly overwhelm us such a disaster as
smote the ancient world when the vandals of the con-
questing theological armies in the fourth century burned
the museums at Alexandria and reduced to ashes the
700,000 written treasures of antiquity—how poor and
shrunken would we instantly become! For in the printer's
skill and art is enshrined and preserved the wisdom, the
culture, the struggles and the achievements of our fore-
bears.

Miss Gillespie, in the pages which follow, outlines the
known stages in the development of the printed word in
Scotland from the time in the beginning of the sixteenth
century when Bishop Elphinstone of Aberdeen (who, by
the way, was also the first Chancellor of King's College
there, a fact which is of some special interest to me)
induced King James IV to issue a printing licence to certain burgesses of Edinburgh. We have historical records,
too, of the monopoly and control years when no printer
might print anything until it was first '*sene, vewit and
examit be sum wyse and discreet persounis*'. Also we know
something of how by the end of the seventeenth century
even the paper criers or newsvendors in our city streets
were controlled; how in Edinburgh they had to wear an
'appron of Blew Linnen' and were forbidden to curse or
swear and had to go to church and to school 'one diet
every week day'. There are humours, too, of these early
control days when an edition of the Psalms was published
with an obscene song as an appendix! But neither Bremner
who wrote his *Industries of Scotland* in 1869—when printing and its allied trades constituted the staple industry of
Edinburgh—nor Coupar in his elaborate (and often

amusing) account of the Edinburgh Periodical Press from
the earliest times to 1800, tells us much about the journeymen or the apprentices, or of the conditions in which they
worked. The Webbs in their monumental *History of Trade
Unionism* have surprisingly little to say about the tramp
compositors, and I remember when writing my *History of
the Working Classes in Scotland* being completely stuck in
my endeavours to trace the origins of the 'chapel' in the
composing rooms.

But now here is Miss Gillespie, sponsored and encouraged by the Scottish Typographical Association, to throw
what illuminations are still possible upon the build-up of
union and security conditions in the typographical section
of the great printing industry during the last hundred
years.

The typographers of Scotland are justly proud of their
hundred years of union achievement, and in June of this
year (1953) they celebrate the century-old continuity of
effort by their Association—partly through the publication
of this record—so that the skilled craftsmen of to-day and
to-morrow will know something of the struggles of the
past and consequently something of the inheritance to
which the present members are heirs. But partly, too, the
Scottish Typographical Association celebrates its centenary by providing an endowment fund from which every
year in future will come prizes to the most outstanding
students at the printing day-classes in the Heriot Watt
College in Edinburgh, the Stow College in Glasgow and
the technical evening schools at Aberdeen and Dundee.
That monetary provision for a stimulus to pride in craftsmanship, for all time coming, is in itself a most praise-
worthy centenary commemoration.

The Trade Union with which I had closest association
for many years—week in, week out—was the Scottish
Typographical, and I came to regard the skilled workmen
and the leaders in that Association with the highest esteem
and regard.

Changes in methods and conditions in this as in other
trades are inevitable; always upon the horizon are new

processes; yet in this, the twentieth century, we are reaching out steadily but surely to full employment, and that
for a surety involves new efforts in co-operation and good-
will in the industry; a pride, too, in good craftsmanship
and an appreciation of the struggles and sacrifices of the
generations which have passed away. And that this centenary record of the Scottish Typographical Association
will provide to its members a fresh guidance and encouragement is the fervent wish of

Yours sincerely,

Thomas Johnston

PART I

THE SCOTTISH PRINTING INDUSTRY AND ITS LABOUR FORCE

1507 — 1853

CHAPTER ONE

SCOTLAND AND THE ART
OF PRINTING

While this book is primarily concerned with the centenary history of the Scottish Typographical Association, founded in 1853, some account of the printing industry in Scotland and of the organisation of its labour force prior to this date, would seem to provide a necessary and fitting introduction. It is, however, obviously impossible, and indeed presumptuous, to review the history of printing in Scotland up to 1853 within the scope of one short chapter. Here, therefore, it is proposed simply to outline the story of its introduction to Scotland, with some account of its early development, and to indicate the main features of its subsequent growth.

The early history of printing largely concerns Edinburgh, which in those days was the seat of government and the centre of trade and commerce. Printing was known on the Continent in the early fifteenth century, and the first printing press was established in Westminster by William Caxton in 1476, but it was not until 1507 that the new art was introduced to Scotland. In that year James IV granted a patent to Walter Chepman and Andro Myllar, burgesses of Edinburgh. The patent authorised them 'to furnis and bring hame ane prent with al stuf belangand tharto and expert men to use the samyne, for imprenting within our realme of the bukis of our lawis, actis of parliament, croniclis, mess bukis and portuus efter the use of our realme, with additiouns and legendis of Scottis sanctis now gaderit to be ekit thairto, and al utheris bukis that shall be sene necessare, and to sel the sammyn for competent pricis be our avis and discretioun, thar labouris and expens being considerit'.

It was William Elphinstone, Bishop of Aberdeen, who urged James IV to issue this patent. His object was to produce a Scottish Service Book to replace the Sarum or Salisbury Use, then the common form of service in Scottish churches. This is revealed by the content of the 1507 patent, which goes on to decree that mass books, prayer books and the like, 'efter our awin Scottis use' be generally used throughout Scotland as soon as they can be printed, and to forbid thereafter the importing and selling of books of the Salisbury Use. The Aberdeen Breviary was produced by Chepman in two volumes, one in 1509, the other in 1510, but the hopes of Elphinstone for its general use were not realised, and it proved impossible to ban effectively the Salisbury books.

The Aberdeen Breviary was long believed to be the first book printed in Scotland and consequently Chepman the first Scottish printer. In the eighteenth century, however, a collection of ballads printed by Chepman and Myllar in 1509 came to light and these are now recognised as the earliest example of Scottish printing. Later a copy of the 1507 patent was discovered, and further investigation has revealed the part played by Andro Myllar in this enterprise; he was the practical printer. Chepman, a merchant of some wealth and a favoured person at court, probably supplied the necessary capital to finance the enterprise, but there is no evidence that he had any previous knowledge of printing. Andro Myllar, on the other hand, like Caxton, had learned the art on the Continent and had practised as a printer in Rouen prior to 1507. Whether Myllar died before the Breviary was produced, or simply lacked the means to share in its financing but continued to work for Chepman, is not known.

Nothing has survived of any printing done by Chepman after the Breviary. This may have been due to the death of his royal patron at the battle of Flodden in 1513. In his later years Chepman built an aisle in St Giles' Cathedral in memory of James and his Queen, and before his death in 1532, he gifted to the Church the property in the Cowgate which had housed his printing press, to provide funds for an altar in this aisle. In 1879 the aisle was restored by Dr William Chambers. By this date restoration was necessary because 'the bad taste of a former generation had converted this interesting memorial to the base uses of coal-cellar and lumber-room'.[1] A brass tablet was placed in the aisle, commemorating both founder and restorer. The tablet bears a facsimile of the device with which Chepman adorned his books—a representation of Adam and Eve in the Garden of Eden.

Although the benefits of printing were first made available to the people of Scotland at a time when 'the love of learning was exercising its benign influence upon their rude minds and hearts',[2] progress in the new industry was slow. The reason is not hard to find. From the battle of Flodden until the middle of the eighteenth century Scotland was the scene of almost continuous turmoil and strife, political and religious—frequent Border skirmishes, the Reformation, the protracted struggle of the Covenanters, the invasions of Cromwell, and the two Jacobite rebellions. The constant strife, the low material standard and the puritanical outlook of a period of religious fanaticism were not conducive to the development of literature or the art of printing. Not until the second half of the eighteenth century did the industry progress and expand, in a period of relative peace and growing material prosperity.

Printing continued in Edinburgh after Chepman's time, but many of the early works were destroyed at the time of the Reformation. It certainly played an important part in that struggle, the medium of satirical poetry and drama being used by the reformers to expose the ignorance of the clergy.[3] As a result of this the first attempt to censor the press was made in 1551, when it was decreed that nothing be printed without a licence. Repeated attempts by Parliament and Church to control the products of the industry suggest that the decree was not completely effective. Nevertheless, the restrictions of this and the later

---

[1] *Scottish Typographical Circular*, October 1879.   [2] ibid.
[3] To this period belongs Sir David Lyndesay's *The Thrie Estates*, which has lately enjoyed a revival through the work of Robert Kemp.

post-Reformation period were sufficient to curtail the output of the printing-press and hamper the development of the industry.

As might be expected, the printing of Bibles formed a major part of the industry's activity at this period. Complaints by John Knox and other reformers of the high cost of Bibles, then imported from England, resulted in the first Scottish production, the Bassendyne Bible. To finance this project every parish in Scotland had to contribute five pounds, in return for which the Privy Council undertook to produce a copy of the Scriptures 'weel and sufficientlie bounde in paist or tymmer'. The contract was given to an Edinburgh printer, Bassendyne, and his partner, Arbuthnot. The work was carried out with the help of a compositor brought from Magdeburg, who is reported to have received 49/– per week. The task was completed by 1579, and the Scottish Parliament then decreed that every householder paying 300 merks of yearly rent and every proprietor worth £500 in lands and goods must purchase a Bible. To ensure that this law was carried out an individual was appointed to visit every parish, and he required to be shown a copy with the owner's name on the fly-leaf.

A folio Bible, noted for its high standard of typography, was produced by Andrew Hart in 1610. In 1637 Robert Young printed a folio Common Prayer Book, subsequently known as 'Laud's Liturgy', of Covenanting 'fame'.

About this time Glasgow received its first printing-press. The industry had hitherto been confined almost entirely to Edinburgh, although there was a small office in St Andrews as early as 1546. It was first introduced to Aberdeen in 1622, but did not reach Glasgow until 1638. The Covenanters have been credited with giving Glasgow its first printer, George Anderson, an Edinburgh man. He came to the city to print for them the proceedings of the General Assembly of 1638.

It is through his son, Andrew, however, that the name of Anderson has most significance for the history of Scottish printing. Andrew Anderson first printed in Glasgow in 1657. He returned to Edinburgh in 1661, and in 1671 received the gift of King's printer for a period of forty-one years. For nearly half a century controversies and legal battles were waged over the Anderson monopoly, which for long crippled the development of Scottish printing. James Watson, an Edinburgh printer of this period, and one frequently involved in these legal disputes, described it as 'a Dead Stroke to the Art of Printing'. The extent of the control granted to Anderson certainly now seems incredible. He was literally given the sole right to print all books in Scotland; nobody could print anything 'from a Bible to a Ballad' without his permission. Anderson shared this gift with four others as partners, but on his death a few years later, his widow acquired all the shares but one. Much has been written for and against the redoubtable Mrs Anderson, who appears to have attacked all comers and spent a considerable amount of time trying to enforce to the full the monopoly granted to her husband. Certainly the records of the period contain many references to complaints about the poor quality of her printing, particularly of Bibles. According to Watson she produced 'the most illegible and uncorrect Bibles and Books that ever were printed in any one Place', and did this rapidly and with the sole object of making money. 'Prentices, instead of the best Workmen, were generally imploy'd,'—a complaint which has a familiar ring. The opposition of other printers eventually succeeded in curtailing this monopoly, Mrs Anderson being granted only the rights formerly associated with the office of King's printer—to print Bibles, Acts of Parliament and the like. Also, in 1683, Robert Sanders, who had succeeded Anderson in Glasgow, acquired the one share in this gift not held by the widow herself. But in spite of these mitigating factors, the monopoly undoubtedly had an adverse effect on the output and quality of Scottish printing.

James Watson, mentioned above as one of Mrs Anderson's most frequent opponents, finally secured the gift of King's printer after the expiry of the Anderson monopoly. This he achieved only after protracted legal battles with Mrs Anderson and others. Watson was

responsible for the printing of several of the early newspapers, and also helped to meet the growing demand for
periodical essays. In 1722 he produced a folio Bible, which
was prized for its fine typography. But his most interesting production was his *History of Printing*, which appeared
in 1713 and was claimed as the first to be published in
Britain. The chief interest here is in the Preface, which
contained a brief sketch of the history of printing in Scotland. Credit for the Preface is sometimes given to John
Spottiswoode, but at least one expert has rejected this in
favour of Watson.[1] Watson was concerned about the state
into which the art of printing had fallen in Scotland.
Some of his comments on this may be of interest. The
chief defects, in his opinion, included the lack of qualified
correctors and of expert pressmen. The latter were more
important for the beauty of the work and should be paid
more than compositors. He advocated the bringing of
presses and pressmen from Holland. There pressmen
were not allowed to work more than eight or nine hours a
day, while here seventeen or eighteen hours was not uncommon. Watson's *History* itself has been described as a
creditable example of good workmanship compared with
the many inferior books issued in Edinburgh at the time,
and with some of the wretched prints coming from Glasgow contemporary presses.

While printers were not unknown to Glasgow by this
time, there was little produced there and the quality was
poor. Some encouragement was certainly given to the
industry by the University with the creation of the office
of University printer, and the provision at the beginning
of the eighteenth century of premises within the College.
But no outstanding contribution was made by Glasgow
until the advent of the Foulis brothers. Whether the
causes were those listed by Watson, or simply the general
poverty of the country, combined with the unsettled religious and political background, or the effect of the
Anderson monopoly, it is certain that by the beginning of
the eighteenth century printing in Scotland was in a poor

[1] Rev. W. J. Couper, writing in the *Circular*, 1913.

state and had deteriorated rather than progressed. Scottish works were then generally printed abroad, and books were chiefly imported from the Continent, particularly from Holland.

During the eighteenth century, however, the industry began to revive. The quality of Watson's own work was evidently good compared with that of his predecessors. A further improvement may be credited to the efforts of Thomas Ruddiman, Keeper of the Advocates Library. Ruddiman was a noted Latin scholar and grammarian, and author of a number of school books. He started his printing activities in 1715 and in 1727, along with James Davidson, an Edinburgh bookseller, he petitioned the Town Council for the appointment of printer to the University. The petition contained reference to the current large-scale importation of books, a state of affairs which the petitioners hoped, by this appointment, to remedy. The appointment was granted, and the work of Ruddiman helped in the improvement of the native industry, although the problem of foreign competition remained for many years thereafter.

It is, however, to the Foulis brothers of Glasgow, particularly Robert, that the greatest debt is due by Scottish printing. 'Few men, since the days of Caxton, have done more than Robert Foulis to raise the standard of printing and to inspire a love for fine books.'[1] Among those who have contributed to the development of the art in Scotland the name of Foulis stands out, and the fame of the brothers extended far beyond their native city or country. Robert Foulis was a barber by trade, but became a scholar and ardent student at the University. His brother Andrew, who became his partner, was a graduate of the University and, for a time, a teacher of languages. The brothers studied and travelled extensively, and in 1741 Robert was appointed bookseller to the University, being granted a room within the College for this purpose. In the same year he started as printer and publisher, and in 1743 was appointed printer to the University. A few years later he

[1] James MacLehose, *The Glasgow University Press*, 1638–1931.

took his brother into partnership. The name of Robert Foulis is associated with the printing of classical works of an outstandingly high quality in every way; each was a work of art in itself; his folio Homer is particularly famous. Care and accuracy and beauty of typography were the hall-marks of his work, and his contribution to the development of Scottish printing.

To the work of the Foulis brothers must also go the credit for the development of type-founding on a similarly high standard. Watson's Preface contained the first reference to type-founding in Scotland. In 1711 Mr Peter Rae, a Presbyterian minister of Kirkbride, near Dumfries, set up a small printing establishment, and he was reported by Watson to be 'making some Advances towards the Founding of Letters'. Nothing more is known of him, however, nor of James Duncan, listed as a letter founder in Glasgow in 1736. In 1740 Alexander Wilson set up a foundry at St Andrews, and later moved to Glasgow, where he worked for the Foulis brothers.

It is not surprising that this major contribution to the development of printing should have come from Glasgow at this period. The middle and second half of the eighteenth century was a period of tremendous commercial activity and expansion. It was the heyday of the 'tobacco lords', and the start of the development of Glasgow and the Clyde as a trading centre. But it was also a period of cultural renaissance. Within the University were to be found at this time a number of outstanding men, of whom Adam Smith was the most distinguished and famous.

Early in his career Robert Foulis transferred his interest from printing to art, and founded the Glasgow Academy of Art within the University. As a result of this venture he eventually suffered financial ruin. After his death in 1776, his son, Andrew, failed to revive the printing and publishing business, and Glasgow, for the time being, faded from the forefront of printing development. To Andrew Foulis, junior, however, must be credited a share in the subsequent development of stereotyping, a process which played an important part in the production on a large scale of cheap editions necessary to meet the growing popular demand. The process was invented by William Ged, an Edinburgh goldsmith, in 1725, but was then rejected by the industry. It was reintroduced successfully by Andrew Foulis and Alexander Tilloch in 1782.

Meanwhile printing in Edinburgh was also expanding. In 1745 there were some five printing-presses in the capital, and by 1779 the number had increased to twenty-seven. This was a period of growing popular demand for books of all kinds, a development from which the printers benefited and which, at the same time, they fostered. About the middle of the century Alexander Donaldson, an Edinburgh bookseller, had taken a leading part in the issuing of cheap editions of popular works, setting an example which was followed by London publishers. In 1771 William Smellie started the first edition of the Encyclopaedia Britannica, which was to be a recurring source of employment for the Edinburgh printers. For Edinburgh, however, the highlight of this fruitful period for Scottish literature came with the publication of the poems and novels of Sir Walter Scott. With him were associated the Ballantynes, noted for their elegant style of printing, and the publisher Archibald Constable. Their association, although it ended in financial disaster in the crash of 1826, forged a link between the Edinburgh printing and publishing trades and the London market. By the beginning of the period with which this volume is primarily concerned, the tide of publishing had set towards London, but the connection between the Edinburgh printing industry and the London market was maintained. Although Edinburgh's share in this market has declined recently, particularly since 1918, it is still important to the Edinburgh industry. During the late eighteenth and early nineteenth centuries Edinburgh became a centre not only for printing and publishing, but also for trades allied with printing—type founding, lithographic printing, engraving, bookbinding, stereotyping and, in the neighbouring Midlothian area, paper manufacture.

Finally, some brief reference must be made to the origin

of that important branch of the printing industry in modern times, the newspaper section. While the development of the newspaper as we know it today dates from the repeal of the Stamp and Paper Duties in the mid-nineteenth century and the subsequent birth of the daily press, the first newspaper known to have been printed in Scotland appeared at Leith in 1653. This was a reprint of a London diurnal, the *Mercurius Politicus*, and the printer was one Christopher Higgins, brought to Leith by Cromwell after the battle of Dunbar. The reprinting was then transferred to Edinburgh and continued there until 1660, when the first legitimate Scottish newspaper appeared. This was the *Mercurius Caledonius*, described as 'Comprising the Affairs in Agitation in Scotland, with a Survey of foreign Intelligence'. This first Scottish weekly survived only ten issues, but the reprinting and republishing of English newspapers continued at Edinburgh until practically the end of the century. In 1699 James Donaldson was authorised to publish the *Edinburgh Gazette*, of which James Watson, the staunch opponent of the Anderson monopoly, was the first printer. Watson's name was also associated with the *Edinburgh Courant*, which first appeared in 1705 and which was transferred to Daniel Defoe in 1710; the *Scots Courant*; and, the *Scots Postman*. In 1718 the *Edinburgh Evening Courant* appeared, and in 1720 the *Caledonian Mercury*, a Jacobite paper which became the organ of the Highland Army in '45, and which was printed and owned by Thomas Ruddiman from 1729. These early papers appeared either twice or three times a week, and it is reported that several respectable women made a livelihood by purchasing four or five copies and lending them at the rate of 2d for first day readers, 1d for second day readers and ½d for third day readers. In 1744 there appeared the first number of the *Edinburgh Weekly Journal*, which was acquired by James Ballantyne in 1806 and in which appeared the *Waverley Novels* of Sir Walter Scott.

It was not until 1715 that Glasgow produced its first newspaper, the *Glasgow Courant*. This appeared three times a week, and in contrast to the 7d of some of the early newspapers, cost only 1d to regular subscribers, and 1½d to non-subscribers. The *Courant*, later renamed the *West Country Intelligence*, survived for barely two years, the smallness of its circulation in a city of some 15,000 inhabitants and the low price doubtless having much to do with its demise. During the rapid expansion of Glasgow in the eighteenth century, however, a number of newspapers appeared. In 1729 appeared the first issue of the *Glasgow Journal*, which flourished for over a century, and by 1793 Glasgow had also a *Mercury*, an *Advertiser* and a *Courier*; the *Advertiser* subsequently became *The Glasgow Herald*.

From the columns of the *Glasgow Journal* of 1746 and 1747 come the following amusing examples of marriage notifications: 'On Monday, James Dennistown, Esq., of Coly Vine, was married to Miss Jenny Baird, a beautiful young lady.'—'On Monday last, Mr. Robert Hamilton, Professor of Anatomy and Botany in the University of Glasgow, was married to Miss Molly Baird, a beautiful young lady with a handsome fortune.'—'On Monday last Mr. James Johnstone, merchant in this place, was married to Miss Peggy Newell, an agreeable young lady, with £4000.'

EARLY FORMS OF LABOUR ORGANISATION

I. THE CHAPEL

The organisation of the workmen within a printing establishment into a chapel is a time-honoured custom, apparently almost as old as the industry itself. The explanation of the term 'chapel' is unknown; some have attributed it to the fact that Caxton set up his press in a small chapel attached to Westminster Abbey; others have seen in it a symbol of the close association of the early industry with the Church and theological writings. The chapel embraced all the workmen in the office; the head or Father of the chapel, in the days of the guild system, was the oldest Freeman, but subsequently was appointed by a vote of the members. The chapel acted as a means of disciplining the men, its weapon being a series of solaces or fines.

The earliest records of the organisation and working of the chapel are probably not directly relevant to Scotland, because of the relatively slow growth of the industry here. The following description is of an Edinburgh chapel, started in 1785, the minute-book of which was the subject of a series of articles which appeared in the *Circular* of 1873. There were, no doubt, chapels in Scotland at an earlier date than this, but this may be taken as a typical example. The chapel described was that of Neill & Co., Old Fishmarket Close, Edinburgh, a printing office established in 1749. The wording of the preamble to the minute-book, combined with the fact that the chapel was not formed until 1785, seems to support the view that, in Scotland at least, it was only as the industry expanded and the size of the individual establishments increased, that such organisation was adopted. The formation of this chapel was justified thus: 'Experience has fully evinced that without Laws and Regulations order never can be observed in any community. The observance of order and regularity is not more necessary in society than in a printing office, and the strict observance of rules becomes more necessary when the members are somewhat numerous: therefore the journeymen and apprentices in Messrs Neill's, observing with regret the little regard paid to order in the execution of the work in the house, and the train of evil consequences attendant thereon, both to masters and servants, with a view to prevent said consequences in future, resolved to erect themselves into a chapel . . . and they also agreed to sign, support and enforce the following rules and regulations.'

There followed a number of rules, with fines for their non-observance, some with reference to the general conduct of the members, others with particular reference to compositors or pressmen in the performance of their work. In the former category was the first rule, to the effect 'That all cursing and swearing shall be punished with a fine of twopence for each offence'. Again, a fine of twopence was levied on anyone leaving the office without extinguishing his candle, and one penny on anyone washing his hands in the pure water trough or taking away the water bowl. These no doubt make strange reading in an age which takes electricity and running water for granted. The compositors and pressmen were liable to a number of fines for careless handling of working materials, the breaking of letters, handling of paper with dirty hands, and the like, and had to make good the value of matter damaged. The duties of the head printer's devil received special mention, and included sweeping the floor, the kindling of fires, and the 'raising of compositors out of bed in the winter mornings'. If any member refused to pay the fines imposed on him, these were deducted from his wages the following Saturday. Earlier records show that attempts by individual members to protest against the rules or decisions of the chapel were dealt with in a much less human manner, often at the peril of life and limb.

The signatures to the rules were headed by those of Adam and James Neill, the heads of the firm who were also members of the chapel and equally subject to its laws. In fact the penalties in their case were greater—'when the masters are convicted of a breach of any of the foregoing rules, they are understood to be liable in double the fine annexed to said rule'.

In the raising of revenue these early printers did not lack resource or ingenuity. A 'benvenue' of 2/6 was levied on a new journeyman member, payable at the end of his fourth week in the office. An apprentice was required to pay an 'entry' of 5/–at the end of his fourth week of 'servitude', and a further 5/– when his indenture was completed. In addition to these entry charges, however, 'taxes' were also levied on marriages and births. The sum of 2/6 had to be paid four weeks after marriage, while four weeks after a birth the sum of 1/– was levied for a boy, 6d for a girl. Nor was single blessedness tax free, it being agreed that 'every unmarried journeyman shall, at the end of each year, pay the sum of one shilling'. Inevitably, with the passage of time, the 'cost of living' in the chapel increased, and by the early nineteenth century the benvenue and entry charges had risen to 10/6. Also, a further levy had been imposed on all members over sixteen years of age, who had to 'pay equally and severally to the treasurer, on their birthday, the sum of one shilling sterling'.

The amount raised by these charges is not usually revealed by the minute-book, although in one year, 1795, there appeared the entry—'Benvenues, births and batchelors—£2 6s. 6d'. The funds of the chapel, however, were often supplemented by authors, publishers and lawyers.[1]

The chapel funds obviously provided the main source of relief to tramps, that wandering band of unemployed printers, in the days preceding the trade society. But some

---

[1] Law work provided an important part of the Edinburgh industry's business in the early days.

further light is shed on the spending of these funds by an account preserved in the minute-book for the chapel's 'annual jollification', held in Mrs Thomas' Tavern on the 2nd January 1807. The details give some indication of the capacity of these hardy old printers, in the days when whisky cost only about seven shillings a gallon.

Dinner	£5	5	0
Punch	3	10	0
Whisky		14	8
Porter		5	
Beer		3	
Fruit		1	6
Biscuits		1	
Servants		5	
	£10	5	2

But habits were changing, at least during working hours. Thus in 1811, it was resolved 'That any member coming into the printing-office intoxicated with liquor, and disturbing his neighbour, shall pay a fine of two shillings and sixpence for such conduct'.

II. THE TRADE SOCIETY

(i) *Edinburgh*

In the *Circular* of May, 1882, there appeared an account of the unveiling of the Burns statue in Dumfries, the occasion of a procession in which the printers and bookbinders took part. This report is of interest because of a flag evidently carried by the printers. This 'venerable relic' was described as the original flag of the Edinburgh Letterpress Printers' Society, incorporated in 1758. The absence of any further information concerning this Society makes it impossible to say whether this was a very early example of a society of journeymen, or a society incorporating both masters and men. While the date of incorporation is rather late for the latter, this might be explained by the delayed development of the Scottish printing industry. On the other hand, while there is evidence to suggest that some early form of trade society existed in Edinburgh before the end of the eighteenth century, including some reference in the above-mentioned minute-book, no specific mention is made of this Society. The nature of the 1758 Society therefore remains a mystery, but, all things considered, it seems more likely that it was a joint organisation of masters and men.

In 1792 it is recorded that the compositors engaged in the Edinburgh book-trade secured a rise of $\frac{1}{2}$d per 1,000 ens,[1] while the rate for law printing remained unchanged. It seems likely that some form of trade society was in existence by this date, and that it was through it the compositors secured this rise, at a time when the book-trade was experiencing a boom.

A specific reference in the minute-book of Neill's chapel, dated April 1799, gives more information about the nature and working of the early society. There it is recorded that 'the chapel being convened, a letter was read from the secretary of the committee of journeymen printers, informing them that new committee men should be elected, as the time for the present committee continuing in office was about to expire'. It is further recorded that the chapel appointed two of their members to represent them on this committee. Other references support the view that the earliest form of the trade society was in fact such a committee, and was called simply 'The Standing Committee'.

Trade unions, as such, were made illegal by the Combination Acts of 1799, but in spite of this the organisation of labour continued, combinations taking the form mainly of friendly societies. The Standing Committee was not a friendly society in any but the literal sense of the words, but continued to function as a trade body during this period, chiefly as a result of the informality of its form and meetings, which earned for it the title of the 'Jolly Standing Committee'. In the early years of the nineteenth century the delegates from the various chapels met annually in the parlour of some favourite tavern. There, round the

[1] From the practice of reckoning letters or types by the letter 'n'.

table, trade matters were discussed, disputes reported, and decisions given which were carried out through the medium of the chapel, as far as the circumstances of the time permitted. When the more serious issues were settled, other members of the trade joined the Committee. The members of the latter then produced 'the white shilling which his chapel had given him wherewith to wet his whistle', and the meeting was opened to all members of the trade. A jolly evening of gossip and entertainment followed. The conviviality of the meeting in fact prevented the authorities from interfering with this trade gathering.

A further look at the chapel minute-book reveals traces of the influence of the Standing Committee, meetings being convened at its direct instigation, or issues raised in the chapel by the members of the Committee. In the latter category, for instance, comes the discussion and decision regarding the habit of 'twicing', pressmen working as compositors and vice versa. In 1807 a particular case of this was dealt with, the culprit being given the opportunity to choose which branch of the trade he wished to follow and forbidden to practise the other in future, under penalty of one guinea. The chapel decided 'that every other member of this chapel who shall be guilty of the like offence is hereby declared to incur the same penalty'. In a similar manner the question of the 'turnover' apprentice was raised in 1812, when it was decided that apprentices coming from another office should 'pay an entry of ten shillings'.

The date at which the Standing Committee was replaced by the first Edinburgh Society is unknown, but the former was still in existence in 1826. At that date the minute-book records the following: 'The chapel being met and constituted, in consequence of a requisition by the preses of the Standing Committee calling upon them to take into consideration the case of the unemployed workmen in London, they came to the following resolution, viz.,—"That each journeyman in the office subscribe the sum of sixpence weekly, to continue for the space of eight weeks; and then to consider further their case at the end of that period." The sum of £4 was accordingly remitted.' At the same time, it is recorded, the sum of 18/– was paid towards the relief of the unemployed in Edinburgh.

The year 1826, it may be recalled, was one of financial crisis and failure for several London publishers. Sir Walter Scott, James Ballantyne and Archibald Constable were involved in this crash, and the repercussions on employment in the Edinburgh printing trade were doubtless serious. It seems likely that this had an adverse effect on the cause of labour organisation in the industry, but whether it had anything to do with the demise of the Standing Committee, or delayed the growth of the Edinburgh Society, can only be the subject of speculation. The first Society was formed sometime between 1826 and 1836, but the cause of union in the Edinburgh trade only gained strength after 1840.[1]

(ii) *The Interlocutor*

While the Edinburgh Standing Committee was undoubtedly in existence at the time of the famous Interlocutor, and was no doubt the prime mover in that event, nevertheless in 1803 the compositors sought authority from the Sheriff to convene a meeting of the craft, thus safeguarding themselves in the eyes of the law. As a result of the meeting, a memorial for an increase in wages was presented to the employers. The case was taken to law, and the initial decision was given against the compositors. The latter, however, took the case to the Court of Session, and in 1804 the Lord President, Ilay Campbell, issued an Interlocutor in favour of the compositors. The employers appealed against his decision, but their petition was dismissed. The 1805 Scale of Prices had, in consequence, the backing of law, and the Interlocutor is an important landmark in the history of the Edinburgh Society. It is also of interest as being contrary to the general trend of the period. About this time attempts were made by the workers in a

[1] See Chapter 3.

number of trades, in England and in Scotland, to revive old laws empowering the justices to fix wages. These were generally unsuccessful, however, and indeed eventually resulted in the repeal of the old laws. Its importance and its interest justify the inclusion here, at some length, of extracts from the detailed and well-prepared documents on which the compositors' case was based. These throw interesting light on the compositors of 1803, as well as on the state of the printing trade and on the general conditions of the period.

'Your Lordships are now requested to decide between the memorialists and their masters, upon the justice of a demand which the memorialists have made for an increase in wages; and they shall endeavour, with all possible brevity, to explain the grounds upon which they hope that your Lordships will sanction the very moderate increase for which they have petitioned.

'A very remarkable change has taken place within the space of the last half century, on the condition of the people in this country, and their mode of life, as well as on the productive powers of labour and the general riches of the community. Independently altogether of the occasional scarcities with which the country has within that period, and particularly of late years, been afflicted, the price of provisions, and expense of all the necessaries of life, have risen at least one third, nay, it is believed, that a fairer proportion would be one half; . . . This increase in the expense of living has made it necessary to augment the wages of workmen in all those trades and occupations in which the condition of the manufacture, the state of the masters' profits, and the prevalence of the demand for the productions of labour, afforded any fund for the augmentation of wages . . . the wages, not only of particular manufacturers, but even of unskilled and common labourers, have been augmented very considerably above the rate at which they stood 20 or 30 years ago.

'During the period now alluded to, the wages of journeymen compositors have not been altered . . . except in the year 1792.

'During those late years of scarcity, which will not soon be forgotten, the memorialists suffered the hardships endured by other workmen; and in order to subsist themselves and their families, were forced to sell or pledge their furniture, and incur debts, which many of them have not been able to discharge yet. . . . The memorialists were sensible that the state of the printing business in Scotland at that time afforded them no reasonable prospect of an augmentation of wages. . . . This depressed state of the manufacture, however, is now at an end. The trade of printing has again become flourishing in Scotland; . . . It is a fact capable of the most distinct and early proof, that there are more books composed and sent forth from this city than from almost all the other cities of the island taken together, with the single exception of London; but even London booksellers have come of later years to employ Scotch printers to print for their market. The Edinburgh work is daily improving in elegance and correctness . . . the memorialists' case comes to this . . . that their wages are the same as those given half a century ago, while the price of living has risen more than one third. But the memorialists think themselves entitled to a rise of one fourth, as required to place them in the same state of comfortable living relative to the price of the articles of subsistence as formerly, as necessary to place them in a relative level with other workmen, both skilled and unskilled, and as fully justified by the particular articles of labour which they are called upon to perform, and the skill, knowledge, unremitting attention, long education, and injury to health, which are the requisites and concomitants of their employment.'

The following is a copy of the Scale of Prices granted by the Interlocutor:

I. That all works considered as Common be cast up at 4½d per 1000, including heads and directions.

II. That Session-Work and Jobs be paid at the rate of 5½d per 1000.

III. That all Dictionaries done in the manner of a Lexicon be paid at 5d per 1000; but not to extend to Dictionaries of Science, or such as, from their nature, can be considered only as common matter.

IV. That Pamphlets of Five Sheets and under be paid One Shilling per sheet above what they come to by letters, for furniture and extra trouble.

V. That all works heretofore paid double (Greek and Scheme) take a proportionate advance according to the first proposition.

VI. That all works printed in a Foreign language, though common type, be paid at 5d per 1000.

VII. That all works done on Nonpareil be paid at 5d per 1000; and on Pearl at 5½d per 1000.

VIII. That Grammars and School Books, where Roman and Italic words occur alternately, with braces, different justifications, etc., be paid at 5¼d per 1000.

IX. That Newspapers be considered as liable to a proportionate advance, according to the first proposition.

While undoubtedly a notable victory at the time, the long-run effects of the Interlocutor Scale on the pay of the Edinburgh compositors was by no means entirely favourable. It now seems fairly certain that it was in an effort to avoid the high charges of the Scale for certain types of work that the establishment or 'stab system of payment was introduced, side by side with piece payment, with a consequent depressing effect on earnings.[1] It is recorded, in fact, that in 1812, in the King's office, alarm at the increase in bills under the new Scale caused the manager to offer 27/– per week to his best compositors and 25/– to the others. A meeting of the trade decided against this 'innovation' as it would destroy the advantages gained from the Court of Session. Attempts to replace the men proved unsatisfactory, and payment according to the Scale was resumed. 'So ended the first attempt to introduce the 'stab.'[2]

(iii) *Glasgow*

While the Edinburgh Standing Committee was probably the earliest example of organisation in the Scottish printing industry, the trade society proper is of much earlier origin in Glasgow than in Edinburgh. The Glasgow Society was instituted in 1817, its objects being: 'First, to provide for such members as require to leave the City for

[1] See Chapter 6.   [2] *Circular*, May 1858.

want of employment, without having pecuniary means: Secondly, to furnish, with facility, money to such strangers as cannot find employment in the City: and, Thirdly, to co-operate with other places in exposing irregular work-men, and maintaining a friendly intercourse throughout the Trade.' This preamble to the Articles of the Glasgow Society is of interest as indicating what was probably the typical form and purpose of Societies at this time: they were concerned mainly with the relief of unemployment under the tramping system, but had a watching brief over wage rates, wherever possible and as far as the law allowed.

Under the tramping system, an unemployed member received a card from his Society, attesting to his position as a member, and armed with this, he travelled on foot around the country in search of work. On presentation of his card to the 'call-house' of the Society at each place visited, he usually received food and lodgings, and in the absence of work, a sum of money to help him on his way. This was often augmented by the charity of members of local chapels. If he failed to obtain permanent work, on the completion of his tour of branches, he returned to his home town and Society.

The Regulations of the Glasgow Society, published in 1820, throw further light on the working of this system and the nature of a Relief Society. A member setting out in search of work received 15/– from the Society, or, if married, 21/–. This sum he was not entitled to receive again until nine months after he rejoined the Society. A tramp visiting Glasgow received 7/–, provided he was a member of a similar Society. The sum of 5/– was paid to strangers who had not had an opportunity of becoming members of a similar Society, provided they were 'free of professional opprobrium', but 'nothing can be granted to brethren in Glasgow who are not members'.

In addition to operating a relief system the Glasgow Society was also concerned with the preservation of stan-dard rates of wages. Reference is made to the scale agreed between masters and journeymen in 1815. Anyone work-ing for less was to be treated as a 'rat', and his name published in a circular, which was sent to corresponding Societies in other towns. The Society was open only to journeymen, and the entry fee was 5/–, or, in the case of a former member of a similar Society, 2/6. The contribution from each member was 6d per month.

CHAPTER THREE

NATIONAL ORGANISATION

I. The General Typographical Association of Scotland, 1836–1844

The first attempt at national organisation in the Scottish printing industry dates back to 1836, a time when Trade Unionism was, in a sense, only in its infancy, when there was a constant battle against legal restrictions, and when many of the new ventures in labour organisation were short-lived. The General Typographical Association of Scotland was formed in August 1836 and continued to function until the end of 1844, when it was replaced by the Northern District Board of the National Typographical Association. Unfortunately no detailed records of this Association appear to have survived. Some indication of its nature and scope, however, can be gathered from the following rather sketchy outline.

Nothing is known of the events leading up to the formation of the Association or of its instigators. It seems likely, however, that the Glasgow Society played the leading part in its formation, although Edinburgh was the main centre of the Scottish printing industry, and the number employed in the Edinburgh industry was far greater than that of Glasgow. Two facts support this. Firstly, the Edinburgh Society was not at this time strong enough to take a leading part. It is recorded that prior to 1840 the printers of Edinburgh 'had the unenviable reputation of being willing to accept work at a reduced rate in almost any town in the United Kingdom'. The writer goes on to add that this was true only of part of the profession, and was the result of want of union.[1] Secondly, the Association

[1] Correspondent in the *Typographical Protection Circular*, November 1850.

was at first located in Glasgow, the Central Board being appointed by and from the Glasgow Branch.

Two major objects of the Association appear to have been to secure more uniform rates of pay and the regulation of the number of apprentices. The latter became a particularly important issue and cause of disputes during the second half of the Association's short life, the policy in this matter being later described as high-handed and tyrannical. But it was on the question of rates of pay that the first major challenge arose. The origin and nature of this challenge is revealed by a circular issued to members in February 1837. The circular begins thus: 'The Central Board beg leave to express the high feelings of pride and satisfaction which they entertain respecting the manner in which the great majority of the Local Societies throughout Scotland have acted, in connecting themselves with the General Association; and likewise of the spirited efforts which many of these Societies have made for the redress of their grievances, since they became thus connected.' Up to this point progress had evidently been made with little sacrifice, but a crisis had now arisen. A fundamental principle of the Association was the equalisation of pay for press and case work, and further to this, the pressmen of Glasgow had drawn up a scale of prices 'in accordance with the rates paid by the principal houses in town for the last ten years'. The employers were opposing this scale, and at the same time, evidently trying to break the new Association. Workmen had received notice to quit from a number of offices, including 'the three most extensive establishments in Glasgow'—Brookman's, Fullarton's, and Khull's. In all, sixty-five journeymen and sixty apprentices were involved. Further, it was believed that the employers had entered into a number of resolutions, including one binding them not to employ any member of the Association.

Appended to the circular is a report of a meeting of the Glasgow Master Printers' Association and of the resolutions agreed to. It is interesting to note that this meeting took place in the Waterloo Tavern on the 21st February at 2 p.m., while the date heading the circular issued by the Association was also the 21st February. Obviously news travelled just as quickly then as now, and the leaders of the Association were not slow to take action.

The resolutions, of which the first three are given here in full, throw further light on the functioning of the early Association. They were: '1st. That, as the Journeymen Printers of this City, by means of the Societies or Associations aftermentioned, and otherwise, have been attempting to dictate to their employers, respecting the scale of prices to be paid by them, and to interfere illegally with their employment of Workmen and Apprentices, the Masters consider it necessary to adopt such measures as shall be best fitted to protect themselves against any unjust and illegal attempt on the part of the Journeymen. 2nd. That, as one means of protecting themselves, the Masters resolve immediately to discharge all Journeymen who are members of "The Glasgow Typographical Society", or "The Central Typographical Association of Scotland". 3rd. That no Master shall give employment to any Apprentice who may have left the office of another without leave, on the present occasion, and that no Master shall take any Apprentice into his employment until he shall have subscribed an Indenture in a form to be approved of by a Committee named at this meeting; and in future all Apprentices shall be regularly bound by Indenture in the same form.'

Other resolutions concerned measures to promote a 'General Association of the Master Printers throughout the United Kingdom', and the appointment of a committee to carry out the resolution.

The Central Board, in the above-mentioned circular, appealed to all members of the profession in Scotland to stand firm against this challenge, which they realised would determine the future, if any, of the Association. They imposed a levy on all members of five per cent of their wages, to assist those losing their jobs during the dispute. Unfortunately nothing further is recorded about this dispute or its outcome, although the latter can be deduced from the fact that the Association survived and thrived for some years thereafter.

The next record of the Association concerns the Rules and Regulations which were adopted by a meeting held in Edinburgh in August 1841. These are of particular interest since they became the basis on which the present Association was founded in 1853. For this reason they are given in detail in Appendix I.

More is known of the closing years of the Association, and extracts have survived from the last two Annual Reports, issued in August 1843 and August 1844. By 1843 a marked improvement had occurred in the affairs of the Edinburgh Society, which then included nearly 500 members. No doubt as a consequence of this, the location of the Central Board had changed, and during these two years at least, the affairs of the Association were conducted from Edinburgh.

From the Report of 1843 we find that the main problem of the period was unemployment, the conditions of the profession being described as most distressing. 'In Edinburgh and Glasgow there has not been for some time past anything like constant employment for even half the journeymen.' Efforts had been made by subscriptions to relieve the unemployed, but the numbers were so great that the relief which could be given made little impression on the distress and suffering. A list of the number of tramps relieved during this year in the main branches showed these to total 755, which was slightly more than the total membership of the Association. The cost of this relief was £121 16s 2d.

The main cause of this unemployment was believed to be the apprentice system. Much good had resulted from the formation of the Association and in many cases the number of apprentices had been reduced, but much still remained to be done. In this, it was suggested, the example of the Edinburgh Society might be followed. In 1842 the Edinburgh Society had concluded an agreement with the employers, restricting the number of apprentices as follows: 'For every master or company, two apprentices, (one at case and one at press); and thereafter, one apprentice for every three journeymen permanently employed in each establishment.' Commenting on this, the Report concludes thus: '. . . it is to be hoped that, ere long, Edinburgh (which was formerly considered the nursery of the apprentice system in Scotland, and the most apathetic branch of the General Association,) will . . . be able at least to give employment to its own journeymen.' It was, in fact, nearly the end of the century before a similar restriction of apprentices began to be effective throughout the area of the present Association.

In the Edinburgh memorial to the employers on this subject, it was claimed that the present state of the trade was due to the mushroom growth of small masters and the consequent fall in the profits of all. This in turn was attributed to the excessive number of boys employed and the consequent dearth of openings for journeymen. Restriction was, therefore, as much in the interests of the employers as the journeymen.

In spite of the problems of unemployment and too many apprentices, however, the Report of 1843 speaks of the growing prosperity of the Association in a year of 'abundant uninterrupted tranquillity'. The number of Branches in the Association totalled 15, including Aberdeen, Dumfries, Edinburgh, Glasgow, Kelso, Kilmarnock, Montrose, Perth and Stirling. The membership of these 9 Branches was 651, while the total membership of the Association was over 700. The balance at the close of the account for the year was £158 16s 2½d. The Report concludes thus: 'Our demands have ever been reasonable and just —we have never asked anything incompatible with the true interests of our employers—and are, therefore, despite the apathy of some, and the undisguised opposition of others, in a fair way to obtaining all for which we have associated—employment, and for that employment a fair remuneration.'

The Report of 1844 paints a very different picture. It records a year of strikes which were 'numerous, vexatious and expensive'. A considerable number of offices were closed, and expenses were heavy. The causes of dispute are not revealed, but it seems likely, both from the content of the previous Report and from comments made in later years on Association policy, that a major one was apprentice restriction. In addition, the problem of unemployment was so acute that a special committee was appointed in Edinburgh to devise means of relief, and an appeal issued to the profession throughout the country.

As a result of these troubles, the finances of the Association were severely strained, and it was recognised that a levy would be required before another year could be faced. The annual meeting of the Association, however, had unanimously decided to adopt the amalgamation scheme proposed at the Derby Delegate Meeting in July of that year. Thus the General Typographical Association of Scotland ended its brief existence, at a time when trade conditions were very bad and strikes numerous. But, although weakened financially and obviously facing a crisis, the Association did not fail, and it was primarily in an effort to take up where it left off that the present Association was formed.

II. THE NATIONAL TYPOGRAPHICAL ASSOCIATION: NORTHERN DISTRICT BOARD, 1844–47

The scheme of amalgamation, sponsored by the old Northern Union,[1] and approved by the Derby Delegate Meeting in July 1844, was put into operation with the creation of the National Typographical Association in January 1845. The Association extended over England, Ireland and Scotland, and comprised five Districts—of which Scotland was one, viz., The Northern District— each governed by a Board.

The functions of the Association were summed up as the support and maintenance of strike members and of the unemployed, and one of its main objects was to replace the old tramping system with a regularised system of unemployment benefit. The evils of the tramping system had

[1] i.e. North England.

been a motive factor behind the amalgamation scheme—
'to annihilate the Arab-like propensities of those who
brought pecuniary embarrassment upon the profession'.[1]
Under the new scheme members paid a weekly subscription of 6d, and the unemployment allowance was 6/– per
week, or where a member was in partial employment but
earning less than the specified allowance, the sum of 8/–
was to be made up. Every unemployed member was to
accept employment in another town when requested to do
so by his own secretary, or be fined 2/6. When a member
lost his employment through 'defending the privileges of
the profession', he would receive, with the approval of the
Association, payment amounting to three-quarters of his
wages for a period of six months. A series of graded fines
for non-payment of subscriptions was adopted, and after
six months of non-payment, the member was expelled.

The Northern District Board was run by Edinburgh,
and the minute-book of its meetings there between
January 1845 and November 1847 still exists, in neat and
legible handwriting. For the first two years the Board met
regularly at least once per week, and often the pressure of
work and lateness of the hour caused an adjournment until
the following evening. That the meeting did not usually
begin until 9 p.m. is probably a fitting comment on the
hours of labour at that time. At the end of the first six
months there were eight Branches in the district—Aberdeen, Dingwall, Dumfries, Edinburgh, Glasgow, Kelso,
Kilmarnock and Stranraer—while many members in
smaller places were attached to one or other of these
Branches—e.g. Arbroath and Montrose were attached to
the Edinburgh Society, while Wick members were ar-
ranging to join the Aberdeen Society. The Board were
active in encouraging the formation of new Societies and
the revival of Societies in areas where they had been
allowed to disband. Thus, during the first year, Societies
were re-formed in Dundee and Perth. Early in 1846 a
Society was formed at Stirling, while later in that year

[1] Address to first Delegate Meeting of N.T.A. by Mr Robert Davies,
Liverpool.

attempts to form Branches at Ayr and Inverness were recorded.

At the outset it was decided that non-members then un-employed would be admitted on payment of five shillings, but that they must make twenty-six weekly payments before they would be entitled to benefit. Compositor apprentices were admitted only from their fourth year, while those of press were admitted from the commence-ment of their apprenticeship.

All matters of dispute in the District were submitted to the Board, and when the question of closing an office arose, the matter had to be sent to the Executive and the deci-sions of all the other District Boards obtained. Similarly, the Northern Board considered and gave opinions on questions submitted by the other Districts.

Within the Northern District, one of the earliest questions cropping up was the perennial one of apprentice restriction, the Edinburgh Society campaigning to get their scale accepted by Glasgow. A case is quoted of one office in Glasgow with thirteen journeymen and twenty-one apprentices. The number of apprentices appears to have been the most common cause of dispute throughout the District at this time. Thus, at the first Delegate Meeting of the National Association, held in London in March 1846, the Edinburgh Society proposed that the ratio of apprentices be equalised in Edinburgh and Glasgow, ac-cording to the scale agreed in Edinburgh in 1842, and in the provinces one apprentice be allowed to every two journeymen. In fact, the Delegate Meeting decided that the ratio be equalised throughout Scotland according to the Edinburgh scale—i.e. two apprentices to every master or company, and thereafter one to every three journeymen permanently employed. Protests immediately followed from Glasgow, and reports of oppostion by the employers to this decision. The Glasgow Society decided that the rule should be modified and one apprentice to every two journeymen be permitted in book houses, although the one to three rule be retained in newspaper offices. This deci-sion received neither the approval nor the sanction of the

District Board. In fact, a crop of disputes appears to have followed the attempt to introduce the new apprentice rule, particularly in Glasgow and Aberdeen, from whose Societies constant appeals for funds were sent to the Board in the closing weeks of 1846. The strike in Aberdeen appears to have been a particularly lengthy one, and the apprentice issue was proving a costly one to the Board. The disastrous Edinburgh strike of 1847 put all other questions in the background, and the only other mention of the apprentice problem is in August 1847, when a Delegate Meeting decided that the ratio be uniform throughout Scotland—one apprentice to every two journeymen.

Later comments on the National Association and the old General Scottish Association suggest that, in the matter of apprentice restriction, these bodies were too high-handed and dogmatic. Attempts to force a rigid policy of restriction, combined with the wholesale closing of offices, was evidently an important factor in the strengthening of opposition from the employers, and in the disputes which culminated in the breakdown of the National Association. The extent of the restrictions proposed was too great, in view of current conditions in the industry, and the rigid adherence to the policy and refusal to compromise unwise, at such an early, and therefore relatively weak, stage in the development of national organisation.

On the establishment of the Northern Board, it had been agreed that minimum wage rates be 25/– per week in all places within ten miles of Edinburgh and Glasgow, and elsewhere 20/–. In October 1846, Aberdeen received the sanction of the Board to press for an increase in wages to 22/–.

The question of pay for 'Sabbath work' was raised in connection with *The Glasgow Herald* Office, toward the end of 1845. It was eventually agreed that the men were entitled to double pay, viz., 9d per hour, and in the case of Sunday night work, 1/– per hour. This was corroborated by the decision of the Delegate Meeting, in 1846: 'That Sunday work be charged double, and that over-time be charged 3d per hour extra.'

A new Edinburgh Scale of Press Prices was approved in May 1846. This included: '4d per hour for attendance after 8 p.m. for proofs', and 'when required to work on beyond 10 p.m., 9d for refreshments, all night 1/6'.

Among the other topics submitted for consideration to the 1846 Delegate Meeting by the Northern District was the evil of the 'settlement' system as it was operated in Edinburgh. Under this system the men received a little more than the standard weekly rate, often only a shilling more, and in return they were required to work as many hours as the employers demanded. This was an evil which spread considerably in Edinburgh in the troublesome times following the dissolution of the National Association in 1847.

Another proposal submitted to the Delegates concerned the reduction of hours in Scotland from eleven to ten per day, but it was decided, 'from prudential motives', not to interfere with existing regulations.

At this first Delegate Meeting, held in White Conduit House, London, it is reported that the business occupied seven days, and that nearly a hundred propositions had been submitted by member Societies. The scale and alleged lavishness of the event, however, found little sympathy north of the border. The expense accounts of the Scottish delegates were the subject of close scrutiny and much wrangling, culminating in the resignation from the Board of at least one member. In one case objection was taken to a claim for board during the journey to London, as 'the steamer fare of £1 17s 6d included provisions during the journey'.

The year 1846 put the National Association severely to the test. Trade was bad, disputes numerous, with growing opposition from employers, and the funds of the Association were seriously depleted. In September the Executive announced that the subscription throughout the Association would be doubled for a period of three months from the beginning of October. The drain on the funds of the Northern District through unemployment was aggravated by the strikes in Glasgow and Aberdeen. In August the

Board had over £400 to its credit, but by December there were no funds in hand and appeal had to be made to the Executive. But the greatest blow was still to come—the epic Edinburgh strike, which, in fact, delivered the death blow to the Northern District and, indirectly, to the National Association itself.

To the existence of the Northern District Board is credited the creation of the Master Printers' Association of Edinburgh. After 1845 growing opposition was offered by the employers to the activities of the Edinburgh Society, and on 28th October 1846, three resolutions were issued under the signatures of thirty-eight employers:

'(1) That no journeyman shall be taken into employment who either leaves or threatens to leave his employer on "Strike".

'(2) No journeyman shall be taken into employment without producing a certificate from his last employer.

'(3) That in all cases Masters shall prefer Non-unionists to Unionists.'

In December the matter was referred to the Executive, and early in January it was decided that the thirty-eight employers concerned be regarded as in dispute, and that members losing employment would be entitled to receive 10/– per week. On the 27th January 1847, the employers demanded acceptance of their Resolutions, on penalty of discharge, and early in February over 150 men received notice.

The men, with few exceptions, stood firm, although their plight in the months which followed was desperate. Funds were contributed throughout the Association and from kindred organisations. Outstanding was the contribution of the Daily Newspaper Compositors Society of London, who had contributed nearly £200 by November 1847. Proposals for a treble subscription were at first vetoed, and later, in June, revived, when the Northern Board issued a circular appeal for funds with the announcement that only if a treble levy were adopted could they continue to support the National Association.

Some of the employers withdrew their names from the resolutions—and some never signed them at all—but the remainder appear to have obtained sufficient non-union labour, much of it from the south, to carry on. Many of the ejected men left Edinburgh and obtained work in London and other parts of the country, but, by October, 30 still remained on the books of the Edinburgh Society. By this time the average weekly payment which could be made to them was only about five shillings.

The financial position of the National Association as a result of heavy unemployment and the cost of the Edinburgh strike demanded a radical revision of the rules and working. A Delegate Meeting in Liverpool in August 1847 created a new organisation on a much more modest scale. The amount and duration of unemployment benefit were reduced, as was also the strike allowance, while the ratio of apprentices recognised was one to every two journeymen. The Northern District Board was replaced by a District Committee, and at its first meeting it resolved to ask the Executive for discretionary powers to deal with closed offices in Edinburgh. This was granted, and on 13th October the Committee terminated the strike with the following resolutions: 'That the members who entered closed offices in consequence of the Association having failed to implement its engagements with them, be now permitted to resume their connection as free members without payment of Entrance Money; and that the members of the Association be allowed to accept situations in any office which was closed in consequence of the Masters' Resolutions.'

Even in its revised form the National Association found it impossible to meet the financial liabilities which it had incurred during the disastrous months of 1847; the Northern District alone had incurred debts of over £300. In November 1847 it was decided to suspend the rules regarding payment of unemployment and strike benefit until the debts of the Association were wholly cleared. The subscriptions of each Society were to be divided among its creditors weekly, unemployed members being included in the dividend, but having no claim for the full amount due under the Rules of the Association. The Minutes of the Northern District Committee end with an appeal to members to continue to support the Association with their subscriptions during the abeyance of benefits. But this decision, combined with the prevailing depression of trade and the consequent heavy unemployment, put too great a strain on the slender ties of allegiance to the infant and evidently premature national organisation.

A combination of circumstances and policy may be held responsible for the overthrow of the National Association. The scheme was too ambitious for this early period. In particular, the commitments in respect of relief to the unemployed were heavy. This was underlined by the fact that the scheme was launched into a period of severe depression and unemployment. Finally, the rigidity of policy for apprentice restriction added to the general distress through an increasing number of closed offices, with correspondingly increased financial responsibilities. Above all, the moral to be drawn was that national organisation, if it is to succeed, must be strengthened and backed by the necessary financial reserves.

CHAPTER FOUR

THE FORMATION OF THE SCOTTISH TYPOGRAPHICAL ASSOCIATION

(i) *The Industry after* 1847

The economic conditions and difficulties of the 1830's and early 40's, to which can probably be attributed alike much of the credit for the formation of the old General Typographical Association of Scotland and the more ambitious National Typographical Association, and much of the blame for their breakdown, continued in the closing years of the half century. The year 1848 has been described as one of the worst the working-class ever experienced. The rapid expansion in coal and iron, and the attendant development of heavy industries, which characterised the peak of the Industrial Revolution in Scotland, did not follow a smooth, uninterrupted course. The 'railway mania' of the 40's was bearing fruit in the form of monetary crisis, to add to the familiar famines and shortages which earned for the period the title of the 'Hungry forties'. The first signs of recovery appeared in 1849, when a good harvest and a revival in trade led to some rise in wages. This appears to have been somewhat offset by a further wave of immigration from Ireland. By 1851, however, a trade boom had set in which lasted until 1854.

The printing industry in Scotland shared in the general experience of depression, recovery only beginning to be felt by 1850. Further, the menace of an increasing number of apprentices appears to have grown steadily after the dissolution of the National Association, leaving the industry with the problem of a surplus labour force even in times of relatively good trade. The industry evidently subscribed to the view, popular at this period, that emigration provided one solution to the unemployment problem. Thus we find the Glasgow Society in 1849, with large numbers of unemployed, contributing towards an unemployment and an emigration fund.

The tramping system had returned; the Glasgow Society relieved 132 cards, and issued 43, between February 1848 and January 1849. Complaints of the evils and abuses of the system again became widespread. In fact, the apprentice question and the tramping system appear to have been the major problems of the trade at this period, and the two were by no means disconnected. The printing industry had expanded, and yet the number of unemployed had increased—and this before the days of large-scale displacement of men by machines. From this the obvious conclusion to be drawn was that the increase in the labour force had been greater than the increase in demand for the industry's products. That this surplus labour force was due to the excessive number of apprentices was borne out by such statistics as were available. An estimate for the Scottish industry at this time was some 1,500 journeymen to 1,200 apprentices, and these were divided between the two main sections of the industry thus: newspapers, 500 journeymen and 350 apprentices; bookwork and jobbing, 1,000 journeymen and 850 apprentices. The effect of this was felt not only in the numbers without employment, but in the relatively low average wage of journeymen; in Scotland the average wage, over the whole country, was about 15/6 per week, and that for a week of at least 66 hours.

The breakdown of the regularised system of unemployment benefit instituted by the National Association, and the expense which such a system had been shown to entail, resulted in a return to the tramping system. The justification for this form of relief was the need to support the surplus labour force to some extent, to prevent it undercutting the existing level of wages. Some, in fact, argued against this view, and maintained that the industry would be better off if the system were abolished. Certainly the extent to which those genuinely distressed through unemployment were relieved by the system appears to have been so small as hardly to have constituted a preventive to undercutting. Abuse of the system, on the other hand, was extensive and widespread.

Another preoccupation of the trade at this time was the campaign for the repeal of the Paper, Advertisement and Stamp Duties, or the 'Taxes on Knowledge' as they were called. Many Societies throughout the country collaborated in the signing of a petition for their repeal, and a Stamp Abolition Committee was formed. While there is evidence that some parts of Scotland joined in this campaign, and it is recorded that a petition was sent from the Glasgow Society, yet, on the whole, there is little evidence that it aroused the crusading fervour experienced in the south.

(ii) *The Aftermath in Union Organisation*

Union organisation in the Scottish printing industry had suffered a severe set-back as a result of the calamitous events of 1847 and the dissolution of the Northern District Board. Many individual Societies appear to have gone under at this time, while those which survived emerged weak and crippled. The Aberdeen Branch had already announced its inability to carry on, because of reduction in numbers, before the Northern Board was dissolved.

The Edinburgh Society naturally suffered most, and had the heaviest burden of debt to carry. In the following years references appeared, from time to time, to the apathy and inertness of the Edinburgh printers, the prostrate conditions of the Society, and to the encroachments and innovations introduced by the employers, without complaint or opposition, which were 'threatening to earn for Edinburgh its former bad reputation'. Not only did the number of apprentices increase substantially, but the misuse of the 'settlement' system gained ground. One case is quoted of a law-printer with a flourishing business, who paid his men 26/– a week, this sum covering all the excessive overtime necessary during the sittings of the Court of Session. The same employer paid off the 'stab or establishment man without the customary fourteen days' notice, sometimes in the middle of a week. The revival of the Society was hampered by the debt which was the legacy of the 1847 dispute; by 1850 this still amounted to some £58. In April 1850, however, a trade meeting in London decided to form a committee to consider plans for the liquidation of this debt, incurred in the name of the National Association. Not until the end of 1851 is the position of the Edinburgh Society favourably reported; then the state of the funds is described as satisfactory, and the membership reported to be over 200.

Elsewhere in Scotland the revival of trade union organisation was slow, hampered, no doubt, by the acute depression of trade and the large number of unemployed. A list of Scottish Societies published in 1849 comprised Banff, Dumfries, Dundee, Edinburgh, Glasgow, Kilmarnock, Perth and Stirling, while 1850 saw the establishment of a Society at Elgin; the re-formation of a Society at Aberdeen did not occur until 1853. That the majority of these were, at this time, merely relief societies, is borne out by the fact that the list of recognised Societies issued by the English Provincial Typographical Association in September 1851, and which did not recognise mere relief societies, included only one Scottish one, viz., Glasgow. Later the Edinburgh Society's cards were also recognised by the P.T.A., its name being excluded from the original published list because of its failure to furnish in time the particulars asked.

The events of 1847 left the Glasgow Society as the strongest in Scotland, and it is a measure of the extent of the blow dealt at that time that the strongest Society was reported, at the end of 1847, to have in hand between £2 and £3 after clearing all liabilities. Recovery, however, was fairly rapid, at least financially, and by the beginning of 1849 the Glasgow Society was 'on reciprocal' with every Society throughout the United Kingdom. Trade, however, was very bad and the number of unemployed large. The position of Glasgow in this respect was aggravated by the large influx of unemployed from other parts of the country. By March 1850 this Society was described as in a comparatively flourishing condition, with increasing membership and considerable surplus funds, but not until the end of 1851 was trade reported to be good.

(iii) *The Association revived*

The first reference to attempts to re-form a Scottish Association came from the Glasgow Society as early as January 1849. This attempt would appear to have been premature, however, and nothing more was heard from Glasgow on this subject until late in 1851. In the interval a few references appeared in print from time to time, emphasising the need for such an Association and urging Glasgow to take the lead, as the strongest and most influential Society. In August 1851 reference was made to a committee, reported to have been formed by the Glasgow Society, whose task was to consider the question of reviving the Scottish Association. Thereafter Glasgow evidently contacted the main Scottish centres, seeking their opinions on an amalgamation scheme. In December a meeting of the Edinburgh Society unanimously approved of the proposal and promised to co-operate in the scheme. By this time favourable replies had been received from Kilmarnock and Paisley, and an unfavourable one from Stirling, while Glasgow had announced its determination to carry out the scheme, even if supported only by one other Society.

By November of the following year Glasgow announced that the formation of the Scottish Typographical Association was all but completed. The rules of the old Scottish Association had been circulated for approval or alteration, and a Delegate Meeting arranged for Tuesday, 9th November. This meeting was held in Angus's Temperance Hotel, Glasgow. Mr Clark, Glasgow, was appointed chairman, and Mr Cooper, Edinburgh, interim secretary. It was reported that five Societies had intimated their willingness to join—Dumfries, Kilmarnock, Paisley, Edinburgh and Glasgow. Stirling had declined, and no reply had been received from Perth, Dundee or Inverness, where, in fact, no Societies existed at that time. Aberdeen had expressed regret at being unable to form a Society; there were then only twenty-two journeymen there and the number of apprentices was so great that they seemed powerless to do anything. The delegates at this meeting unanimously approved of the formation of an Association, on similar lines and with similar rules[1] to the old Scottish one. It was agreed that it be called the Scottish Typographical Association. Thus the present Association came into operation on the 1st January, 1853, the Central Board being located in Glasgow and elected by the Glasgow Branch.

[1] See Appendix I.

PART II

THE FIRST FIFTY YEARS
1853 — 1902

CHAPTER FIVE

A GENERAL SURVEY

I. The Industry

A few years after the formation of the Association conditions of general depression prevailed in Scotland. Industry and employment were affected firstly by the impact of the Crimean War, and then, a few years later, by the serious and wide-spread repercussions of the American Civil War. The years 1855 to 1857 were ones of monetary and industrial crises; the outbreak of the American War in 1861 was followed by a dearth of cotton and extreme depression in the textile industry; while the years 1866 and 1867 were again characterised by financial and industrial crises and failures, largely the result of speculation and over-expansion. The end of the American War was followed by a new period of expansion, particularly in the heavy industries and shipbuilding. Scotland, as a large-scale exporter of capital goods, was intimately concerned in the development then taking place in overseas countries. Improved means of transport resulted in the opening up of vast food-producing areas overseas, and the subsequent capital construction in these areas provided, at the same time, a market for the products of Scottish industries and an apparent gold mine for Scottish investors. Much of this investment was highly speculative and rash, and the industrial expansion which accompanied it excessive and unstable. The inevitable reaction came in 1873 when the boom was replaced by depression, to which a railway crisis in America and unsuccessful speculation in Australia contributed. The notorious City of Glasgow Bank failure in 1878, the result of fraud, added to the general depression which reached its nadir in 1879. The period from 1873 to 1896 is often referred to as 'the

Great Depression', but while prices fell throughout, the period in fact contained three depressions separated by two short spells of recovery. After 1879 conditions improved and recovery lasted until 1882; a second period of recovery started in 1886 and lasted until 1890. General recovery returned in the closing years of the century.

There is, naturally, a close parallel between the cycles of general industrial activity and the fluctuations experienced by the printing industry. The products of the industry inevitably bore part of the burden of reduced demand and spending during periods of unemployment. But printing is not directly tied to the capital industries, in which the fluctuations are greatest, and so it tended to suffer relatively less. Nor had it a large stake in the export market, but catered primarily for the home market, where demand was more stable. These factors tended generally to modify the swings. In addition, however, activity was influenced by events of direct and peculiar concern to printing. These sometimes modified the general trend, sometimes accentuated it.

Two major examples of particular events reacting on the general trend occurred early in the period. The repeal of the Stamp Duty in 1855 tended to increase employment in a period of extreme general depression, although only to a limited extent and for a very short time. In fact, the hopes of the trade regarding the effects of the repeal on employment were short-lived. Several cheap daily newspapers were started, particularly in Glasgow, although the provinces reported little increase because 'the publishers in London and Glasgow supply our booksellers with printed penny newspapers at a cheaper rate than what they can be done for here'.[1] Many of the new ventures were, however, short-lived, their discontinuance being attributed to the general depression of industry. The second event of particular importance to the industry was the repeal of the Paper Duty. This got off to a false start in 1860 when a Bill for repeal was passed by the House of Commons. Printing activity was largely suspended for some six

[1] Report from Dumfries Branch, June 1855.

months, pending the passing of the Bill by the Lords. The Lords, however, rejected the Bill, and the Duty was not finally repealed until the autumn of 1861. Again hopes were high and again these were disappointed. The immediate effect was a rapid multiplication of the number of dailies published, increases in size, and reductions in price. Fierce competition followed and the death-rate among newspapers was high; Edinburgh reported in 1863 that no fewer than 12 newspapers started during the last four years had been discontinued. The *Newspaper Press Directory* for the same year reported an increase of 41 in the number of newspapers published in the United Kingdom, while those published in Scotland totalled only 142, of which 9 were dailies, compared with 150 before the repeal of the Paper Duty. The keen competition of this period resulted in the extinction of many weeklies, unable to compete with cheap dailies. In provincial areas the local press suffered a similar fate, hastened by improved transport. The book-trade did not escape unscathed. Much of the increasing demand for reading matter was satisfied by new forms—magazines, periodicals and newspapers— while the Scottish book-trade suffered as a result of the growing tendency of publishing to gravitate towards London. In fact, in 1863 Edinburgh reported that many offices were kept going with work from London publishing houses.

The widespread depression of industry generally, as a result of the American War and the cotton famine, both contributed to and aggravated the situation which followed the repeal of the Paper Duty. Depression persisted until 1864 and returned again in 1866 and 1867. Because of the printing work resulting from the enlargement of the Electoral Rolls, following the extension of the franchise, and from a General Election, prosperity had returned to the industry by 1868, while the general depression lasted until the end of 1869. For the next few years boom conditions prevailed and the unemployment problem virtually disappeared. By the mid-70's, however, general depression had returned and was shared by the printing industry, although not until a slightly later date and then on a more modified scale. The City of Glasgow Bank failure in 1878 actually brought some temporary increase in employment to both Glasgow and Edinburgh. In 1879, however, trade was described as reaching its lowest ebb in living memory, the only comparable period being that prior to the repeal of the Paper Duty, when unemployment, although severe, was neither so widespread nor so lasting. Thereafter recovery was slow, and dullness persisted for another two years—in Glasgow longer, chiefly because of the large number attracted to the city in search of employment. In the following years the industry shared in the general fluctuations from depression to recovery and back to depression. In the closing years of the Association's half-century trade was good and employment regular.

The fluctuations and unrest of the last two decades of the nineteenth century were general and the causes various. In the case of the printing industry an additional factor was the introduction of machinery. The composing machine had been a constantly recurring feature of the period, but progress was slow and the threat to employment for long a distant one. By the last decade, however, the machine had become an accepted fact and was soon widely adopted. While the effects on employment were, on the whole, much less harmful than had been feared, there was inevitably some displacement of labour in the very short period.

II. THE ASSOCIATION

Slow but steady progress characterised the early years of the Association. In fact, with very few exceptions and these not general, the history of its hundred years is largely a chronicle of peaceful growth. Here the danger to the historian is that of boring the reader with a welter of dull facts. A turbulent period of disputes and strikes no doubt makes more exciting reading, but has harmful effects for both sides of industry; in terms of solid achievement more stands to the credit of steady, peaceful plodding. This certainly appears to have been the view of the founders of the Association. Their aim was strength through union, their purpose defensive—to protect the privileges of the profession and secure better pay and working conditions. In this the use of and need for the strike weapon were realistically recognised, but a determination to avoid disputes and seek a peaceful settlement of differences was frequently expressed and characterised the actions of the Association's early leaders. The complete absence of any major collisions with employers during the early life of the Association was most marked. During its first decade an article in the *Circular*, advocating an increase in benefits to members from the funds then accumulated, justified this on the grounds that no one could seriously expect the funds again to be threatened by a major dispute—a prematurely optimistic assumption, as the events of a few years later proved. The caution which marked the forward movements of the young Association was in sharp contrast to, and probably a reaction from, the aggressive and tyrannical methods imputed to the earlier national organisations. The events of the period 1836 to 1847 were still alive in the minds of many—particularly the tragic year 1847—and probably strengthened the determination to avoid the arbitrary methods, the large-scale closing of offices, and the lengthy and costly disputes, which had contributed to the breakdown of the earlier Associations. The motto was 'gang warily'.

The rules and policy of the Association were determined originally by biennial Delegate Meetings, but these were discontinued in 1864 on grounds of economy, and thereafter issues were decided by a vote of the whole membership, a method which, it was felt, gave the individual members a greater influence. A special Delegate Meeting was held in 1870 to consider particular questions of importance to the trade—chiefly the apprentice problem and the relief of tramps—and again in 1877, when the development of the Association as a friendly society was first considered. Thereafter regular Delegate Meetings were held every four years, with the exception of one lapse of six years from 1889 to 1895. In addition to these regular reviews of policy and rules, special meetings were held from time to time as urgent questions arose and when the majority of the members expressed a desire for them. Thus special meetings were held in 1878 and 1891, the former in connection with the introduction of the Sick Scheme, the latter the Superannuation Scheme. But on the whole the feeling was that a Delegate Meeting, while periodically necessary, was a much too expensive method of settling questions, where these could equally well be dealt with by the issue of voting papers.

At its formation the Association consisted of five Branches—Glasgow and Edinburgh, with Dumfries, Kilmarnock and Paisley. To these others were gradually added—Banff in 1853 and Dundee in 1854, while by 1855 Aberdeen, Arbroath, Cupar (Fife), Greenock and Perth also figured on the list. The question of missionary work to extend the Association naturally formed an important part of the business dealt with at biennial Delegate Meetings, and in 1858 a special campaign was launched. The Executive Council and the Branches co-operated in visiting areas not yet represented. In the following two years the number of Branches increased from fifteen to twenty-four. This particular phase of missionary zeal extended also to Edinburgh, where the Society was evidently still suffering from the effects of the 1847 lock-out. Only one third of the trade were Society members, but in the two months following a meeting addressed by a deputation from the Executive Council, 100 names were added to the membership. As part of this campaign of extension efforts were made to collect statistics of the trade, and although this appears to have been done annually from about 1860, and passing references were made from time to time to the changes during a year, it was not until 1873 that they were published in the annual reports.

The missionary effort continued, with varying degrees of intensity, throughout the period. Mention was again made of special campaigns in 1875 and 1882, when circulars were sent to Branch Secretaries urging their support. In 1893 a committee was formed by the Executive Council to aid in missionary work, and in the following years visits to Branches were made with the object of helping to strengthen them and to bring in non-members. The Branches, too, played an active part in organising the outlying districts. As a result new Branches were added from time to time, although naturally not at the spectacular rate of the earlier years. By the end of its first fifty years the Association embraced thirty Branches, covering a total membership of 3,775.

The work of the Association was carried out by a Central Board as Executive Council, consisting of thirteen members. The location of the Board was decided every two years—until 1864 by the Delegate Meetings, and thereafter by a vote of the members. The Board, in fact, remained in Glasgow, although suggestions that it should be located in the main centres in rotation cropped up occasionally during the early years. Originally the members were appointed by and from the Glasgow Society, but the basis of representation was widened by the decision of a Delegate Meeting in 1877 that every Branch with over 200 members be allowed two representatives. Only the Edinburgh Branch accepted, however, both Aberdeen and Dundee intimating that they would not have the Board located in their city, nor did they wish to be represented on it. The right was exercised by Aberdeen between 1886 and 1888, when the two representatives were withdrawn on account of the distance they had to travel and the expense. In 1895 attempts were again made towards increased representation, Edinburgh's membership being increased to four, while Dundee provided two members. It was not until 1900 that Aberdeen again exercised its right to elect two members.

Apart from an initial ruling regarding hours of labour and payment for overtime, the Association, during the first decade of its existence, did not launch any general forward movement. Rather was it concerned with extending and consolidating its position through missionary work, with the gradual amassing of information concerning the state of the trade, and with the checking of further encroachments on its fundamental principles. Conditions naturally varied widely in different parts of the country, and the securing of minimum standards for members of the Association was a major aim. But here the policy adopted was flexible and the attitude realistic. Support was given to Branches in their efforts to protect their privileges or improve their conditions, but no attempt was made to force a rigid policy of action on a Branch. In the case of the apprentice question, for instance, while a maximum ratio was adopted, it was left to the Branches to fix their own ratio within this, and where the existing numbers were substantially in excess, policy was usually aimed at preventing further deterioration and seeking agreement with employers not to take on any more until the ratio was the permitted one.

Not until 1863 was a general movement for increased wages in the provinces inaugurated. For the next ten years or so advances were gradually obtained throughout the whole Association, in some cases with little or no opposition, in others only after a struggle. The disputes in the main were slight and local in character. In relatively few cases were offices closed. A few local disputes also occurred at this time over the apprentice question, which was gradually being more actively grappled with. In general, the second decade may be described as one of increasing activity and growing confidence. By 1870 the question of shorter hours was taken up, and in the next two years, with one exception, all the Branches reported a forward movement.

The acute depression of the 80's was essentially a defensive period for the trade unions, and in many industries much of the ground gained earlier had to be given up. In this respect the Association fared relatively well. A few local disputes occurred over attempts to increase hours or pay less than the recognised wage, but such encroachments were in general successfully resisted. With the return of more prosperous times a new advance movement was in-

augurated in 1891, and during the following years spread
throughout the Branches. In some cases the increase in
wage was accompanied by a reduction in hours. Attempts
were made to secure greater uniformity throughout the
Association. The close of the century brought a further
general forward movement in wages, while the Association's Jubilee was marked by a renewed campaign for the
reduction of hours.

The peaceful relations which prevailed during the most
of its first twenty years enabled the Association to grow in
financial as well as numerical strength. By 1866 the funds
exceeded £1,000, and by the end of 1871 totalled over
£1,500. The following year, however, brought the first,
and only, major test. As was the case with the Northern
District of the National Association, again the challenge
came from Edinburgh, where a strike over the reduction
of hours involved between 700 and 800 men, and lasted
for three months.[1] The total expenditure incurred was
over £5,300. A special levy was imposed on members,
while the balance was received in the form of gifts and
loans from other Societies in the printing and other trades.
The Association ended 1872 with a deficit of £860. Ironic-
ally, while the Edinburgh strike was pending, a conference
of representatives from Aberdeen, Dundee, Edinburgh
and Glasgow Branches was held to consider revision of
the rules of the Association. One decision of this conference was that the Association should aim at a minimum
consolidated fund of £3,000, to achieve which the rate of
contribution was doubled.

Unlike the events of 1847, the blow of 1872 was not a
fatal one, but there followed an inevitable period of relative
inactivity while the weakened Association recovered its
strength. By the end of 1875, however, the debts had all
been cleared and a balance of £400 remained. The following year brought appeals from various sources for a return
to a more active policy. Unrest appeared to be simmering
throughout the Branches, and the conviction gained
ground that a Delegate Meeting was long overdue. Since

[1] See Chapter 10.

the last meeting in 1870, and particularly since the
Edinburgh strike, dissatisfaction with the policy of and control over the Central Board had grown, and matters were
brought to a height by the Board's decision to discontinue
payment of the annual grant of £12 to the *Circular*, the
Scottish trade journal founded and managed by the Edinburgh Society. The Edinburgh Branch deducted the sum
from the funds due to the Association, and the Board
retaliated by refusing to grant a receipt for payment made.
The Board adopted delaying tactics towards increasing
appeals for a Delegate Meeting, and even attempted, on
the grounds of non-payment of subscription, to exclude
Edinburgh from the meeting which was finally held in
August 1877. A vote of the members decided against this,
but the first decision of the meeting was to extract a pledge
from Edinburgh that the balance due would be paid
immediately, as a condition of allowing the Branch's
delegates to take part in the proceedings. Thereafter, the
Circular question was, surprisingly enough, disposed of
without discussion and the grant renewed.

While the immediate pretext of the 1877 Meeting thus
proved a damp squib, the real business transacted by the
delegates concerned an issue of far greater significance,
namely, the nature and function of the Association itself. For
some time the feeling had been growing throughout the
membership that the time had come for a new departure.
The need for new services of a provident nature had found
expression in the formation of special funds by individual
Branches, and the proposal now considered was that such
services should be provided by the Association for the general membership. As the schemes eventually adopted will
be the subject of more detailed study in a subsequent chapter it will suffice to say here that, as a result of the decisions
of various Delegate Meetings between the years 1877 and
1891, the Association emerged as a full-scale provident
society, providing sick and funeral benefits, unemployment allowances, and superannuation. The pattern of development which emerges from this is typical of the craft
unions. The Association's purpose at the outset was prim-

arily defensive, although some assistance was granted to Branches for the relief of tramps, by a refunding of part of their subscriptions where calls on their funds for this purpose were excessive. Only after twenty-five years of existence as a defensive organisation did it begin to add the functions of a friendly society, and only relinquished these to government agencies as and when the dictates of the welfare state demanded.

After recovery from the cost of the Edinburgh strike of 1872, the financial history of the Association was an almost unbroken record of steady advance; its stability was never again seriously threatened. By 1887 the Protective Fund had passed the £3,000 target set by the Rules Committee of 1872, while at the same date the total funds exceeded £4,000. The new benevolent functions assumed by the Association brought new financial responsibilities, but while the particular funds of the various schemes suffered fluctuating fortunes, and at times required to borrow from the Protective Fund, the general policy followed was to make each separate fund financially sound. By the end of the first fifty years the total at the credit of the Association was £12,264, of which £4,729 was due to the Protective Fund.

In this introductory chapter the object has been to survey very briefly the broad trends of development, both in the industry and in the Association during the fifty-year period. Particular aspects of the Association's history will be taken up and dealt with in more detail in subsequent chapters. It is sufficient here to mention that in addition to progress achieved in improving wages, hours and conditions of work, the Association was concerned during this period with the problems of the tramping system, eventually replaced by the scheme of unemployment benefits, the apprentice question, which was a constantly recurring theme throughout, and the appearance of two new factors —the machine and the female compositor.

CHAPTER SIX

ADVANCE MOVEMENTS—HOURS
AND WAGES

I. General Advances

The complexity of any detailed study of wage movements in the printing industry, over such a long period and covering such a wide area as that embraced by the Association, makes some broad generalisations both necessary and inevitable. It must be said at the outset that the aim here is to trace the general progress over the period in outline, filling in only the milestones of that progress, and to avoid the mere tabulation of scales and rates. The task may be simplified by considering the Association as divided into two main areas; firstly, Glasgow and Edinburgh, to whose rates a number of Branches have come to conform, by reason either of their size or their proximity; and, secondly, the provinces. Further, the method of payment falls into two categories—the weekly rate or 'stab, and the price or piece scale. In the case of the provinces and of Glasgow it is the former which is of most concern, while the piece system is of particular and peculiar importance to Edinburgh. Finally, the level of wages is different in the two main sections of the industry —the newspaper section and the book and jobbing section.

Reference has already been made in the previous chapter to the forward movements which occurred during this period. In fact the fifty years can be roughly divided into six stages or periods: (1) a period of little change lasting throughout most of the first decade; (2) a general forward movement starting in 1862; (3) a further wage movement, merging into an hours movement, starting in 1870 and reaching its peak with the Edinburgh strike of 1872;

(4) a period of general quiet lasting until 1891, with the exception of limited advances in a few of the larger Branches in the late 70's; (5) an advance movement in the early 90's; (6) a campaign for the reduction of hours, launched in 1901.

In the matter of wages, the rule adopted by the Association at its formation in 1853 was that of the earlier General Association, that the minimum wage for Glasgow and Edinburgh be 25/– per week, and for the provinces 20/–. For ten years thereafter this remained the ruling wage. Indeed, in some of the country Branches the rate remained below the stipulated 20/–, in spite of the efforts of the Association to secure uniformity. In Edinburgh, where the piece rate predominated, the scale remained that of the famous 1805 Interlocutor. As has been already noted, the Association moved cautiously during the early years. Thus, the Delegate Meeting of 1854, dealing with a proposition to raise wages in the provinces 'thought it advisable, seeing that they had recommended the reduction of the hours of labour, extra pay for night work, and the probability of the abolition of the taxes on knowledge, to delay in the meantime'. Again in 1858, when a proposition was submitted that wages in the provinces be 22/– per week, the Delegates decided that the Branches should do all in their power to secure this, but were opposed to arbitrary action to enforce it. Indeed, the main achievement of this period was the stamping out of a practice which had grown in Edinburgh out of the weak and disorganised conditions following 1847, namely, that of paying a man on the 'stab system a little more than the recognised minimum, in return for which his hours were at the pleasure of the employer. The success of the Edinburgh Society in dealing with this question is recorded in the first report of the Association. The only other wage activity concerned the revision of newspaper scales in Edinburgh and Glasgow, following the repeal of the Stamp Duty in 1855. This and the subsequent repeal of the Paper Duty in 1861 brought the question of payment for those employed on daily papers to the forefront. Again, in Glasgow payment was mainly by time rates of 6½d per hour or 32/6 per week, while in Edinburgh a piece rate of 6½d per 1,000 ens prevailed. This higher rate of payment, however, was considered inadequate in view not only of the inconvenience and strain of constant night work, but also the unceasing pressure of work on dailies. The need to increase pay and reduce hours of work in this section was widely discussed in the following years, and indicated what was to be the subsequent trend of development.

The second stage of the wage history started in 1862, a year which must be regarded as an important milestone in the progress of the Association. It marked the start of the first general forward movement, a movement which continued over the following five or six years, and spread throughout the entire Association. The movement started in Edinburgh, but Glasgow quickly followed, and in a series of moves between 1862 and 1867 the two cities obtained similar advances in 'stab and piece rates in all sections of the industry. Thus the 'stab rate for book and jobbing became 27/6, the piece rate 5½d per 1,000, while in the newspaper section the 'stab wage for morning dailies was 35/–, for evening dailies 30/–, and the respective piece rates 7d and 6d per 1,000.[1] The final stage of the movement in Edinburgh, in 1866, was completed only after a short, sharp struggle and after some two-thirds of the journeymen had given notice. During the same period a general advance was secured in the provinces, and by 1869 the original claim of a 22/– minimum had been exceeded in many areas. Here the advance was most marked in the area around Glasgow, the 'stab rate being as high as 25/– in Airdrie, Dumbarton, Greenock, Hamilton and Paisley.

The third stage of development, which followed hard on the heels of the second, was a short one, being confined almost entirely to the three years from 1870 to 1872, but it was a period of intense activity and of considerable

[1] While rates were practically uniform in the two cities, the piece scale in Edinburgh was a more complicated one. Also, there being no evening dailies in Edinburgh, the rates here apply only to Glasgow.

importance in the history of the Association. The course of events in Edinburgh and Glasgow differed sufficiently to justify separate consideration here. Glasgow started the movement by securing an advance for the daily newsmen in 1870, followed the next year by a similar advance for other sections. Attention was then turned on the question of hours, in which Edinburgh had given a lead. This was the first move in this direction since 1854, when a Delegate Meeting had decreed that the hours be 10 per day, with payment of 3d per hour for overtime between 9 p.m. and 6 a.m. In 1872 Glasgow joined in the general movement for a 9-hour day. The original claim was for a 51-hour week, but the agreement eventually reached granted this only to morning dailies, while the other sections were granted a reduction to 54 hours, with corresponding adjustments to piece rates. The day's work was to finish not later than 6 p.m., and overtime was to be paid at the rate of 1/– per hour for morning dailies, and 10d per hour in all other departments. The outcome of this movement in the book and jobbing section was a 'stab wage of 30/– and a piece rate of 6¾d per 1,000, for a 54-hour week. The newspaper section had received a corresponding advance in wages, with a greater reduction in hours. The relative position of this section was further improved in 1874, when wages were again increased, bringing the rate for morning dailies to £2 for a 51-hour week, and that for evening dailies to 34/– for a 54-hour week.

In Edinburgh attention was concentrated on reducing hours rather than increasing wages. Here hours had been reduced to 57 per week in 1865, and in 1871 the Society presented a memorial for a reduction to 51. A reduction to 54 was accepted temporarily, with an increase of ½d per 1,000 on piece rates. The hours of work were from 8.20 a.m. to 7 p.m., closing time on Saturday being 2 p.m. Again the newspaper section secured a relative advantage, hours for night work being reduced to 48, and for day work to 51. In 1872 the attempt to secure a 51-hour week for the other sections, with an increase of ½d per 1,000, was renewed with a claim for increased pay for overtime.

The outcome of this was the strike, which provided the first and only major test of the Association's strength.[1] Some 750 men were involved and the dispute lasted for fully three months. It was defeated by the use of non-union men, chiefly from England, apprentices and female compositors. In the end the men accepted the employers' offer to increase the 'stab wage and the overtime rate. The position in the book and jobbing section was thus less favourable than in Glasgow, with a 'stab wage of 30/– and a piece rate of 6d per 1,000 for a 54-hour week. In the newspaper section the reduction in hours was greater, but the increase in pay less, only one advance of $\frac{1}{2}$d per 1,000 being secured compared with the advance of 5/– per week secured for morning dailies in Glasgow.

The provinces shared in the wage movement of 1870, and by 1871 fully half of the Branches had secured an advance. Here too the wage movement merged into an hours movement, and by the end of 1872 the Annual Report of the Association showed that 'at no period . . . since its formation in 1853 has there been such a general and marked upward progress'. Only one Branch, Alloa, still operated a 60-hour week, while in Aberdeen, Dumbarton, Dundee and Perth a reduction to 51 hours had been secured. For the remainder, hours varied between 54 and 56. Some 18 provincial Branches had secured an increase in wages, including Greenock which had secured the Glasgow 'stab rate of 30/–.

The activity which had characterised the years from 1862 to 1872 was in marked contrast to the subsequent period, in which little change was the keynote. For nearly twenty years, with one slight interruption, policy was concerned with consolidating and defending the gains already made. At the beginning of this period the dullness of trade, combined with the weakened financial position of the Association as a result of the Edinburgh strike, made any other policy impossible. In 1877, however, a short forward movement occurred, affecting Glasgow, Edinburgh and a few of the large Branches. As a result of this

[1] See Chapter 10.

Glasgow gained a further advantage over Edinburgh, securing a 'stab rate of 32/6. Edinburgh's claim for an increase of $\frac{1}{2}$d per 1,000 on all rates in the book section was only partly successful. The position in the newspaper section in Edinburgh was slightly improved by the guarantee of 5$\frac{1}{2}$ hours composition each night, and of 33 hours per week to day hands, the former at 1/1 per hour, the latter at 10d. At this time, however, the conditions of trade were against any general forward movement. In many industries some of the ground gained by organised labour had to be yielded and wage cuts accepted. The fact that the Association maintained wage rates and hours during this period was in itself an advance, although it did not escape the toll of unemployment. A few isolated cases of attempts to increase hours or pay less than the recognised wage were reported and dealt with, usually successfully, but there were no concerted or major attempts at encroachment.

The next stage of development concerns the forward movement started in 1891. Glasgow took the lead and the outcome, after some minor disputes, was a 'stab wage of 34/– for a 52$\frac{1}{2}$-hour week. Edinburgh followed, securing a 'stab wage of 32/– for a 52$\frac{1}{2}$-hour week, and a rise of $\frac{1}{4}$d per 1,000. The small rise in the piece rate meant a further deterioration in the relative position of the Edinburgh piece-worker, particularly in offices where a mixed 'stab and piece system was worked. The provinces again shared in this forward movement, particularly the larger Branches, most of whom obtained both an increase in wages and a reduction in hours. Of these, both Greenock and Paisley secured the Glasgow rate of 34/– for a 52$\frac{1}{2}$-hour week. The movement in the provinces continued throughout most of the decade. In 1895, as a result of a decision of the Delegate Meeting, the Branches were circularised urging their co-operation in an effort to secure greater uniformity throughout the Association, and the closing years of the century saw a further wave of peaceful advances in both wages and hours.

The last stage in the fifty years' development, a movement for the further reduction of hours, was launched in 1901. The question of an eight-hour day had been occupying the attention of a growing number of industries since about 1880. While expressing itself in favour of this movement, particularly as one possible solution to the problem of surplus labour created by the introduction of machinery, the Association took the view that, until the fifty-one hour week became universal in the printing industry, any movement for a forty-eight hour week would be premature and inadvisable. This was one of the reasons given by the Association for its rejection in 1888 of an invitation from the Glasgow Trades Council and the Amalgamated Society of Lithographic Printers to co-operate with them in such a movement. The other reason, however, was that this movement aimed at an appeal to Parliament to legislate on the question of hours, a policy to which the Association was opposed. It was contrary to trade union principles, and opened the door to the regulation of wages by Parliament, perhaps in favour of the employers. In 1901, however, a general movement for the reduction of hours was started. Glasgow endeavoured to secure a 48-hour week, but eventually accepted a reduction to 50, with $48\frac{1}{2}$ hours for night shifts, and a five per cent increase in piece rates. Other Branches followed, and by the end of the period more than half the membership enjoyed a 50-hour week, while in one Branch, Ardrossan, hours had been reduced to $49\frac{1}{2}$. Here, however, Edinburgh fell behind, the hours remaining at $52\frac{1}{2}$ per week at the end of 1902.

Finally, no résumé of the fifty-year period would be complete without mention of the arrival of the composing machine. Although the subject of experiment and discussion throughout most of the period, in Scotland it only became a factor to be reckoned with during the last decade, when the Linotype invaded offices in practically all parts of the Association, affecting first of all the newspaper section, but soon spreading to the book department. The Association was represented at Delegate Meetings called by the Provincial Typographical Association at Sheffield in 1893 and Manchester in 1897, and reported that Scotland

was not falling behind in the matter of conditions and
pay for the operators of these machines. The 'stab rate of
pay was at first paid, then the task of drawing up scales
was undertaken by the various Branches. Eventually the
machines were worked mainly on piece rates, the hours of
work were generally shorter than for hand compositors,
and the average earnings higher. Thus the Glasgow scale,
finally approved in 1898 after several years of negotiations,
secured a rate of $3\frac{1}{8}$d per 1,000 for morning dailies, and
$2\frac{5}{8}$d per 1,000 for evening papers, hours being reduced to
48 for day work and 42 for night work. Edinburgh was
not concerned in this question until much later, the Linotypes being introduced at first only into newspaper offices,
which were closed to the Association.[1] By the end of the
period, however, the machines had begun to invade the
book offices, and steps were being taken to draw up a
special scale. In the provinces development was on similar
lines, but in some cases the machines were worked on a
'stab wage. In these cases, the rate fixed was in advance of
the recognised rate of the Branch, and the hours shorter.
Thus, in 1898 Dundee secured approval to operate Linotypes at a rate of 45/– for night work and 37/– for day
work, the hours being 48 per week.

II. Comparative Advances

The outcome of the various movements described in the
previous section may be briefly summarised. Over the fifty
years wages advanced on an average by 8/9 per week,
while hours were reduced by about ten per week. The increase obtained by Glasgow was 9/–, compared with 7/–
in Edinburgh. In the provinces the increases varied from
14/– in the case of a few Branches near Glasgow, such as
Greenock and Paisley, to 5/– in one or two smaller
Branches. The position of the piece-worker was relatively
less favourable, chiefly due to the fact that the majority of

---

[1] *Scotsman*—closed in 1872 as a result of a dispute over the division of
work. *Evening News*—closed in 1877 as a result of refusal to pay guarantee
for waiting time.

those on piece work were to be found in the Edinburgh book houses, and there the mixed system of payment tended to depress their earnings. The wage level of the newspaper section remained above that of book and jobbing, the difference being slightly less at the end of the fifty years. In Glasgow the wage rate for morning dailies increased by 7/6, compared with the increase of 9/– on the general 'stab rate. In this section, in fact, no advance in wages had been secured since 1874, although a greater reduction in hours of work had been secured. Also, this was the one department most immediately and directly affected by the introduction towards the end of the period, of composing machines, for which earnings tended to be higher.

Only a very inadequate picture of progress can emerge, however, from a review of changes in money wage rates alone, or even in earnings. In endeavouring to secure a more complete picture, some indication of the relation of such wage changes to the cost of living and to the changes which occurred in other industries is necessary and relevant. Lack of information about the early part of this period, particularly for Scotland, makes any detailed or exact statistical comparisons impossible. Some relevant facts are revealed in the records of the Association and the industry, however, and these, along with such official statistics as exist, are sufficient to indicate the broad trends of progress in this respect.

References to changes in the cost of living are made in most of the early wage memorials. The famous Edinburgh memorial of 1803 referred to this in general terms.[1] According to this document the rise in the cost of necessities over the previous fifty years had been between a third and a half. Meanwhile the pay of printers had varied little. The rate in 1774 was 3d per 1,000, rising to $3\frac{1}{2}$d by about 1780, and apart from a temporary rise to 4d in the book trade in 1792, remained at $3\frac{1}{2}$d until 1805. The memorial also gave examples of average weekly earnings over the period, these being estimated at 14/2 in 1774, 19/8 in 1792, 18/5 in 1802, and 17/11$\frac{1}{2}$ in 1803. The request for

[1] See page 22.

an increase to 4½d per 1,000 was therefore justified on the grounds of the rise in the cost of living. As a result of this increase average earnings were estimated to rise to 20/3.[1] Nearly fifty years later, in 1862, an Edinburgh memorial again refers to the increased cost of rent, food and clothing, rent having risen in many cases by as much as twenty-five per cent. Subsequent references from time to time to the position of the Edinburgh printers relative to the cost of living concluded that their position was probably less favourable than it had been some thirty years earlier. Earnings in the Edinburgh book trade were, of course, affected by the mixed system of payment and the large numbers on piece-work. Further, it was admitted that conditions of work and hours of labour had vastly improved.

In fact, prices generally rose throughout the 1850's and 60's, and sometimes fairly sharply, as during the Crimean War in the 50's. It has been concluded that, in general, increases in money wages at this period were to a large extent offset by rising prices.[2] It seems likely that this was particularly true of the printing industry, since no forward movement occurred until 1862. In the 1870's, however, prices fell rapidly, while in the printing industry no reduction in wage rates was inflicted. Thus there would be a rise in real wages at this period for those who remained in employment. Again, from 1880 until about 1896 the cost of living fell, with a few interruptions, and real wages rose.[3] Once more unemployment was an important factor, particularly in the early part of that period, but the advances of the 90's represented real gains. The last few years of the nineteenth and the beginning of the twentieth century were marked by an upward movement of prices, and during this period the industry did not secure any general advance in wages, although hours were reduced. Thus, in the matter of wages alone relative to the cost of living, the position of the Association by 1902 was prob-

[1] Webb, S., *Labour in the Longest Reign*.
[2] G. H. Wood, 'Real Wages and the Standard of Comfort since 1850', *Statistical Journal*, 1909.
[3] A. L. Bowley, *Wages and Income in the United Kingdom Since* 1860.

ably rather less favourable than in the mid 1890's, but considerably more favourable than in 1853.

The wage memorials also contained a few references to the position of the printers relative to workers in other industries. Thus in 1803 it was noted that during the previous twenty or thirty years the wages of skilled and unskilled labour had risen 'very considerably', and the increase sought was regarded 'as necessary to place them in a relative level with other workmen'. In 1862 reference was made to the increases in the wages of other skilled workers throughout the country during the last few decades. In Edinburgh alone, it was claimed that the increase had been between 15 and 20 per cent, and in some cases as high as 25 to 30 per cent. Examples were quoted of the wages of joiners and masons. The former had risen from 13/– in 1826 to 22/– in 1861. Masons were receiving 5½d per hour, or 27/6 for a 60-hour week, which was fully 50 per cent more than the rate of thirty years earlier. Again in 1876, the Glasgow memorial for a 'stab wage of 32/6 for a 54-hour week noted that the building trades were receiving 9d, 9½d and 10d per hour. At the same time it was pointed out that printers had once been foremost in the matter of wages, and that this advance would help to reduce the gap between printing and other industries. About the same period, Cupar (Fife) reported difficulties experienced by one office in obtaining apprentices, and attributed this to the fact that the prospect of earning 25/– per week, after a seven years' apprenticeship, had little attraction in view of the 8d, 9d and 1/– per hour earned in other trades.

In fact, one of the notable features of wages in the printing industry is their relative stability over fairly long periods. There was also a tendency, at least in the early period, to lag a little behind other industries in a period of general advances. Thus, while wages in general were increasing in the 1850's and 60's, the printers did not secure any advance until 1862. It seems reasonable to assume that their relative position at this time did deteriorate. On the other hand, the stability of wages in the industry was an advantage in a period of falling prices, and the ability to maintain wage rates when other industries were forced to accept cuts, as in the late 70's and the 80's, improved their relative position. Thus, by the time of the Wage Census in 1886 the position of printers was reasonably comparable with that of other skilled trades. The rate in Glasgow was 32/6, in Edinburgh 30/–. At the same time, the rate for masons, on summer hours, was 29/9 in both Glasgow and Edinburgh, while engineering fitters in Glasgow were paid 27/6. From 1894 onwards the wage rates of the industry can be compared with rates in these two skilled trades as published by the Labour Department of the Board of Trade. Taking the case of Glasgow only, for simplicity and example, by 1894 the rate for compositors was 34/– for book and jobbing, and 40/– for morning dailies. Compared with this, the rate for masons was 36/2, and for engineering fitters 30/4$\frac{1}{2}$. Between 1894 and 1902 wage rates remained the same in all sections of the printing industry, while those of masons increased to 40/4$\frac{1}{2}$ and engineering fitters to 36/–. From this it would appear that, by the end of the fifty years, in a period of rising prices, the industry was again tending to lag behind other skilled industries in the matter of wages. The rate for morning dailies appears comparable, but in fact it had always enjoyed a relatively higher rate, involving as it did night work, and by 1902 masons, for a fifty-one hour week of day working, were earning slightly more.

III. Piece and 'Stab—The Edinburgh System

The question of the relative merits of the piece and time systems of payment was not one of active concern to the industry, apart from the special case of Edinburgh, and was not one with which the Association was at any time required to deal. That the time method was preferred, there seems little doubt. Apart from the traditional argument that piece rates tended to depress average earnings, and the attraction of security of employment under the 'stab system, the complexity of the piece-scale required by the industry gave ample scope for anomalies and disputes over interpretation—a fact particularly demonstrated by the complicated Edinburgh scales. Further, the system of payment 'per 1,000 ens' rather than according to the time and labour involved, made no distinction between 'fat' and 'lean' work, thus making possible abuses in the distribution of work. But while the 'stab rate was the general rule outside Edinburgh, there was little evidence of active opposition to the piece system. Thus in 1878 it was reported that *The Glasgow Herald* had decided to change over to the piece system, and that the Glasgow Branch had no objections to this since the employers had agreed to pay the recognised rates. Nevertheless, in the prevalence and persistence of the piece system, Edinburgh was an exception to the general trend. The most likely explanation of this which suggests itself is that it was a consequence of the 1805 Interlocutor. The Court of Session's decision seems to have given the Scale a sanctity which it lacked in other areas.

The outstanding feature of the Edinburgh book houses, however, was not simply the prevalence of a piece system, but the existence of a peculiar and pernicious system whereby both piece and 'stab rates were paid in the same establishment—i.e., the mixed system to which passing reference has already been made. This practice appears to have originated early in the nineteenth century, and there is some evidence to support the view that it, too, was a consequence of the Interlocutor. Some of the charges in this Scale were too high, and the employers sought to avoid them by the introduction of a number of men on an established wage basis, by whom the highest priced work was executed. An attempt to mitigate the effects of this aspect of the Scale was made in 1866, when some reductions were offered in return for an increase in the rate for common type. The mixed system, however, became firmly established in the Edinburgh Branch, and prevailed throughout the entire fifty-year period here considered. Indeed, only during the last few years of the period did the Branch begin active attempts to end it, and no success in this direction could be reported by 1902. Further, the system was confined solely to Edinburgh, although a brief reference was made very early in the life of the Association to the ending of it in one office in Aberdeen.

The chief evil of this mixed system was the unfair division of fat and lean which it fostered. The most remunerative work was given as far as possible to the 'stab men, and the poorest to the linemen. In consequence, the work performed by the 'stab men, calculated at piece rates, was worth more than the 'stab wage, while that done by the linemen gave an average wage considerably below the 'stab rate. As a result of this system, favouritism in the distribution of work became a constant source of grievance, and feelings between the two sections were bitter. The 'stab man was, in fact, obliged to 'earn' more than his wage, and suggestions of unfair practices and cheating of the lineman to secure this end were not uncommon or without foundation. Also, when trade was slack, efforts were made to keep the 'stab men fully employed at the expense of the linemen. The position of the latter was made worse by the fact that preferential treatment in the distribution of work was also given to apprentices, and, after 1872, to female compositors. Further, the system provided a strong incentive to employers to increase the number of apprentices, these generally being employed on the simplest work, which was often also the best paid work, in return for a relatively small rate of pay.

The effect of the system was to depress the average earnings of the majority of compositors in the Edinburgh book houses considerably below the level of the recognised 'stab wage. A few examples over the period illustrate this. Prior to the advance of 1862, when a 'stab wage of 25/- was enjoyed by some 70 compositors in book houses, the remaining 260 earned an average of 15/2 per week. This was actually less than the wage secured by the Interlocutor.[1] Again, in 1875 the 'stab man was virtually working for 4½d per 1,000, while the lineman was prevented from

[1] See page 70.

accepting less than 6d. In 1877 it was reported that, in one book house, 'Good average compositors, working a 54-hour week, can scarcely reach the modest sum of £1 per week'. And, at the time of the advance in 1891, the average wage for a good man under the piece system was estimated at 24/–, while the 'stab worker enjoyed 32/– per week.

The evil consequences of the mixed system formed a recurring topic of letters and articles throughout the period, and the remedies proposed were many and varied. Some advocated a scrapping of the complicated Interlocutor Scale and a greater levelling of charges. Others argued that such a process would make the position of the linemen worse, as it would deny them what little fat they occasionally got under the existing system. To many the only possible solution was the abolition of the piece system and the universal adoption of a time wage. Finally, it was suggested that a necessary first step towards this was the abolition of the mixed system, without any decision on the relative merits of each method of payment by itself.

The Society was slow to make a move in this question, and the extent to which the mixed system became an established practice owed more than a little to the fact that it was accepted apparently without protest. Thus, in 1869 a sub-committee set up by the Branch to consider the question of abolishing piece-work, reported that the general feeling of the membership was to leave well alone, and their unanimous decision was 'that it was inexpedient and impolitic to interfere with the existing mode of working in Edinburgh printing offices'. It was not until 1898 that any active attempts were made to remedy the situation. Then the policy adopted was to seek the complete abolition of piece-work, and a memorial to this effect was presented to the employers, with a proposal for a uniform time rate of 7½d per hour. The employers replied that they could not accept such a revolutionary proposal, but were willing to discuss the grievances of the present system. No progress was achieved, however, and the matter was dropped, partly as a result of the apathy of the Branch members. The Society returned to the attack in 1901. This time it was urged that, while the substitution of time for piece payment was the ultimate aim desired, more hope of success lay in a less drastic policy. Thus a memorial was presented to the employers requesting that steps be taken to abolish the mixed system, each employer being asked to choose a time or piece system, but one method of payment to apply to all in any one establishment. To this the employers again replied in the negative, but promised to remedy grievances about favouritism and the unfair distribution of copy, if supplied with concrete evidence of particular cases. Again the matter was dropped, not surprisingly, through the failure of the Branch to produce the necessary evidence. But thereafter some improvement was reported in the conditions of the linemen, which suggested that the attempt to secure a remedy, although unsuccessful, had not been entirely useless.

CHAPTER SEVEN

PROVIDENT SCHEMES

I. The Tramping System and Unemployment Relief

Perhaps the most important of all the provident schemes is that concerned with the relief of unemployment. The tramping system of relief was an established feature of the industry long before the formation of the Association. Indeed it might be said that by the 1850's the beginning of the end of this system was in sight. It was a well organised and widespread method of relief, and evidently had a long history in printing and other crafts, although its origin is obscure.[1] On this, an article in the *Circular* of July 1862 states: 'Tramping is an ancient institution. It existed long before the introduction of the art of printing, and was frequently resorted to by scholars and men of genius, for whose abilities and learning society in those days presented an insufficient demand ... but tramping, as a recognised institution, has descended to, and become part and parcel of the approved benevolent agencies of, the industrial orders.' In an earlier period it was regarded primarily as a method of relieving strike funds and so strengthening the bargaining power of labour. Thus we find that cards issued to compositors on strike, coloured cards, carried with them the right to double the normal amount of relief.[2] By the nineteenth century, however, the system was regarded mainly as a method of relieving the unemployed, and the discussion which raged around it during the first twenty or thirty

[1] E. J. Hobsbaum, 'The Tramping Artisan', *Economic History Review*, 1951, Vol. III, No. 3.
[2] See Rule 14 of the Scottish General Typographical Association, Appendix 1.

years of the Association's existence emphasised this. As
has been already noted, the main justification for it was
the belief that it was necessary to provide some support for
the surplus labour force and keep it moving, to prevent it
competing for the limited work available at less than the
recognised wage. That such a system was a central feature
of the early Typographical Societies is illustrated by the
Articles and Regulations of the Glasgow Society of 1817.[1]
Indeed, during the period of the Combination Laws it
provided the main function of and justification for these
Societies. But the heavy unemployment during the first
half of the nineteenth century, particularly the hungry
forties, put a severe strain on the system and gave rise to
general dissatisfaction with and criticism of it, which culminated in its abolition by the Association in 1877. As
early as the 1830's agitation against it was started by the
London Society of Compositors, and, as already noted, the
premature National Association endeavoured to replace it
with a scheme of unemployment relief in 1842. The system was reinstated, however, on the breakdown of this
Association, and incorporated in the present Scottish
Association in 1853.

The early years of the Association saw growing attention given to the question of tramping and its evils. The
system evidently produced a number of 'characters', reg-
ulars who toured the country, nothing farther from their
thoughts than work. Thus in 1856 the Banff Branch reported: 'It is to be feared that many of these who take to
the road do so, not because they have no work to do, but
because they have no will to do it.' References appeared
from time to time to particular cases of abuse of the system
by the presentation of cards containing false entries. The
'flying brethren', as the Alloa Branch called them, not infrequently found an outlet for their talents in the faking of
cards. The evils of the system formed the topic of articles
and correspondence in the *Circular*, and repeated complaints were made by several of the smaller Branches of
the drain on their funds through relieving tramps.

[1] See page 25.

The subject was first seriously considered by the Association at a Delegate Meeting in 1860, on the initiative of the Glasgow Branch. In a lengthy and eloquent statement Mr John H. Cooper put forward the case for some amendment of the system. The attitude towards tramping expressed here appears to have been typical of this period, similar views emerging from most articles on the subject. The plight of the unemployed was fully recognised and the need to give them some means of support acknowledged. The latter course was justified partly on benevolent grounds, but partly also on the aforementioned economic grounds—the need to prevent the unemployed undercutting the labour market. Growing attention was given, however, to the large proportion of rascals among the tramps, to the iniquity of the indiscriminate provision of relief, by those in employment, to all cases whether deserving or not, and to the inevitably demoralising effect of such a method of providing relief for those unfortunate enough to be without employment. 'When a man once acquires the habits of the road, he is compelled, through force of circumstances, to adopt it as his calling.'[1] By 1860 several areas in England and Ireland were already operating schemes of home relief of the unemployed, and Mr Cooper cited the schemes of London, Dublin, Leeds, Manchester and Sheffield. While expressing the belief that the day must come when tramping would be entirely superseded by home payments, nevertheless he felt that the time was not yet ripe for such a change in the Scottish Association. The tramping system could not be at once abolished. 'It has grown with the growth of our various bodies—forms a portion of the groundwork upon which the foundations of our unions rest.' But, anticipating the day when the Societies operating a system of unemployment benefit for their own members, would cease to pay relief to the cards of other Societies, some steps towards reform were immediately necessary. For this purpose the following propositions were suggested: '(1) That from and after the........day of........, the present system of

[1] *Circular*, July 1862.

tramp relief shall be so far altered and modified, that no
card of ordinary issue shall be relieved twice in a less period
than two years. (2) That all strike cards shall be entitled to
double relief for the first year only of such period; for relief
equal to one and a half for the first six months of the second
year; and to the ordinary relief for the remainder of the
full time. (3) That no relief whatever be given to any card
—whether strike or ordinary—except the statutory allowance; and that Fathers of Chapels and Society Delegates
be instructed to see that this is strictly enforced.' A further
proposition concerned the establishment of a special Committee of the English Provincial Typographical Association to consider cases where the holders of cards 'acted in
such a way as to merit reprobation', with power to with-
hold payments on such cards. It was unanimously agreed
that these propositions be submitted for consideration to
the Branches of the Association, and also to the London
Society of Compositors, the London Union of Pressmen,
the Leeds, Manchester, Birmingham and Oxford Societies, the Provincial Union of England, and the Associations of Dublin and Belfast. Further, a committee was to
be set up by the Central Board, along with the Secretaries
of Glasgow, Edinburgh and Aberdeen, to consider the
question of the home relief of unemployment, a vote being
taken of the entire membership.

In fact, the propositions were never put into practice,
although some Branches were in favour of them; nor is
there any record of the proposed Committee on the question of home relief. The next move came from the English
Provincial Association. A Delegate Meeting in 1861, attended by several Scottish members, considered the propositions, along with others on the same question, and
decided to appoint a Committee to draw up a system of
mileage relief. Mr Cooper of Glasgow was appointed to
this committee. The system adopted at the beginning of
1863 provided relief at the rate of 1d per mile, with a
maximum of 120 miles per week. Contributions were 1d
per week from all members of Societies joining the scheme.
Members of non-conforming Societies were to receive $\frac{1}{2}$d

per mile. The Scottish Association, however, at its Delegate Meeting of 1862 had unanimously decided against the scheme. Besides being intricate and expensive, it was believed that the system would simply foster and perpetuate tramping. The Glasgow delegates alone had been instructed to vote for the scheme, but they yielded to the general feeling of the meeting. At the same meeting, as a result of a complaint from Dumfries regarding the heavy burden of expenditure on relief in that Branch, by reason of its geographical position, it was agreed that the reimbursement of expenditure at present granted by the Association to small Branches, be granted to all Branches heavily burdened by tramps. About the same time it was reported with regret that the Falkirk and Arbroath Branches had been dissolved, because it was impossible for them to meet the numerous demands of tramps without being a continuous burden on the Association.

For the next few years trade was fairly good and little was heard of the tramping question. In 1867, however, when an increase in the number of tramps was reported, the Glasgow Branch proposed that a vote of the membership be taken on the question of joining the English Relief Association. The vote subsequently produced an overwhelming majority against this. In this and subsequent years, the Ayr Branch also repeatedly urged that the Association reconsider the question of revising the relief system. Ayr, like Dumfries, suffered by reason of its geographical position, receiving calls from most of those travelling between Scotland and England. The question was raised again at the Delegate Meeting in 1870, when the Board was asked 'to devise some means of equalising the system of tramp relief'. It was subsequently reported that this was receiving consideration, but no scheme was produced.

The mid 70's brought renewed discussion of the evils of the existing system, and of the pros and cons of an out-of-work scheme. The question was closely linked with the general dissatisfaction with the conduct of the Association at this period and the growing feeling that the time had come for a new departure. At the same time, the number of tramps was again increasing. In 1875 the number relieved was 714 at a cost of nearly £76; in 1876 the number increased to 915 at a cost of £102. At the Delegate Meeting which was eventually called in 1877, the memorable step was taken to abolish the tramping system entirely. While the proposal to adopt an out-of-work scheme was shelved on this occasion, a system of removal grants was adopted. Under this scheme payment was made to unemployed members leaving town at the rate of 4/- per year of membership, up to a maximum of £3, but no relief was given to the unemployed coming in from other areas. At a Special Delegate Meeting the following year a proposal to form an out-of-work scheme was again rejected, but the substitution of removal grants for tramping relief was re-approved. Meantime the abolition of tramping unfortunately coincided with a period of growing unemployment. Glasgow was particularly afflicted by this, the position being aggravated by the large influx of unemployed from other parts of the country. The result of this was an attempt by Glasgow to get some form of tramping reintroduced, and an unsuccessful appeal to the Board to hold a special delegate meeting on the subject. A break in the ranks of the Association was then threatened by the action of Glasgow in approaching the Provincial Association of England, with a view to affiliation. The threat never became a reality, however, and the ultimate solution adopted was that of self help. In 1878 steps were taken by the Branch to relieve the distress of the unemployed. Relief was at first paid from Society funds to unemployed members of twelve months' standing. Then in 1879 a levy of 6d per week for six weeks was imposed on the Glasgow members for this purpose. Finally the Branch appointed a committee to draw up a regular scheme of unemployment benefit. As a result of this, 1880 saw the adoption of a scheme whereby benefit of 8/- per week was paid for six weeks in any quarter. The scheme was financed by an extra contribution of 1d per week from members. The hope was expressed that this step would provide an example to be copied by the rest of the Association. In the meantime other Branches were faced with the same problem. Thus, in 1880, the Kirkcaldy Branch decided to pay men on the road 6d from the funds, with 6d extra on Saturdays, and to augment the Association removal grant by a further 4/–.

The hope of the Glasgow Branch in fact, was realised in 1881, when a Delegate Meeting adopted an Association out-of-work scheme. The subscription to this fund was fixed at $1\frac{1}{2}$d per week, and benefit was payable at the rate of 7/– per week for six weeks in each quarter of the calendar year. Payments were to start, after a six months' probationary period, in July 1882, and the removal grants were to be paid from the same fund. The scheme was compulsory for all members.

II. OTHER PROVIDENT SCHEMES

The development of the funeral, sick and superannuation schemes was on similar lines. As might be expected, the friendly society functions of the Association all originated in the Branches, the larger centres taking the lead, and only after they had been proved as local schemes were they gradually taken over by the Association. There were, in fact, two stages in the development of such local schemes. In the first instance, friendly societies existed separately from the Branches, although with their approval and support, and these were open to all members of the profession. Later, the Branches themselves started similar schemes available only to their own membership. Thus the Edinburgh Compositors' Benefit Society falls into the first category and was founded in 1824. This was a comprehensive scheme covering sickness, old age and life assurance. In 1855, the Edinburgh Society started its own funeral scheme and in 1857 a sick scheme. In 1859 a sick and funeral scheme was established by the Aberdeen Branch, and in 1860 a friendly society was formed by Glasgow. The details of the Edinburgh scheme may be taken as typical. Originally the subscription was 6d per month, and sickness benefit was paid at the rate of 5/- per week. Later the subscription was increased to 9d per month for the first four months and 6d for the remainder of the year. Sickness benefit was increased to 6/- per week, and the sum of £5 was paid on death.

The Delegate Meeting of 1877, which substituted the payment of removal grants for tramp relief, also adopted sick and funeral schemes. A committee of the Glasgow Branch had prepared detailed schemes, and these formed the basis of the proposals actually adopted. The sick scheme provided benefit of 12/- per week for the first thirteen weeks, 7/- for the second and 6/- for the third thirteen weeks, with 2/6 per week for the remainder of the illness. Under the funeral scheme the relatives of members of one year's standing were to receive £2; for three years' membership, £4; five years, £6; ten years, £10. The total subscription for all purposes was increased to 5d per week to the Association, and it was estimated that another 1d per week would probably be sufficient to cover the working expenses of Branches. The chief difficulty raised by these new schemes concerned the question whether they should be made compulsory to members. Compulsory membership seemed desirable if they were to be operated successfully, but there was a general feeling against coercion. The Delegate Meeting decided that this question be put to a vote of the members, with a strong plea for compulsion. The result of this vote showed a majority in favour of compulsion, although some Branches protested against it.

In the next few months, however, opposition to the new schemes increased, many Branches reporting difficulties in collecting subscriptions and reductions in membership. The Dumfries Branch seceded from the Association. Aberdeen reluctantly agreed to try the schemes after protest, while Inverness, Cupar (Fife), Ardrossan, Kilmarnock and Hamilton all appealed to have them on an optional basis. The greatest opposition, however, came from Glasgow, which had been unanimously in favour of the schemes at the time of the Delegate Meeting. The chief cause of grievance here appears to have been the fact that the proposals adopted put old men on the same footing as younger ones. The Branch sent a letter to the Fathers of Chapels in Edinburgh, presumably seeking support in their opposition to the sick and funeral schemes, against which feeling in Glasgow was growing and towards which little in the way of contributions had been received. They also appealed to the Board to take a new vote on compulsion, and on whether the schemes should be adopted at all and if so, when eligibility should begin. The outcome of all this opposition was the decision, by a vote of the members, to hold a Special Delegate Meeting to reconsider the whole question. The meeting was held in Edinburgh in May 1878, and decided against the establishment of a sick scheme. The funeral scheme, however, was approved, the sums payable being reduced to £2, £3 and £5 according to length of membership.

Thus the provident development of the Association proceeded at this time on the principle of two steps forward followed by one step backward. This, however, proved to be only a temporary delay. Almost immediately following the Delegate Meeting, a vote was taken of its members by the Edinburgh Branch on the question of adopting a compulsory sick and funeral scheme. The result showed a majority in favour and such a scheme was at once put into action. This example, too, was eventually copied by the Association, a sick scheme being adopted by the Delegate Meeting of 1881, at the same time as the out-of-work scheme was approved. The subscription to the sick scheme was 1½d per week, and benefit was payable at the rate of 10/– per week for the first thirteen weeks, 5/– for the next thirteen weeks, and 2/6 per week for the remainder of the illness. A compromise was adopted regarding the question of compulsion. The scheme was optional for the present members, but was to be compulsory for all new members after 1st January 1882. Distinction was also made between old and young members. Those over fifty years on entry were to receive only 7/6 instead of 10/– per week during the first period, while those over 60 years received only two rates, 5/– per week for the first thirteen weeks and 2/6 for the remaining weeks. The same meeting increased the rates of funeral allowance to £3, £5 and £7 according to length of membership.

The final stage of development concerns the adoption of a superannuation scheme. In 1872 Edinburgh announced the formation of a branch of the Provincial Printers' Pension Fund, the object of which was 'to grant pensions to decayed printers and their wives'. The question of an Association scheme was raised at the Delegate Meeting in 1881 but was rejected; it was raised again in 1885, when a committee was appointed to consider the matter. The next Delegate Meeting, in 1889, adopted a superannuation scheme, for which the subscription was to be 1d per week. The question of compulsion again became a bone of contention. An optional scheme was deemed impossible and a majority of the members voted in favour of a compulsory scheme. But opposition came from several Branches, most persistently from Edinburgh, whose members had decided not to contribute to this scheme at all. Glasgow, wholeheartedly in favour of the scheme, nevertheless found difficulty in enforcing it and exacting payments. The outcome of this was a Special Delegate Meeting held in 1891. On this occasion the scheme was finally approved, three grades of benefit being provided according to years of membership and payable from the age of 60 years. For 25 years membership benefit was at the rate of 6/– per week; for 30 years, 7/–; for 35 years, 8/–. Payments were not to start until January 1893, by which time it was hoped to have accumulated a fund of £1,500.

III. The New Association

With the adoption of a superannuation scheme the transformation of the Association was completed and it emerged in a new form. Founded as a purely protective organisation, it had now assumed all the functions of a full-scale provident society. In this respect, its development was not untypical of the time. Further, the course of this development followed a definite pattern. The origin of the general provident societies is not relevant here. In so far as the early trade societies were also benefit societies, they were concerned mainly with tramp relief. Nevertheless, it was from the local societies that the modern provident schemes were devised. The growing need for such services first found expression in Branch schemes, but as the need became greater and the demand more widespread, the Association was faced with the alternative of following their lead or seeing its influence diminish. The fear was expressed that increased services from and subscriptions to the Branches would make members more reluctant to continue to subscribe to the Association, unless some more obvious and direct benefit were received in return. Under the new arrangements the Association's commitments in the sphere of provident schemes far exceeded, at least financially, those of a purely protective nature. This was at the same time a symptom and a cause of its strength as a trade union.

That the schemes were not perfect in their original form is not surprising and the years following 1881 saw some modifications. Thus, it was complained that the out-of-work scheme, permitting as it did the full amount of benefit to be received in each quarter, tended to encourage chronic idleness. To mitigate this, and at the same time limit the drain on the fund, the weekly allowance was reduced in 1889 to 6/–, 4/– and 2/– in the second, third and fourth quarters of the year respectively. Prior to this the estimated expenditure on out-of-work relief had been 8/4 per member, while the income had been about 6/3. At the same time the position of those in part-time employment was improved by the decision to make up their earnings to 12/– per week for six weeks in each quarter, thus removing the anomaly that the unemployed received no monetary advantage from a single day's work in the week. In spite of these modifications, however, the drain on the fund through the large numbers unemployed continued, and in 1892 it was decided to raise the subscription from 1½d to 2d per week. This appeared still to be inadequate and many Branches reported the need to augment Association payments from local funds. In 1893 the Glasgow members decided to pay ½d per week to such a local fund, which was used to make up the weekly benefit to 8/– for six weeks in each quarter. Glasgow at this time was suffering once more from an influx of unemployed, and in 1894 £100 was transferred from the general fund to this special fund. In that year the Branch reported that benefit had been paid to 363 members, and the total amount paid out, from the Association and the local fund, was £981. In 1895 the contribution to the Association fund was further increased to 3d per week. This increase finally put the scheme on a sound financial basis. Between 1889 and 1894 it had been almost continuously in debt to the protective fund, the debt amounting to £627 before the increase in subscription in 1895. Thereafter improved trade also helped to restore financial stability, and by the end of 1902 the amount at the credit of the scheme was £5,693.

The sick scheme fared better in its early years, and in view of the increasing balance, the Delegate Meeting of 1895 decided to increase the benefits paid. The allowance for the second thirteen weeks was increased to 7/6, and that for the third grade, or permanent illness, increased to 5/–. At the same time it was decided to offer to those permanently disabled the choice of a sum not exceeding £30 or continuation at the lowest grade of allowance. Payments from the superannuation scheme were likewise increased. Age eligibility was reduced from 60 to 55 years, and benefit increased to 6/–, 8/– and 10/–, according to length of membership. The Edinburgh Society was opposed to these changes, and the following years proved that their objections were justified. Almost immediately deficits began to appear in the sick scheme. The fund which had accumulated over the years was steadily reduced, and by the end of 1902 amounted to only £138. The burden on the superannuation scheme also began to increase, as had been expected. The fifty-year period closed with a warning note about the unsound financial position of both funds. A situation in which the income to the schemes annually fell short of the expenditure obviously could not continue indefinitely.

Between the start of the schemes and the end of 1902 the total amount paid in benefits was as follows: out-of-work £18,615; removal grants £2,710; sick £21,600; funeral £5,110; and superannuation £6,146. This compared with a total on protective purposes of £12,791, of which £5,102 had been paid since 1878 when the first of the above schemes was started. The total contribution to the Association had been increased to 7½d per week. Thus, in spite of a temporary financial instability in some of the schemes, the end of the fifty years saw the Association firmly established in its new and wider role.

CHAPTER EIGHT

THE APPRENTICE QUESTION

Under the old guild system and the practice of indenturing apprentices, the problem of restriction was simple. With the breakdown of this system, the removal of restrictions, and the expansion of trade, the threat of an excess supply of labour and fear of competition from cheap boy-labour in some industries made apprentice restriction an important feature in the policy of the young trade unions. While the ending of Anderson's monopoly in 1711 opened the way for greater development in the Scottish printing industry, the most marked expansion appears to have been during the late eighteenth and early nineteenth century. From this expansion emerged the apprentice problem. Apparently only during the first two or three decades of the nineteenth century did the problem of an excess supply of cheap boy-labour become a vital one for the compositors. No suggestion of it appears in the lengthy document accompanying the appeal for an increase in wages in 1803, but apprentice restriction formed a major—if not the major—purpose of the General Scottish Association of 1836, and of the later National Association. The other main problem of this period, tramping, was regarded, in fact, as a symptom of this. The recurring large-scale unemployment of the nineteenth century focused attention more and more on the apparent surplus labour supply and its root cause, unlimited increase in the number of apprentices.

The remedy adopted at this time was one of restriction, and reference has already been made to the attempts of the two early Associations in this direction, and the extent to which attempts to enforce a too rigid and extreme restriction probably contributed to their demise. Typical of this period was the Edinburgh memorial on the apprentice question presented to the employers in 1842. This attributed the problem to the mushroom growth of small masters and the consequent fall in the profits of 'respectable employers'. It pointed out that while printing had increased rapidly, the work had gone to the growing number of boys rather than to the journeymen, to the detriment of the latter. The consequent dissatisfaction experienced by the journeymen resulted in many setting themselves up as masters, which had a ruinous effect on prices. Thus, it was argued, the adoption of apprentice restriction would be of benefit to all. A considerable degree of success evidently attended the Edinburgh campaign at this time, and later attempts were made, under the National Association, to secure a similar restriction throughout Scotland, namely, one apprentice to every three journeymen. This policy, however, met with opposition from both branches and employers. Its success was limited and at the cost of many closed offices. Towards the end of its life a weakened N.T.A. relaxed the restriction to one apprentice to every two journeymen, and following its breakdown, there was, in effect, no real restriction. Thus, in 1850 it was recorded, by Mr Edwards in his prize essay on this subject, that there were 954 journeymen and 550 apprentices in six Scottish towns—Dundee, Edinburgh, Glasgow, Kilmarnock, Perth and Stirling—while for the whole of Scotland the approximate numbers were 1,500 journeymen and 1,200 apprentices.

The policy of restriction adopted by the early Association had provided only a temporary brake, and when the present Association was founded in 1853 the rate of increase of apprentices was as great as, if not greater than before. In this, as in other questions, the policy of the new Association was at first a cautious one. The question was discussed at the first Delegate Meeting in 1854, but it was decided to delay giving a ruling on it, and in the meantime attempt to obtain more complete information about the extent of the problem. Subsequent Delegate Meetings in 1856 and 1858 took up the question, and the rule was finally adopted: 'That Branches shall fix the ratio of apprentices for their own guidance, but in no case shall the minimum be lower than two apprentices to a firm, and one apprentice to every two journeymen thereafter'. At this time in Glasgow there were 330 journeymen and 192 apprentices, which gave a ratio of 10 to 6, after deducting the numbers allowed to firms. The position in Aberdeen created a special problem, the number of journeymen being 48, while apprentices numbered 81. This matter it was decided to leave in the hands of the Aberdeen Branch, and in 1859 the Branch reported that a memorial on the subject, described as 'exceedingly respectful and temperate', had met with silent contempt and had cost the local secretary his job. On this occasion the Central Board advised Aberdeen to exercise forbearance and give no occasion to the employers for collision. Nevertheless, after the formation of the Association, one or two Branches did succeed in putting a brake on the increase in numbers of apprentices. Thus, in 1856 Dundee reported success in 'thinning out the ranks of apprentices, where previously employers took on boys ad lib.'. With few exceptions, this was mainly achieved by protesting at new encroachments, and little attempt was made to secure universal application of the Association rule of one apprentice to two journeymen. The rule, in fact, was largely ignored, and in consequence, the problem remained.

Attention was again concentrated on it in the 60's, when the extent and danger of the problem, its causes and remedies were widely discussed. In 1860 a Delegate Meeting proposed that the term of apprenticeship be reduced to five years, but the feeling of the Branches was unanimously opposed to this. There were broadly three approaches to the problem at this time. Firstly, it was believed, evidently by the majority, that the only solution was the old one of restriction. That this had seemingly failed in the past was due not to defects in the remedy, but to failure to apply it. Some, however, sought a solution in the reduction of the term of apprenticeship. By thus depriving the employers of the years in which an apprentice was capable of performing the work of a journeyman, it was argued that the incentive to take on an unlimited number of boys would be removed. Finally, a minority favoured the complete abolition of apprenticeships, as an unnecessary restriction. The main debate, however, waged around the first two—restriction and the length of apprenticeship.

The subject was exhaustively dealt with in articles and correspondence. Of particular interest are a series of articles in the *Circular* of 1862–63.[1] Here the above views were examined at some length, and an eloquent case made out for the second. The views of the French economists and Adam Smith were frequently quoted, particularly the latter. 'The arts', said Adam Smith, 'contain no such mystery as to require a long course of instruction. In the common mechanic trades, the lessons of a few days might certainly be sufficient.' But he also acknowledged that dexterity required 'much practice and experience'. From this it was concluded that Smith's writings supported, not the abolition of apprenticeships, but their reduction. Fully recognising the need to restrict the number of apprentices, it was argued 'that apprentices can be restricted only in accordance with the conditions and requirements of the business'. Changes in technique and the subdivision of processes had simplified the tasks of the printer and made a seven years' apprenticeship obsolete. '. . . under the name of apprentices, it creates an ever-increasing staff of workmen, who, at half, or less than half, the ordinary prices, execute work which would otherwise be executed by the general body.' The fact that journeymen complained of the inroads made by boy-labour was itself proof of their ability, after a year or two, to compete successfully for journeymen's work. 'The apprenticeship should cease. when learning gives way to proficiency.' Thus, it was concluded, the only possible solution to the apprentice problem was the reduction of its term, by graduated stages, to 'a minimum period'.

That the problem had not, at this time, abated, is

[1] November and December 1862 and January 1863.

demonstrated by the current statistics. In the six Scottish towns referred to by Mr Edwards in 1850, the number of apprentices had, by 1862, increased to 917, while journeymen totalled 1,380. In other words, the percentage of apprentices to journeymen had increased from 58 to 66. In Edinburgh the percentage was 60 compared with 55 in 1850, the position in the smaller offices being much worse than in the large ones. Thus, it was reported that in 1860 some 33 small book and jobbing offices employed a total of 133 journeymen and 136 apprentices, while 7 small newspaper offices employed 47 journeymen and 52 apprentices. The custom in the provinces was to dismiss a man on the completion of his seven years' training and replace him 'not infrequently, by two boys'. That this expansion of the labour supply was greater than the requirements of the industry was held to be demonstrated by the continuing presence of unemployed journeymen.

Another aspect of the same problem, which was also the subject of concern at this time, was that of 'turnover apprentices'. The practice of employing turnovers had been condemned by the Association from its formation, and in 1855 Edinburgh reported that, as a result of a circular issued by the Society, the problem there had slightly abated. By the 1860's, however, the practice was evidently widespread and particularly associated with the many small employers. These often carried on mainly, or even entirely, with the aid of boy-labour, and by the offer of a shilling or so extra, enticed apprentices who had already served four or five years, away from the employers who had trained them. Such a practice was made possible by the large number of apprentices, and at the same time, fostered an increase in that number. These small offices, rarely employing journeymen, could outbid the larger firms and make it impossible for them to compete if journeymen were employed. Here also, it was argued, the solution lay in a reduction of the term of apprenticeship, thus cutting off the supply of turnovers to the small firms.

While discussion of these problems continued throughout the 60's, it was not until 1870 that action was taken by the Association. At a Special Delegate Meeting of that year a proposal to reduce the term of apprenticeship to five years was again considered. It was decided to communicate with the English and Irish Societies on this question, but when these subsequently replied, almost unanimously, in the negative, it was decided to take no further action. The same Delegate Meeting, however, ruled that in future the systematic employment of turnover apprentices was to be regarded as sufficient reason for withdrawing Association members. A memorial to this effect was issued to all employers, and by the end of the same year it was reported that action by the Glasgow Branch had already succeeded in stamping out the practice. In the following years a firmer stand was evidently taken, particularly by the larger Branches, in this and in the question of restricting the number of apprentices. In 1872, when the rules were revised by a special committee, that concerning apprentices was altered to allow one to every three journeymen and one to the firm. At the same time, it was reported that the statistics of the trade showed 'a flattering reduction' in the number of apprentices and turnovers. The question of reducing the length of apprenticeship was again raised, at the Delegate Meeting in 1877, by the Aberdeen, Dundee and Stirling Branches. Opposition to this, led by Glasgow, was based on the belief that it would merely increase the number of journeymen more quickly. The majority were in favour of retaining a seven years' apprenticeship, and renewing attempts at restriction. It was admitted that the rule here was 'systematically winked at', particularly in the smaller Branches.

Except in a few of the larger towns, the position remained essentially unaltered until the 1890's. In the intervening years the larger and stronger societies were more successful in enforcing the Association rule and opposing attempted infringements of it. Disputes over this were reported from time to time, and in some cases, offices closed, but some headway was certainly made by the larger Branches. One notable exception to this was Aberdeen which, as late as 1886, proposed a special delegate meeting 'to consider and devise means which would check the increase of apprentices in Scotland'. The proposal was rejected on the grounds of expense and the lack of practical proposals. 'What is wanted is the general application of the principle of restriction,' was the comment of the Annual Report. In 1888 the Aberdeen Branch was instructed to try to prevent the employment of any new apprentices until the numbers were in the correct ratio of one to three. The greatest infringements of the apprentice rule, however, continued in the provinces. Thus, in 1884, Kirkcaldy reported: 'Here, as in most provincial towns, there is a great preponderance of apprentices over journeymen. This growing evil is getting to so large dimensions that the members of this Branch will need to take steps very soon to eradicate this preponderating element.' Again in 1886 the same town commented on the growing problem, particularly in newspaper offices, where in some cases fourteen or fifteen apprentices were employed to only two journeymen. The following year the number of apprentices in Kirkcaldy was described as nearly as many as any two towns of similar size. Another bad spot in this respect was Ayr, which had something of a reputation as a nursery.

A decision of the Delegate Meeting of 1889 marked the beginning of a new phase. The Executive Council were instructed to carry out the apprentice rule more energetically, and a circular was issued to the Branches requesting that infringements be immediately reported. In the following years the Association came more closely to grips with the problem. In 1890 Aberdeen reported that an arrangement had been made with the employers which should eventually lead to a reduction in numbers. By 1895 the numbers had been reduced by sixty, and further reductions were reported in succeeding years. In 1892 Paisley reported that the apprentice problem was now solved, and in 1893 Glasgow announced that after several conferences with the employers, a satisfactory agreement had been signed by both parties. Reductions were reported by Ayr, although in 1896 the numbers were still large. Dundee, Dumfries, Perth and Kilmarnock all tackled the problem with some success, while in 1901 Stirling reported that 'apprentices were seemingly becoming an almost disappearing quantity'.

The apprentice problem was regarded as one of the main grievances of the trade throughout most of the nineteenth century. Further, in spite of reasoned attempts to introduce a more revolutionary policy, the remedy adhered to throughout was that of artificial restriction. Yet until the last decade of the century the success of this policy was limited. Why did the same policy produce such a different result at this time? Certainly until then the apprentice rule had been more honoured in the breach than the observance. Also, the Branches and the Association made a more vigorous attempt to enforce the rule at this period, and being stronger as unions were more capable of enforcing it. But the records do not suggest the absence of a genuine and earnest desire for a solution in the early attempts to deal with the problem. Also, the establishment and strength of the Association was surely beyond question at a much earlier date than 1890. Something more seems to be necessary for a complete explanation of the decline in numbers at this time. This would seem to be supplied by the introduction of machinery, which became widespread in the composing-room at this period. (Associated with the increased mechanisation of the industry, a new factor appeared about this time in discussions of the apprentice question, namely, the need for more and better training, particularly of a technical nature.) Earlier criticisms of the policy of restriction were based on the grounds that it was in fact artificial; that, so long as it was of advantage to the employer to have a large number of apprentices, the restrictive devices of trade societies would be ineffective. It would appear to be in this respect that the position had changed by the end of the century. The Reports show that the introduction of composing-machines was not accompanied by the large-scale displacement of men which had been feared, but rather by a reduction in the number of apprentices. This was particularly the case in the provincial Branches, where the apprentice problem had been greatest. Thus, mechanisation, combined with a vigorous policy of a strong trade union, finally made effective this apprentice rule, for so long almost a dead letter of the Association statutes.

CHAPTER NINE

FURTHER PROBLEMS OF THE PERIOD: FEMALE LABOUR AND MACHINES

Two remaining issues of this fifty-year period merit separate consideration. These were the introduction of the female compositor, and the introduction of machinery. It must be said at the outset, however, that consideration of these two factors in the same chapter is largely a matter of convenience. While in many industries the introduction of machinery might be said to have resulted in a greater use of female labour, this, in general, was not the experience of the Association during this period. A few cases were certainly recorded of attempts to introduce both at once. Thus, as early as 1875, before a successful type-composing machine had been perfected, Edinburgh refers to the introduction of females to the composing room as of doubtful success, even where females and machines were introduced together. Again, in 1890, Ayr reported that the proprietor of the *Advertiser*, after promising not to take on any more apprentices, had installed a typesetting machine and two girls. In general, however, the widespread installation of composing machines in the last decade of the period was not followed by any marked increase in the number of women employed, and the Association was, by that time, strong enough to defend its members against the encroachments of cheap labour. The two problems are, in fact, separate, that of female labour arising some decades before the composing machine became an accepted fact.

I. THE FEMALE COMPOSITOR

The early history of the struggle to introduce women to the composing-room is not, strictly speaking, part of the

Association's history, although the story summarised here was obtained from the columns of the *Circular*. To the established body of compositors the movement was simply a wild scheme of social reformers and cranks, and represented no threat to their position. During the first decade or so of the movement the facts appear to have justified this attitude and the subject was not of direct concern to the Association. Whether, or how long, this state of affairs would have continued can only be the subject of speculation, but, in fact, the situation was changed by the events in Edinburgh in 1872.

The movement was started under the auspices of the Social Science Association about 1860, as part of a campaign to promote the employment of women and absorb the surplus female population. No less a person than Mr Gladstone appears to have set the ball a-rolling, when, in an attack on the strong combination of printers, he accused them of excluding women, 'although we all know that women are peculiarly adapted, from their small fingers, to the delicate handling of type.' In 1860 Miss Emily Faithfull, backed by the Society for Promoting the Employment of Women, established the Victoria Press in London, where the composing work was done entirely by women, working, evidently, under ideal conditions. In 1861 the Caledonian Press was established in Edinburgh by the Scottish National Institution for Promoting the Employment of Women in the Art of Printing. The patrons in this case were said to include 'dukes, earls, bishops and lords', but it was subsequently reported that the promoter was, in fact, a Miss Thomson of Lasswade. In 1862, the Caledonian Press produced a monthly magazine, called *The Rose, the Shamrock and the Thistle*, to gain greater publicity for the venture and, at the same time, provide some regular employment for the establishment. The object of the publication was, in the words of the prospectus, 'to give assistance to women walking the rugged road of life alone, flints and briars beneath their feet, and scowling clouds above their heads.'

These events are of particular interest in the history of

the employment of women, of which a new phase started at this period. In the early Victorian era the women employed in industry were recruited mainly from the poorer classes, and employment was confined to the unskilled trades. By the second half of the nineteenth century, however, social reform and factory legislation were tending to improve the conditions of such employment and mitigate the exploitation of female and child labour, which had occurred at the beginning of the industrial era. The subsequent improvement in the lot of the working classes was accompanied by an improvement in the position of women compelled to seek paid employment. At the same time a new class of women was seeking entry to the labour market. These women were not primarily of the lowest income group nor was their employment dictated solely by necessity or poverty. This was the start of the modern 'emancipation of women'. Further, it was no longer the unskilled, but the skilled trades and the professions to which entry was sought.

This trend is borne out by the experience of the printing industry. While the practice of employing girls in the press room was dying out, women were seeking entry to the supposedly less arduous, but more skilled tasks of the composing room. Thus the *Circular* of 1862 commented that 'although the practice of employing girls at printing-machines is fast and deservedly going into disuse, they must be tried at the "light and genteel" operation of picking up type'. Further, that these new recruits were, to a large extent, from a higher income group is borne out by the comments in the *Circular* of a female correspondent, herself a compositor. Taking up her pen 'to vindicate the cause of "Woman, lovely woman",' she writes of the small amount of time spent by most women on domestic duties and the ready availability of plenty of domestic servants. Women, she argues, spend most of their time idling, reading periodicals, or 'gazing listlessly at their lily-white hands'. She concludes—'La, me, Sir, it is just encouraging idleness to throw any obstacle in the way of young ladies who wish to become useful artizans.' Thus, it was for 'young ladies' that employment was sought in the second half of the century.

The subject was debated at length and with no little eloquence on the platform and in the press. Opposition to the movement was at first based on the conviction that women were unsuited to the mental and physical strains of the work. Again, woman's place was in the home. 'Home and home duties are the sphere and the work for which she was designed.' Nor were the moral arguments omitted— 'the indiscriminate mixing of the sexes soon rubs out all natural modesty, and the consequences to morality may be inferred.' Finally, but by no means of the least importance, the eventual effect of success would be to cheapen labour. Such competition, it was ingeniously argued, could only add to the number of young workmen already leaving the old country, and thus further increase the surplus female population. Nor was the subject always treated in serious vein. A poet from the ranks of the compositors, in a contribution entitled 'Coming Events Cast Their Shadows Before', visualised the reforming effect of the entry of women to all spheres of life, and concluded thus:

> But, oh, if they should emigrate!
> We'll soon sink to a waefu' state;
> Then ye young chaps, ere it's ower late,
>   Rin, tak a wife!
> Implore the dears at hame to wait,
>   Save Britain's life!

Some limited success was claimed for the Victoria Press, although this seems to have been largely the result of special patronage. A total of eighteen women were employed and these were supervised by eight journeymen compositors. The women worked under special and ideal conditions—'this pampered, velveteen system', as the *Circular* described it. Less evident was the success of the Caledonian Press, where eight apprentice girls were employed with three journeymen to tutor them, and thus calling forth the comment—'it actually employs fewer females than any single respectable milliner of whose philanthropy the world takes no note!' The survival of the movement was at this time doubted, with good reason, and there seemed justification for the final sweeping condemnation of the *Circular* : 'Take away benevolence, sympathy, and patronage, and all institutions for promoting the employment of women in the art of printing will very soon go quietly to Hades.'

The position, however, was radically altered by the unsuccessful struggle of the compositors against the employers in Edinburgh in 1872. The positions of the men on strike were filled by non-union labour and by women, and one important legacy of the struggle was the establishment of women in the Edinburgh printing industry. Thus, by 1875, it was reported that some hundred females were in direct competition with journeymen. The subject continued to be fiercely debated, but the tone of criticism changed. The threat was no longer hypothetical, but real. The old arguments were repeated, and special emphasis laid on the harmful effects to health of such work. On one instance, an American Government Inquiry into this subject was cited, and medical evidence quoted, to prove the disastrous and awful effects on the female constitution following a period of work in a composing-room. But the women survived and persisted, and discussion had to begin with their presence an accepted and accomplished fact. Edinburgh remained the chief problem area, and there the numbers were greatest. But in 1877 Aberdeen reported the return, 'after an absence of 30 years', of women to the industry. Here they were paid 8/– for a 54-hour week, thus the fear of cheapening labour was realised. Some of the provincial Branches were also affected, although on a smaller scale.

Criticism became most vocal in the periods of heavy unemployment which followed, and the female compositor was always included in the list of causal factors. Thus, in 1878, the *Circular* admitted that in Edinburgh they had had some success, and were proving a menace to the pieceman, since they received preferential treatment in the distribution of work. Until this time their influence had not been much felt because trade was good, but with the start of depression, more attention was focused on them as a threat to the employment of journeymen. The subject was raised at a Delegate Meeting in 1881, when it was resolved that the Executive Committee should draw up a statement of the injurious effects of female labour on the printing profession and appeal to the working men of Scotland to co-operate in 'dissuading females from adopting it as a profession'. Again, in the Annual Report of 1884, a discussion of the causes of depression cites the introduction of women as an unfavourable factor. 'This is ostensibly done under the cloak of philanthropy, but its real intention is to lessen the work and wages of men, and to increase the profits of employers.' Proof of this was found in the fact that women doing the same work as men were not paid the same rate of wages. 'Is an accident of birth an economic reason for a differential rate of wages to men and women?' Here it is suggested, for the first time, that the solution should be union organisation of female labour. The subject was also raised at a General Typographical Conference of the principal unions, held in London in 1886. The meeting resolved that females should be admitted to the unions on the same conditions as journeymen, provided they were paid in accordance with the scale. Commenting on this resolution, Edinburgh, while approving of the principle, protested that it would be difficult to put it into practice, at least in the Edinburgh area. There the employment of women had rapidly developed since 1872, and was now deeply rooted and widespread.

In the following years little direct action was taken in the matter. A few isolated cases were reported from time to time, when members were withdrawn because of the employment of cheap female labour. Thus, in 1887, Falkirk reported an unsuccessful attempt to reason with an employer who had introduced two female compositors at a low wage. The men were withdrawn, but it was reported that the office managed to carry on with the help of the President of the Edinburgh Machinemen's Society and his three daughters. In 1890 a Glasgow office was closed for similar reasons. In Edinburgh, however, the size of the problem was too great for such direct action. Other methods had to be sought. In 1896 the Branch sent a resolution to the Secretary of the Treasury protesting at the employment of females on Government printing contracts. Two years later an Edinburgh Female Compositors' Society was formed under the auspices of the Branch, and with financial assistance from Branch and Association. Of this it was said: 'If it will be the means, as is anticipated, of improving the position of the male compositor, there will be no lack of well-wishers in this and every Branch of the Association.' In the Report of the following year, however, it was briefly recorded that the Female Compositors' Society had ceased to exist about the end of the year.

Another town where this problem was evidently not inconsiderable was Perth, and about this time attempts were made to reduce the number of women employed. Thus, in 1899 attempts to introduce female compositors to a formerly male establishment were successfully opposed, and at the same time, it was reported that the number of females in the Branch had been reduced by seventeen during the past year. The following year another attempt was made by a Perth firm to introduce female compositors, and other firms maintained that they had to follow suit, if they were to compete. A lengthy dispute followed, which put the Association in something of a dilemma, since they had so recently given financial support to the Edinburgh Female Compositors' Society, whose members certainly did not receive the full journeyman's wage. It was decided, however, to adhere to the former decision to admit women provided they were employed under the same conditions as men, but to oppose underpaid female labour. Edinburgh was, by the size of its problem, recognised as a special case. With two of the Perth offices negotiations were unsuccessful, and a strike followed which lasted from July until November, and culminated in the closing of the two offices.

The Perth case is of interest, representing as it does an

attempt to introduce female compositors at a time when the type-composing machine was generally in use. That similar attempts were made in some of the smaller Branches seems likely, but the records suggest that few attempts to operate the machines with female labour were made in the main Branches, and that when these occurred, they were successfully opposed. The Association was not opposed to the employment of women provided they were paid the rate for the job. Edinburgh remained the one major exception to this rule. There the facts of the situation had to be faced and a not inconsiderable problem of cheap female labour remained at the end of the fifty-year period.

II. The Advent of Machinery

The pressmen of the newspaper section were the first to be affected by the introduction of machinery. Here the replacement of hand-labour by machines occurred fairly early in the life of the Association. There is, in fact, little detailed comment on this event in the records, but the impression gained is that the change occurred relatively smoothly and quietly and with remarkably little displacement.

The introduction of the mechanical printing press occurred about the 1860's and by 1872 a high degree of perfection had been achieved. Thus, in 1862, the *Circular*, in an article entitled 'Pressmen, Look Out!', described an electro-magnetic printing-press featured at the London Exhibition of that year. This was described as 'a hand printing-press, worked by electro-magnetism', and was the work of an English inventor. About a year later, the same journal contained a description of Wilkinson's Rotary Printing Press, of which it was said: 'it will throw off with ease twenty thousand sheets an hour, printed on both sides, cut and folded, ready for immediate delivery.' Thereafter the invasion of machinery progressed steadily in this department. In 1872 a detailed account appeared of the Walter Press, two of these machines being in use in the *Scotsman* Office in Edinburgh. These were the only two in use outside of *The Times* Office, London, whose manager, Mr Macdonald, was the inventor. For these machines a productive capacity of 12,000 copies per hour, capable of increase to 15,000 or 17,000 copies was claimed, with printing of first-rate quality. The manual labour required was described as being 'ridiculously small', only three attendants being necessary for each machine in addition to the supervision of skilled machinists. The Edinburgh Branch's report on this machine concluded thus: 'The high perfection attained in machine printing seems to leave little room for further improvement in mere speed. Probably, by the addition of another cylinder or two, it may yet occur that these wonderful machines will be made to deliver copies of the paper at the door of the subscriber each morning with mechanical regularity; or, by the addition of a few extra tapes, be enabled to produce the leading matter of the journal.'

About this time Edinburgh reported that, while employment for compositors was good, the position of pressmen was much less favourable and that this branch had become an extremely precarious means of livelihood. 'When the smallest printing office now boasts its one or more machines, this fluctuating employment of hand-labour cannot be wondered at.' The aged and the less competent were being cruelly forced out of the trade, while 'the young, the energetic and the aspiring must acquire a knowledge of machine printing in time, if they would follow out the profession, in gaining a knowledge of which the brightest years of their lives were passed'. A Glasgow report contained passing reference to a similar state of affairs. The absence of further comments, however, suggests that the displacement of labour did not become a major or a lasting problem, probably because of the expansion of the industry.

Much more appeared in the literature of the industry about the composing machine, although it was not until the last decade of the century that this was finally perfected and widely adopted. Although the earliest recorded attempt to devise a mechanical compositor was noted in the

Edinburgh *Journal of Science* in 1822, the invention being the work of a Mr Church of Birmingham, the first to attract the serious attention of the industry in Scotland was the Hattersley machine. In December 1859 this machine was exhibited and described to the Edinburgh employers in the office of Messrs W. & R. Chambers. A subsequent article in the *Circular* described it as 'the most simple, ingenious, and successful of any that have yet been invented'. There followed a detailed account of its working, and a reasoned consideration of its utility and practicability. The conclusion reached was that as at present developed, the action of the machine was limited. It could only perform work devoid of all extras. 'It can put type into a composing stick as quick again as a man can; but that is all.' Further, the labour of the operator was not lightened, since types had to be distributed in the usual way. Far from ridiculing the possibility of a mechanical compositor, however, the article concluded thus: 'Experience has taught us, that whatever increases production is generally beneficial, and ought rather to be desired than resisted; and if this machine, or rather improved tool, can be so perfected as to supplant hand-composition with advantage, we are sure it will be welcomed by every thinking member of the trade.'

Less moderate were the comments of the same journal on the Young type-composing machine demonstrated at the 1862 Exhibition. 'We are not afraid of that thing!' was the comment. The saving of time, it was claimed, was slight. Young's composing and distributing machines, operated by four men and four boys, would be capable of distributing and composing 12,000 to 15,000 types per hour, while the same amount of hand-labour could produce 12,000. Also, the speed of the machine was possible only with straightforward copy. During the following years many variations of the composing machine appeared and were similarly greeted, the hand-compositor being assured that he still had nothing to fear. Thus the demonstration in Edinburgh in 1872 of Mackie's composer and perforator called forth an article entitled 'Composer versus Compositor', in which the compositor was assured that 'threatened folks live long'. Again, in 1876, a new arrival was greeted by the usual comments under the heading 'Still They Come'. The justification for scepticism in these cases was not so much that the machines did not do what was claimed for them, although the claims were often proved extravagant, but rather that they were not economic propositions, and the saving, compared with hand composition, was not large enough to justify the capital invested. Thus, by 1880, in spite of the rapidly increasing number of inventions appearing, compositors were advised to 'find a grain of comfort in the reflection that after half a century of close application, the inventors have now almost reached the point from which their first start was made'.

Although none of these early machines proved generally successful as an economic proposition or were widely used, they were tried in a few cases. In Edinburgh, as already noted, some were in use in 1875, operated by women, but no great success could evidently be claimed for them. In 1876 Glasgow announced, with some derision, the arrival of a new machine in one office there, but no more appeared about it. As late as 1884 Dundee referred to a type-setting machine introduced some years earlier to the *Advertiser* office, and reported that this had now been relegated to the lumber room. This report concluded that this was the last that would likely be heard, at least for a long time, of 'these expensive and destructive toys'.

The position changed, however, with the arrival of the Linotype machine, which proved to be not only workable, but economically practicable. The machine was first used in America in 1886. There is no specific reference to exactly when or where these machines were first used in Scotland. The first reference to them in the Association records, however, occurred in 1890, when a dispute arose following their introduction to the office of the *Scottish Leader* in Edinburgh. The dispute concerned the efforts of the proprietor to get the journeymen in his employ to

sign a contract binding them, after a training period of
two months, to continue in employment for two years on a
piece scale of 3d per 1,000 produced on a Linotype.
Further, three months' notice of intention to leave had to
be given by the journeyman, while the proprietor reserved
the right to dismiss the men on one month's notice. This
was opposed by the Association, but all attempts to negotiate an agreement failed. The outcome was that the members were ejected from work and prevented from working
their fortnight's notice. Considerable publicity was given
by the Association to this case in view of 'the advanced
Liberal opinions of the *Leader*'.

The Association Report of the same year commented
on the attempts made during the previous forty years to
replace hand-labour in the composing room with machines,
and concluded that so far these had not been the financial
success claimed, and 'that the time when hand labour will,
to any appreciable extent, be supplanted by machines is
remote indeed. What we have to fear, and against which
we must protest with all our energy, is the introduction of
unskilled labour to work the machines, thereby supplant-
ing the technically educated compositor.' The same Report
contained a notice from Aberdeen of the introduction of
the Thorne composing machine. Again in the same document, the Glasgow Branch reported: 'The introduction
of type-composing machines is an accomplished fact. It
remains to be seen what effect they will have on the trade
and the Out-of-Work Fund; but the Branch have taken
steps so that, whilst giving every facility for a fair trial of
the machines, the interests of the members may be con-
served.' This was a reference to the introduction of
machines in the *Citizen* office. Until the end of 1892 the
men working these machines received the 'stab wage, but
then an attempt to change to a piece-system led to a dispute
which culminated in the lock-out of some sixty men.[1]

During the following decade the use of composing
machines became widespread, and the Association had, of
necessity, to concern itself with the question of conditions

[1] See Chapter 10.

and pay for those operating them. The Delegate Meeting of 1891 allotted the task of preparing working rules to the Executive Council and representatives of the Aberdeen, Edinburgh and Glasgow Branches. Mr Johnstone, the Association Secretary, attended a Conference in Manchester on the subject, and after receiving his report, the Executive Council adopted the following 'tentative' rules for the working of composing machines:

1. That Type-Composing Machines be worked exclusively by Journeymen Compositors and duly-recognised Apprentices, such Apprentices to be reckoned in the total number allowed to each office, as agreed to by employers and employed.

2. That no Compositor shall be required to undertake piece-work on Composing Machines until he is able to earn the 'stab wage of the Branch.

The Association also sent representatives to Delegate Meetings of the English Typographical Association at Sheffield in 1893 and Manchester in 1897, when the composing machine, particularly the Linotype, was the special subject of discussion. Thereafter it was reported to the members that the Association was certainly keeping pace with their English brethren in the matter of hours and wages for the machine operators. Meantime, as the machines were introduced, the various Branches individually concluded agreements with the employers for their working, subject to the approval of the Executive Council. In 1900 it was proposed that a conference be held with the Linotype Users Association with the object of drawing up a uniform scale for all. In view of the fact that all the employers were not represented by this Association, however, and bearing in mind difficulties which had arisen in England over a similar project, it was decided to continue the method of fixing scales between local Branches and individual employers.

Towards the end of this period attention was also drawn to the question of protecting the health of those operating the new machines. In 1898 it was noted that in England nearly all the machines were provided with 'hoods' to carry off the noxious fumes, and the hope was expressed that the employer in Scotland would not be

behind in providing this necessary addition or some similar improvement. Again, in 1900, it was reported that
enquiries had revealed that a general instruction had been
issued to Inspectors of Factories in 1895 to enforce the
use of hoods in connection with Linotypes, and that this
instruction applied to Scotland as elsewhere. Redress
could therefore be obtained in this matter where necessary,
but, about this time, an improved type of machine was
introduced from which no fumes were emitted and for
which hoods were unnecessary.

Throughout this period additions were reported annually to the number of machines in use throughout the
Association. These were chiefly Linotypes, although the
Thorne machine was also in use in one or two areas, and
by 1899 Glasgow announced the introduction of the
Monotype to the *Mail* office. The larger Branches were,
naturally, the first to be affected in this development, but
by the end of the century most of the provincial Branches
also had their quota of machines. The introduction of the
machines was accompanied in the first instance by the displacement of labour. The announcement by Aberdeen in
1895 of the introduction of eight Linotypes and the displacement of sixteen to twenty men was typical. In 1897
Edinburgh reported that the *Scotsman*, which was closed
to the Association, had then some twenty machines and
that the men displaced were being paid a solatium by the
employers, according to their length of service. By the end
of the century, however, it was generally agreed that the
effect of the machines on employment had not been so bad
as feared. The expansion and prosperity of the trade was
absorbing the men displaced, while the provincial Branches
experienced a reduction in the number of apprentices
taken on, rather than a displacement of journeymen. By
the end of the fifty-year period, therefore, the machines
were well established in the composing room, and the
working conditions and wages agreed were not unsatisfactory to the members of the Association.

Summing up on the introduction of machinery to the
composing section of the industry, one or two special

features are worthy of comment. These mainly concern the attitude of the compositors to the machines. Threatened with displacement by machinery, the craftsmen of the nineteenth century reacted in different ways. Some at first scoffed at the machines, but soon all came to fear them and many tried to oppose their introduction. The hand-loom weavers actively opposed it by wrecking the early machines; many refused at first to operate the machines, but were forced by unequal competition to accept machine work at the employers' terms; while some retained their position alongside the machines by reducing their numbers and greatly improving the quality of the hand-made article, as did the cordwainers (hand bootmakers). As events appeared to prove the inevitability of mechanisation, the attitude of the trade unions changed. The machines were accepted and the unions adapted to them. In some cases, when the machines were not operated by the craftsmen, the operators were admitted to the union; in other cases the hand craftsmen encouraged the machine operators to organise themselves. The most favourable situation was that in which the machines were taken over by the craftsmen, who were able to adapt themselves to the new skill called for by the machines. Here the efforts of the union were concentrated on preventing an influx of cheap labour and safeguarding the position of its members in the matter of pay and working conditions. In the case of the compositors there is no record of attempts to wreck the machinery or refuse to operate it. This was due partly, if not mainly, to the failure of the early machines. Even where they were operated by cheap labour, as, for example, in Edinburgh with the introduction of women, there is no record of marked success, a conclusion which seems to be reinforced by the absence of any widespread movement to follow Edinburgh's example. When a perfected composing machine eventually arrived, it was operated by Association members, who were successfully protected against any general influx of cheap labour. Much of the credit for this situation was evidently due to the long heralded, but much delayed, arrival of the composing machine. In spite of the derision which greeted many of the early inventions, responsible members were eventually forced to conclude that it could only be a matter of time before a successful machine appeared. The compositors were not, therefore, unprepared for its arrival, nor had they failed to learn, from the example of others, the futility of opposing it. Further, the timing of its arrival mitigated the problem of displacement, a problem which could be serious for a highly skilled craft where mobility of labour is apt to be low. Underlying the periodic fluctuations, the broad trend throughout the period was one of expanding demand for printing, to which expansion of population, extended education, and the growing development of newspapers and periodicals contributed. Further, the introduction of machinery coincided with, if it did not cause, a more rigid restriction of apprentices, so that the rate of growth of the labour force was reduced. As a result of these factors, and of the fact that the late 90's witnessed a recovery of trade in general, the introduction of machinery was soon offset by an expansion of demand. Some expansion of the industry also occurred in consequence of cheaper production. Thus Aberdeen, in 1899, reported that, as a result of the introduction of machines, a greater amount of composition was being done and there was an increase in the numbers employed in the machine room.

CHAPTER TEN

DISPUTES

I. THE EDINBURGH STRIKE, 1872

Referances have already been made to the events in Edinburgh in 1872, and to their repercussions. The importance and uniqueness of this strike in the history of the Association, however, justify the inclusion of the story in some detail here. The history of the Association is a remarkably peaceful one. Many local disputes did arise during the first fifty years, but these were, in the main, small affairs with few lasting repercussions. The Edinburgh strike stands out in contrast to this; it alone involved an entire Branch. Between 1853 and 1901 the total spent by the Association on Strikes, Compensation, etc., amounted to £12,782, of which sum £6,135 was spent in 1872–73, chiefly on the Edinburgh struggle. Occurring as it did before the Association had 'attained its majority', it was in fact a challenge to its ability to survive, and the only major test to which the Association was submitted.

The trouble arose in connection with the short-time movement. A memorial was presented in September to the employers for a 51-hour week, with an increase of $\frac{1}{2}$d per 1,000 on piece rates. At the same time advances were requested for overtime and for authors' corrections. Finally, the terms of the memorial were made conditional on the revision of the 1867 compositors' scale, about which considerable difficulties were constantly arising regarding the charging of extras. On pressure from the employers, however, the latter condition was removed. In spite of this, the employers refused to consider the proposals, and the reply received from them in October was signed by thirty-seven

of their number, as members of the Master Printers' Association. To the Edinburgh men this action was reminis-
cent of the ejection of 1846, and they decided to stand
firm against it. At a largely attended meeting the journeymen unanimously resolved to adhere to the terms of the
memorial. Overtime was to be discontinued pending a
settlement, and with the approval and backing of the
Executive Council, notices were to be tendered on the 1st
November. Further, if no settlement was reached before
the end of the fortnight's notice, an advance of 2/6 on the
'stab wage was to be made a condition of any subsequent
settlement. The 'stab wage in Edinburgh at this time was
27/6, while that in Glasgow had already been advanced
to 30/-.

Towards the end of the fortnight's notice, no settlement
having been reached, the men tried to meet the employers
by proposing some modifications to their requests. They
offered to take the reduction in hours by instalments over
a period of eighteen months, with a reduction of one hour
taking effect immediately. Their claim for an advance in
overtime rates was also modified, but, to offset these concessions, the 'stab wage was to be increased to 30/-. In
reply to this the employers offered to concede the 30/-
wage and the modified advance in overtime rates, but
absolutely refused to consider any reduction in hours or
advance in piece rates. The notices having expired, some
750 men came out on strike, their number including
compositors, pressmen and machine minders.

In fact, some twelve employers had conceded the terms
of the men, and, it was claimed, others had indicated their
willingness to do so, although as members of the Masters'
Association they had to accept the decision of the majority
in it. While the Edinburgh men, and in general, the Scottish men, remained loyal, the employers were able to fill
the places of the strikers with non-union men, chiefly imported from the south, with apprentices and women compositors. By the middle of February it was reported to the
Association that there were now over 700 non-union men,
women and boys in employment, and defeat had to be

admitted. The Executive Council advised the Edinburgh Society to accept the employers' terms offered at the start of the strike. This was put to the men at a meeting in Edinburgh and only agreed to reluctantly and by a small majority. Most of the strikers were immediately re-employed, although in some cases the non-union men had been engaged on three months' contracts. By the beginning of April only some twenty of the strikers remained idle, and it was decided to discontinue the payment of strike aliment from the 1st May.

At the start of the strike it had been agreed to pay benefit at the rate of 1 5/– per week to married men and 1 3/– to single men, with a payment of £3 to members leaving the town. These were less than the usual Association allowances, the reduction being decided as a precaution against a protracted run on funds. Events proved this action to be justified. During the weeks of the strike a total of £5,321 was paid out. During the first fortnight alone £300 was paid to men leaving the town. The finances of the Association unaided could not have borne the burden of this expenditure, but substantial assistance was received in the form of loans and gifts from other trade unions and Typographical Societies. Particular mention was made of the assistance received from the London Society of Compositors, who, during the greater part of the strike, contributed £50 per week, half as a gift and half as a loan. In all, £500 was received from this Society. The many other organisations assisting included the Machine Minders' and Press Society, London, the Manchester Branch of the P.T.A., the Glasgow Society, and the Ironmoulders', Masons' and Bricklayers' Associations of Scotland.

One by-product of the strike was the establishment of women in the Edinburgh printing industry. In June 1873 some fifty women compositors were employed in the city, and in the following years the numbers steadily increased. Another interesting offshoot, of a very different nature, was the formation of a Co-operative Printing Company. Early in the struggle a weekly paper, called the *Craftsman*, was produced by the men on strike, under the auspices of the Society. This was continued for a time after the end of the strike, but by June 1873 it was reported to be making a loss of £6 per week and it was decided to discontinue it. It was suggested, however, that a Co-operative Printing Company be formed to take over the office, and by August this was successfully achieved. Although handicapped by the fact that Co-operation in Scotland was at this time in its infancy, and also by its limited capital, the Company nevertheless survived and thrived. By 1875 it was reported that a profit of nearly 25 per cent had been made, and a dividend was paid at the rate of 10 per cent per annum.

II. The Glasgow 'Evening Citizen' Lock-out, 1893

Although not in any way comparable in its extent, duration or cost, to the Edinburgh Strike of 1872, the dispute in the *Citizen* office over the terms of working composing machines involved about sixty men and had one interesting sequel.

The proprietors, Messrs Hedderwick & Sons, had introduced machines to this office in 1890. The Glasgow Branch, foreseeing the probability of other firms adopting the machines, suggested a conference on the subject with the various newspaper proprietors in the city. Given the choice of a joint conference with the other proprietors or a direct conference with the Branch, the proprietors of the *Citizen* expressed a preference for the latter. The proposed conference, however, never took place. The Branch wished the *Citizen* employees to be represented at the meeting, but the employers were evidently reluctant to have their own workmen present. The machines were operated for about two years at the 'stab wage, with which arrangement the Branch was content. By the end of 1892, however, the employers expressed a desire to put the machine operators on piece-work, while retaining the other compositors at the 'stab wage. The Branch decided that such a mixed system was 'one not to be readily adopted, as it was inimical to the interest of the workmen'. The employers then proposed to put all compositors on piece-work, but the Branch took objection to the rate proposed for machine workers as being inadequate. It was claimed that at the end of the first week of piece-work only one operator earned an adequate wage, and some earned considerably less than the recognised 'stab rate. The Branch sought an interview with the proprietors to request an increase of $\frac{1}{2}$d per 1,000 for machine operators, but when this interview finally took place, the employers announced their intention of returning to the former system of payment at the 'stab wage. This decision was received with satisfaction. Some ten days later, however, the men were informed that the office was to be made non-union immediately. In most cases, the first intimation of this was received by the men when they arrived at work on the morning of the first day under non-union rules. The lock-out affected not only the machine operators, who were directly concerned in the dispute, but all members of the Society, including those employed in the jobbing department. Almost the entire staff remained loyal to the Society.

The interesting outcome of the lock-out was the starting of a new evening paper by the Society. This was originally done to publicise the Society's case in the dispute, since they lacked access to the normal channels of the Press, and was backed up by public meetings. At one such large meeting in the City Hall, however, the view was expressed that the time was ripe for starting a newspaper on behalf of the working classes. A prospectus was issued for the forming of a company with £30,000 of capital, and within six months a new evening paper under the title of the *Glasgow Echo* appeared. Described as 'one of the most important developments of trade unionism in recent years', the venture received support from other trade unions, who, along with the Branches of the Association, took up the shares of the new company. By the end of the year it was announced that in addition to the evening paper, the Company were now also publishing a weekly, and that the venture had enabled employment to be found for all the staff locked out. The following year the Association, after a vote of the membership, decided to invest £500 in the company. In 1895 the Association invested a further £500, but the managers were unable to carry on and the company went into voluntary liquidation. The shareholders were paid one-fifth of the purchase price in cash, the remainder becoming a charge on the new firm at 5 per cent. As a result of the change in ownership, the office was enlarged and more men employed. The *Glasgow Echo* was replaced by the present *Daily Record*.

III. The Secession of the Edinburgh Machinemen

The period under review also witnessed one important internal dispute, resulting in the formation of the Edinburgh Press and Machinemen's Society, not affiliated to the Association. This movement resulted from a feeling of dissatisfaction evidently prevalent among the members of this section, who felt that their affairs and interests were not receiving adequate attention under the existing framework of the Association. The feeling was first manifest in the Glasgow Branch in 1866, at the time when machinery was being introduced to this department on a large scale, a fact which probably had much to do with the following revolt. In that year it was reported that a large number of the press and machinemen of the Glasgow Branch had formed themselves into a separate Society and applied to the Executive to be admitted as a Branch of the Association. The Executive refused the application, affirming a belief in the view that to have only one Branch in a town would best preserve union and promote the efficiency of the Association. Further, the application, in the opinion of the Executive, did not contain any valid reason for secession, while the policy adopted by the Glasgow Branch in 1862 entirely removed the necessity for a separate Society. This was a reference to the following motion, adopted unanimously by the Glasgow Branch on that date: 'That, as a feeling very generally prevails that the interests of the Press and Machine departments of the profession have not

hitherto received the attention to which they are entitled
the Society recommend that a Committee of Press and
Machinemen be appointed to deliberate on affairs connected with their departments, previous to submitting
them to either a Committee or General Meeting of the
Society.' Further resolutions in favour of the machinemen
were subsequently passed by the Glasgow Branch, including the appointment of a press or machineman to the
post of assistant secretary of the Branch, the same official
acting as secretary to his own section. On this basis reconciliation was eventually achieved.

It was not until 1874, the year following the great strike,
that a similar secession occurred in Edinburgh. An application to the Executive for recognition as a separate
Branch was refused, the Executive acting on the precedent
of the Glasgow case and adhering to the principle of one
Branch to one town. With the exception of a small minority, however, the machinemen remained in their own
newly formed union, and appeals for conciliation failed.
This move was particularly regretted at a time when the
Edinburgh Branch and the Association were still strug-
gling under the financial burdens left by the 1872 strike.
The main reason given for it was that the interests of
the press section received insufficient attention and were
subordinated to those of the compositors. It was also
suggested, however, at the time of the secession and
during the protracted period of separation, that some of
the grievances were of a purely personal nature.

The first of many attempts to effect reconciliation occurred in 1877, when the question of admitting the
Machinemen's Society to the Association was raised at a
Delegate Meeting. The meeting again decided that there
should be only one Branch in one town, but also appointed
a small committee to try to secure a settlement between the
two sections of the trade in Edinburgh, on the lines of the
Glasgow system. A subsequent meeting with the machinemen proved unsuccessful, however, as they would not consider anything short of recognition as a separate Branch,
and this the Delegate Meeting had decided against. A

similar result was recorded in 1881, when, on the initiative of the Edinburgh Branch, a deputation, including representatives from the Executive and the Glasgow Branch, again approached the machinemen with a view to reconciliation. On this occasion the Edinburgh Branch offered the following terms to the machinemen: when they numbered fifty, the right to elect four members of committee, the president every alternate year, and the clerk every year; when their numbers were above a hundred, equal representation on the committee.

In 1883 the Executive Council again tried to enter into negotiations for a settlement of the dispute. A conference was proposed, but no reply was received from the machinemen. In 1884 the Edinburgh Branch announced the formation of a Press and Machine Section, and it was hoped this would aid them in their attempts to bring the machinemen back into the fold. In 1886 the dispute formed one of the topics of discussion at the meeting of Typographical Societies held in London, and a small committee, consisting of one representative from Manchester and three from London, was appointed to investigate it, and act as arbiters. At the start of the meeting held the following year in Edinburgh, the representatives of both sides, after discussion, pledged themselves to accept the award of the committee. The findings of the committee were in favour of amalgamation of the two sections, with the establishment of a joint committee to settle the details, any points of disagreement to be submitted to the arbitrators. The Association accepted the terms of the award, but the Machinemen's Society refused, reaffirming a resolution passed at an earlier meeting to the effect that 'on no account could the Members entertain the idea of amalgamation with the Edinburgh Typographical Society'.

During the advance movement of 1891 the existence of two Societies in Edinburgh proved an embarrassment and a hindrance. It was stated that the employers played one off against the other, and to the attitude of the Machinemen's Society in this was attributed the relatively small advance obtained. The following year the Machine Section of the Glasgow Branch received permission to meet the Edinburgh Machinemen's Society in an endeavour to persuade them to rejoin the Typographical Society. A resolution to this effect, however, was said to 'act as a red rag' on the Edinburgh men, and they put and carried a counter proposal to the effect that an Amalgamated Scottish Press and Machinemen's Association should be formed. Later the same year, at a Conference of the Printing and Kindred Trades Federation, the question was reopened and it was agreed that the Federation try to bring about a reconciliation, in spite of the assurances and protests of the Association delegates that this would be futile in view of the recent experience of the Glasgow Machinemen. The decision of the Conference resulted in the withdrawal of the Association delegates.

In 1895 the position deteriorated further. The Machinemen's Society endeavoured to increase its membership at the expense of the Typographical Society. As a result of its campaign some twelve members of the latter seceded, while the Branch had to cope with several complaints from its members about alleged persecution by members of the rival body. In 1897 the Machinemen's Society started a movement for a reduction of hours. No approach was made to the Machine Section of the Edinburgh Branch, and there was every indication that the Society still intended to act independently. Their request, however, was refused and when a strike was imminent, they appealed to the Branch for support. The Branch, however, after consultation with the Executive, decided that, in view of all the circumstances of the relations between the two sections, the most they could see their way to do was to prevent their members from filling the places of those on strike. The advance movement failed and no reduction of hours was received, a fact which, it was felt by the Association, demonstrated the advantages of union and strength, and proved their case for reconciliation. The position at the end of the fifty years, however, was a stalemate, and it was not until 1907 that the breach was finally closed and union achieved.

CHAPTER ELEVEN

RELATIONS WITH KINDRED UNIONS AND OTHER MATTERS

Before leaving the first fifty-year period, mention may be made of one or two other items emerging from the records. While none of these is long enough to merit a separate chapter, together they help to complete the picture. The most important of these concerns the Association's relations with kindred unions, culminating in the National Printing and Kindred Trades Federation towards the end of the period. The history of the *Scottish Typographical Circular* also deserves a place in this record. A story of a different kind is that concerning the Association's emblem, which is more in the nature of a curio. Finally, a number of brief items mainly concern working conditions and politics.

I. Relations with Kindred Unions

For some fifty years after the failure of the 1843 attempt at national union, relations between the main typographical unions of the United Kingdom were maintained on an informal but friendly basis. From time to time representatives of the Scottish Association were invited to attend delegate meetings of the English Association, when major issues affecting the trade were discussed, such as tramping and the mileage system of relief. Further, during the Edinburgh strike in 1872 considerable financial assistance was readily given by kindred societies south of the border. It was not until the 80's, however, that the possibility of a closer and more formal connection became the subject of discussion, and not until the last decade of the century was organisation on a national scale finally achieved by means of federation.

The subject of federation was first raised by the Parliamentary Committee of the T.U.C. in 1879. Here the ultimate object was a general federation of trade unions, but it was proposed that a first step might be the formation of a series of federations composed of trades of a kindred nature. While the majority of the workers were evidently not ready for such national organisation and the project came to naught on this occasion, yet the subject was fully discussed in current issues of the *Circular*. The pros and cons of federation within the printing industry were aired in the same columns the following year, on the occasion of a proposal by Glasgow that the Association seek the co-operation of the London Society of Compositors and the Provincial Typographical Association on the question of making provision for the unemployed. No action was taken on the Glasgow proposal, the feeling being that the Association should first take steps to provide for its own unemployed, as the other two organisations already did. The next step towards co-operation came in 1886 when, as a result of a resolution of the 1885 Delegate Meeting, the Association took the initiative in convening a general Typographical Conference in London, 'to consider questions affecting the welfare of the profession and establish closer relations'. Mr John Battersby, Association Secretary, acted as chairman of a meeting at which the English Typographical Association, the London Society of Compositors, the London Machinemen, the London Pressmen, the Dublin Society and the Leeds Society were represented. Among the resolutions approved by this meeting was one to the effect that the various unions concerned be asked to consider the advisability of forming a National Association and send in replies. No replies, however, were received.

The next attempt at national organisation came with the proposal to form a Printing and Kindred Trades Federation, first discussed at a special meeting in Manchester in 1890, at which the Association was represented. The following year the Association decided to join the new organisation, with which it was reported some eighteen Societies had 'now thrown in their lot'. This was the first step towards national organisation, although London had its own separate federation. It was not purely typographical, as the earlier National Association had been, but embraced all branches of the printing industry. Also, in the early stages it was a fairly loose federation, designed to secure joint action in matters concerning the trade, but not involving any close amalgamation or financial commitments.

In fact, the Scottish Association's connection with the new Federation lasted, in the first instance, for barely one year. In 1892 the Federation held a conference in Glasgow, on the occasion of a meeting of the T.U.C. in that city, and during the course of this the Association withdrew from the Federation. The cause of the break was a decision of the Conference that the Federation should endeavour to secure a reconciliation between the Association and the Edinburgh Machinemen. The Association objected to this because of the rebuffs they had received in their repeated and recent efforts to secure this end. It was not until 1895 that the Association rejoined the Federation, after agitation from Glasgow and Edinburgh about the disadvantages of remaining aloof from it. In particular, it was argued that membership would help in the campaign to get 'unfair' or non-union offices opened to the Association, as in many cases other members of the Federation were employed in these offices. In fact, in 1894 the Glasgow Branch sought permission to join the Federation on its own. While this was refused by the Executive Council, a Delegate Meeting the following year resolved that the Association should rejoin.

Shortly after this the question of closer federation came up, and in 1897 the first draft scheme of financial federation was produced. About the same time the T.U.C. again took up the question of a general federation of trade unions, and action on the scheme for the printing trade was postponed pending a decision on this. The General Federation of Trade Unions was formed in 1899, but despite this the question of a new national federation for the printing industry was reconsidered. In 1900 a conference was held with the London Federation with a view to

I   S.T.A.

amalgamation. The following year a scheme for a National Printing and Kindred Trades Federation was approved and came into operation at the beginning of 1902. The Scottish Association had taken an active part in the discussions and negotiations leading up to this event, and Mr John Templeton, the Association's secretary, was appointed vice-president of the new organisation.

One other case of co-operation within the industry, with which the Association was closely concerned, is worthy of mention, viz., the scheme for reciprocal payment of benefits. In this the Scottish Association could claim to be the prime mover. As early as the 1886 London Conference, the Scottish delegates had proposed the adoption of such a scheme. The resolution was rejected on this occasion, and the subject was allowed to drop for a number of years. It was taken up again by the English Association in 1899, and after a number of conferences, a scheme for the reciprocal payment of benefits came into operation at the beginning of 1901. The benefits covered by the scheme were unemployment relief and strike allowances.

II. The 'Scottish Typographical Circular'

The *Scottish Typographical Circular*, referred to in earlier chapters as simply the *Circular*, was first published on the 5th September 1857. The Association was then in its infancy and union organisation, except in Glasgow, was weak. Yet it was as a result of the efforts of a few members of the Edinburgh Society that the *Circular* appeared, under the auspices of, and at the risk of, that Society. The *Circular* was to be devoted to 'the discussion of questions of trade interest and the dissemination of trade news'. In an early editorial note the claim was made that: 'Our ship is thoroughly cosmopolitan, and orthodox or heterodox are alike welcome to claim a nook in it, if so be there is ballast in their argument, and a little regard to propriety in their grammar.' In addition to leading articles, reports and correspondence on matters of interest and concern to the trade in Scotland and other countries, the columns of the early *Circular* frequently contained original verses of contributors, and occasionally serial fiction such as 'The Court-ship o' Patie Cauldshouthers; Or, the Unco Surprise'.

As issued originally, for a trial period of six months, the *Circular* consisted of four pages quarto. The sales during the trial period were regarded as sufficient to justify an expansion, and the size was increased to eight pages. Thereafter, however, the income never proved sufficient to meet the added cost. The *Circular* was subsidised annu-ally by the Association from 1858, with the exception of one year, 1876, when the legality of the annual payment, in the absence of authorisation from a Delegate Meeting, was questioned. On this occasion the dispute with the Edinburgh Society was amicably settled by the Delegate Meeting of 1877,[1] and thereafter the annual subsidy con-tinued. The original hope that the *Circular* would even-tually become self-supporting was never realised. By the 1880's renewed appeals were being made for greater sup-port, and the financial difficulties of the *Circular* were causing concern to the Edinburgh Society. In 1883 it was proposed that the management be undertaken jointly by the four largest Branches, Aberdeen, Dundee, Edinburgh and Glasgow. Aberdeen and Dundee both declined to share in this venture; Glasgow was reported to be willing to consider the proposal, but evidently not with Edinburgh alone. Dundee proposed that the Executive take over the *Circular* and run it on behalf of the Association, but this was rejected. The journal continued to be the responsi-bility of the Edinburgh Society until 1908, when it be-came the official organ of the Association.

In spite of periodic financial difficulties, the *Circular* did a good job in providing a forum where questions of vital interest to the industry could be freely discussed, and the working of the Association, between annual reports, made known to and criticised by the membership. Much of its value lay simply in the fact that it was an independent, not an official, organ. By the time it was taken over by the Association it had expanded to sixteen pages and had been given a cover.

[1] See Chapter 5, page 58.

III. The Emblem

The suggestion that the Association take steps to secure an emblem was first made in a letter appearing in the *Circular* in August 1879. The suggestion was evidently not a new one, but had been inspired on this occasion by the fact that the English Typographical Association had recently acquired an emblem. In the latter case a premium of ten pounds had been offered for the best design, and the *Circular* decided to take up the suggestion that the Scottish Association should follow this example. The Editor announced that he would receive and publish notice of contributions from members and friends towards the building up of a similar premium fund. Two years later it was announced that the premium had now been fully subscribed, and further action was left to the Association. At the Delegate Meeting of September 1881 it was resolved that the Executive should secure a design for the emblem by a competition which was to be confined to Scotland. The conditions finally approved by the Executive included the following: '(a) To be drawn by a draughtsman residing in Scotland. (b) To represent Johannes Gutenberg and William Caxton, the Royal Arms of Scotland, and the Scotch Thistle—artists being at liberty to introduce at discretion the Rose of England and Shamrock of Ireland, in blend. (c) To represent the Composing-Room and the Machine-Room—in the latter the hand-press, as well as the most modern printing-machine.' In addition it was agreed 'that competitors be left free scope in symbolising the rise, progress, influence of the art of printing, and in introducing contrasts to these'.

The competition and its conditions were advertised in the *Circular* and in the daily press of Aberdeen, Dundee, Edinburgh and Glasgow. At the end of the allotted four months, however, only one entry was received. This was the work of John D. Carmichael, draughtsman with Messrs Nelson & Sons, Edinburgh, who was subsequently awarded the second premium of five pounds. His work was evidently good, but the design did not contain all that the Executive felt it should, and it was agreed that he produce another design incorporating their joint ideas. While the original entry conformed to the stipulated conditions of the competition, the Executive felt that 'many features could have been introduced to show the influence of printing on civilisation, such as symbols of science, mechanics, engineering, painting, music, architecture, the drama, peace, and plenty.' They also felt that stereo- and electrotyping, book-binding, and lithographing should be represented, but hastened to add that 'these will not be introduced unless there is ample room and sufficient justice done to the claims of our own profession'.

The outcome of this was the elaborate emblem, reproduced as the frontispiece of this volume, with which the Executive found it necessary to issue the following points of explanation:

'1. The four corner pieces—representing Asia, Africa, America and Europe—are taken from the marble sculpturings attached to the Albert Memorial in Kensington Gardens, London.

'2. The winged figure standing upon the key-stone of the arch represents the attribute of Justice. The wings are a novelty, but the style is after the usual drawings of Mercy.

'3. The left medallion is a drawing of Johannes Gutenberg showing his first printing in 1444; the centre one is the Royal Arms of Scotland; and that on the right is a sketch of William Caxton exhibiting the art of printing to Edward IV, his Queen, and their son.

'4. Sectional views of stereotyping and electrotyping, book-binding and lithographing—three cognate branches of labour.

'5. Three bust drawings of Robert Burns, David Livingstone, and Sir Walter Scott—the representatives of poetic genius, discoveries on the dark continent, and mediaeval and modern Scottish literature.

'6. The central figure upon the platform of the pyramid is Literature, with Astronomy on her left and Engineering on her right hand. The four figures, reckoned downwards, on the right, are Architecture, Agriculture, Music, and Peace. Those to the left, reckoned upward, are Plenty, Drama, Painting, and Mechanics—all of which, with the exception of Architecture and Painting, have derived new life from the development of printing.'

By the end of 1883 the emblem was available for sale to members at a cost of 2/6. The annual report of the following year announced that the Executive Council, in view of the large stock of emblems still on hand, had decided to insure them for the sum of £200. A further comment appeared in the report of 1897 to the effect that there had been little demand for the emblem and the price had now been reduced to 1/–. The fate of this elaborate piece of draughtsmanship may be gathered from the fact that few of the present members probably even know of its existence.

IV. WORKING CONDITIONS AND POLITICS

The question of working conditions and their effect on the health of members deservedly received attention during the period. To this matter attention was chiefly drawn by the *Circular*, which also assumed the role of critic of the various Factory Acts, underlining their weaknesses in practice and as applied to the printing industry. The industry, in fact, had a high death-rate; in 1878 it was claimed that 'one-half of the members of the printing profession in Scotland are cut off before they have reached half the allotted time of man's pilgrimage on earth'. The scourge of the industry was consumption and the toll was heaviest on those in the under-thirty age-group. From 1880 onwards the annual reports of the Association contained an obituary column, giving age and cause of death, and these two facts stand out clearly from these columns: fully half of the deaths recorded were due to pthisis and the majority of the victims were in their early twenties. In addition to overcrowding and lack of air and light in the workshops, many of which were underground, the large amount of stone-work necessary to the book compositor contributed to the prevalence of this disease. As late as 1899 the Glasgow Branch is recorded as recommending to the Health Committee of the Town Council the abolition of underground workshops and artificial light, and more regular visits from factory and sanitary inspectors. On this occasion the Health Committee 'expressed surprise at the very large proportion of deaths of our members from pthisis'.

In the sphere of politics the important issue towards the close of this period concerned direct representation of Labour in Parliament. Support for this movement was urged in the annual reports at the end of the century and regret expressed at the opposition to the new Trade Unionism from the ranks of workers, including some within the Association. In 1900 a vote of the membership on the question of joining the Committee on Labour Representation resulted in 831 for and 728 against, out of a total membership of 3,730, the small proportion voting making the result null and void. In 1902 the Glasgow Branch decided to support the movement and to impose a levy of $\frac{1}{4}$d per member per week for this purpose. The Association was urged to take another vote of the membership, and this was done the following year. Again the result was in favour, but the smallness of the number voting left the Executive Council with no alternative but to let the matter drop in the meantime.

Throughout the period, in fact, the attention and interest of the Association and the Branches were given to a variety of matters, national and local, industrial, political and social, affecting the general well-being of the members. As an example of the purely local activities may be mentioned the provision by the larger Branches of libraries for their members; in Glasgow the Society's library dated from 1852, in Edinburgh from 1858, while that of Banff was started some time between these two dates. In contrast to this, action by the Branches to secure the printing contracts of public bodies for union offices, while local in its immediate effect, had implications for the entire industry, and even for industry in general, since it may be regarded as an important step in the movement towards recognition of a standard minimum wage. In the question of Government contracts the Scottish Branch concerned was, naturally, Edinburgh, and this Society in the 1890's devoted a great deal of its energies to securing recognition of the 'fair wages clause' in the printing of Blue Books. Most of the Branches were similarly active over a long period in the question of printing contracts with local public bodies, school boards, and the like. Where the volume of employment was threatened, the Association and Branches were equally vigilant. Thus, the American Copyright Bill of 1888, which granted copyright to British authors if their books were printed and published in America, gave rise to mass meetings of protest; an appeal was made to the Cabinet; and, in 1891, after the Bill had become law, the Executive Council joined a deputation to the Board of Trade to express the industry's fear of its effect on employment—fears which events proved to be unfounded.

PART III

THE SECOND FIFTY YEARS
1903 — 1952

CHAPTER TWELVE

THE BACKGROUND

I. GENERAL

To the historian looking back, the years of the nineteenth century seem incredibly peaceful in contrast to the first half of the present century. The outstanding feature of the last fifty years is the extent of disturbance and the rate of change in all spheres of life, economic, political and social. Twice during this short time the world has experienced the horrors of modern warfare, in contrast to which all previous wars become mere skirmishes; the slaughter in the trenches of the first world war, and the civilian bombings and the atom bomb of the second, are the peculiar products of twentieth-century civilisation. The end of the period finds the world again engaged in an armaments race.

In the sphere of economics, the two world wars and their aftermaths have created special problems and, at the same time, accelerated inevitable and fundamental changes. Contemporaries of 1902 no doubt considered the industrial revolution complete and the age of mechanical progress well advanced. Yet looking back from the vantage point of the present, mechanisation appears to have been only in its infancy at the beginning of the century. Coal, which was the main source of power and the basis of Britain's prosperity, has yielded ground to electricity and oil, while the future holds the possibility of the development of atomic power. The old emphasis on basic heavy industries has diminished, and what was formerly a source of strength is now a cause of weakness in Scotland. A rising standard of living has been accompanied by a steadily increasing variety of consumers' goods; the essentials of bare existence to-day include products and gadgets unheard of in 1902. These changes are reflected in the economic structure and position of Britain. The relative decline of the heavy industries and expansion of light consumers' goods industries changed not only the structure but the location of industry. Thus were born the depressed areas, one of which included the main industrial district of Scotland. Agriculture, Scotland's second line of defence, suffered in the inter-war period from the relatively large-scale importation of cheap foodstuffs, the consequence of which was poverty rather than unemployment. In industry, the result was a continuous high level of unemployment, regarded in the 30's as permanent and insoluble, on to which were superimposed the increasingly severe trade cycle fluctuations. Abroad, Britain's trading position deteriorated. The gold standard and free trade were abandoned. At home, the 'dole' was introduced, and Commissioners for the Special Areas were appointed. Recovery started in the mid-1930's, but only with rearmament and war did unemployment disappear. In contrast, the period since 1945 has been one of full and over-full employment, a situation for which there was no peace-time precedent. At the same time, the problems of balance of payment deficits and rearmament have been accompanied by inflation and recurrent crises.

In the social and political spheres the changes have been equally far-reaching. The gradual discrediting of the tenets of *laissez-faire* has been accompanied by increasing State responsibility in economic affairs. Even the most reactionary now accept a measure of economic planning. The Labour Party, which has grown along with the trade union movement, has achieved several spells in office, including one with a substantial majority. Taxation and the social services have combined to reduce the inequalities in income distribution; the Welfare State has grown from the '9d for 4d' of 1911 to the all-embracing National Insurance of 1948.

The trade union movement has shared in the general change. The legal and political position of the unions has been repeatedly challenged, but is now more secure than ever before. Their industrial position has been tested by frequent and increasingly heavy attacks of unemployment. Craftsmanship has been further replaced by the ubiquitous machine. Increased organisation of unskilled and semi-skilled labour has given rise to the large, general unions and to industrial unions, which, in many cases, have threatened the position of the smaller craft unions. Where organisation was weak, the Government has instituted Wages Boards and Councils. Wages are now negotiated on a national scale, and machinery has also been created for joint consultation. Finally, full employment and nationalisation have presented a new situation and challenge to the unions, which originated and were built up as defensive organisations, with restriction their major weapon. This new-found power is in marked contrast to their lowly beginnings, and brings with it problems as well as privileges.

In all this it is hard to find any pattern or unity, unless it be the unity of continuous and all-pervading change. In the face of this, the survival and strengthening of the Association is in itself a notable achievement. The completion of its century as an independent and continuous organisation is a tribute to the ability and adaptability of its leaders and members.

II. The Industry

Throughout the period the fluctuations in the printing industry followed closely the movements in industry and employment in general, although on a slightly modified scale. As in the early period, depression usually affected printing a little later and a little less severely than other industries.

Signs of recession in trade appeared early in the period, and varying amounts of unemployment were reported for the years 1904 to 1909. The recovery which started in 1910, and was to some extent stimulated by rearmament, continued until the outbreak of war in 1914. In the first instance, war brought a reduction of demand for printing, since the industry was to some extent a luxury one. This, combined with raw materials difficulties and shortage of newsprint, produced considerable unemployment and short-time working. The labour surplus, however, was soon absorbed by the numbers volunteering for the Services, by the transfer of labour to munitions industries, and finally, by conscription. From 1916 onwards there was a shortage of labour and the efforts of the Association were directed towards the problems of threatened dilution and infiltration of cheap labour.

The inter-war period started with a brief spell of prosperity, which enabled the demobilised members to be reabsorbed into the industry fairly well in all areas except Edinburgh, where a contraction in the staple book-trade had reduced the openings available. A reaction to this post-war boom, however, quickly set in, and the years from 1920 to 1923 were ones of heavy unemployment and considerable short-time working. Conditions started to improve in 1924 and from then until 1929—excluding the disturbance of the General Strike in 1926, in which the Association took part—employment could be described as fair, and although some unemployment persisted, conditions in printing compared favourably with other industries. The year 1930 was one of great depression in Scotland, but in printing the position was still described as 'not so bad as in some industries'. Thereafter unemployment increased, the worst years for printing being 1931 and 1932; never before had so many members been affected. In 1933 it was again reported that unemployment in printing was not so serious as in some industries. Thereafter conditions improved, but a fairly high level of unemployment appears to have been accepted as normal, the problem, attributed in part to increased mechanisation, being regarded as insoluble. Improvement, as a result of rearmament, started in 1936, but a hard core of unemployment persisted until 1938, when the amount paid by the Association in unemployment relief was the lowest for eighteen years.

As well as sharing in the general trade fluctuations of this period, the printing industry also experienced certain internal changes. On the demand side two main trends can be distinguished. In general, the demand for the industry's products increased, as might be expected with the extension of universal and compulsory education and a rising standard of living. Expansion in the newspaper section in particular was considerable. At the same time, however, certain changes in reading habits tended to reduce the demand for books of a high quality. The growing production of cheaper periodicals and magazines, cheaper editions of books of all kinds—in some cases with only paper covers—and the extension of public and circulating libraries, all tended to reduce demand for high quality productions. Edinburgh, as the principal centre of book-production in Scotland, and having a high reputation for quality work, suffered most in this respect. In consequence, there was a steady decline in the numbers employed there on this work in the 1920's. Between 1921 and 1931 the numbers employed in the Scottish printing industry generally increased, the increase being particularly marked in the newspaper section. In Edinburgh the numbers employed in the production of newspapers and periodicals increased by some fifty per cent, but the total employed by the industry had declined by nearly eight per cent. In addition to the factors already mentioned as affecting book production, there was also, during this period, a definite southward drift in this section of the industry. The book trade of both Edinburgh and Glasgow continued to cater to a large extent for the London market, but there was a relative decline in their share of that market, more being employed and more produced in England, particularly in towns in the south within easy reach of London. While this drift was typical of the changes in industrial location at this period, it has also been suggested that wage differences provided a special stimulus in the case of printing. Certainly the rates in Glasgow and Edinburgh were exceeded only by London, and were higher than those of many of the English towns competing for the London market. A further factor concerns productivity which tended to be higher in the south. Here the size of establishment is important, and on an average, the size in Scotland was smaller.

Changes on the production side were mainly the result of increased mechanisation, which was considerable in this period. The introduction of the composing-machine towards the end of last century was achieved with relatively little displacement of labour, because of the expansion of trade. The increased mechanisation of the inter-war period, however, tended to increase the number of unemployed, particularly in Edinburgh. While over all, and ignoring the short-term fluctuations, the total labour force of the industry increased in the twenty years, the numbers in certain highly skilled sections tended to decline. Thus, the total number of compositors in Scotland, according to the 1921 Census Report, was 4,556, while by 1931 the number had fallen to 4,221. A similar trend is discernible in the membership of the Association, although this is, of course, also affected by changes in the list of union offices. The peak membership of journeymen was in 1925, when the total was 4,905, of whom 3,356 were compositors; in 1938 the total was 4,222, of whom 2,694 were compositors.

As before, the outbreak of war in 1939 at first caused considerable unemployment and short-time working. By the end of 1940, however, the call-up of members to the Services and transfers to war industries had eased the position, while from 1941 onwards there was an acute labour shortage. Again the attention of the Association was directed towards a limited and controlled relaxation of its rules to meet the shortage, and, at the same time, the prevention of large-scale encroachments via dilution and cheap labour.

In the post-war period the industry has shared in the general experience of full employment. Demand for its products has again expanded. Higher incomes and the scarcity of alternative spending outlets in the war and post-war years evidently increased the demand for books. This trend has been slightly reversed during the last few years, with the disappearance of many of the wartime shortages and the rising cost of living, and also the high cost of printed products. Nevertheless it seems likely that demand will remain considerably above the pre-war level. Fully twenty per cent of the Scottish industry's products are exported, many to hard-currency countries, and overseas demand, particularly in the Dominions and Colonies, remains high.

On the supply side the industry has been faced with shortages of raw materials and a tremendous increase in costs, particularly in the price of paper. As a result of the changes in the industry in the inter-war period, and the restriction of apprentices which these changes seemed to demand, there is now a shortage of skilled craftsmen. Within the Association, a 'bonus' increase of apprentices has been negotiated. Overtime working increased steadily, rising from 192,676 hours in 1945 to a peak of $457,847\frac{1}{2}$ hours in 1950, since when there has been a slight reduction. In the closing years of the period a slight increase in unemployment has been reported by a few Branches, but mostly of short duration. In so far as it depends on the general economic position of the country, the outlook for the industry is uncertain, but evidence suggests that demand should remain at a higher level than in the pre-war period. Within the industry, however, the big uncertainty concerns the raw materials position and the tremendous rise in costs. The size of the market in future will depend to a large extent on the industry's ability to overcome these problems.

III. The Association

By the beginning of this period the Association had already reached maturity. The first fifty years were the formative years, and from them it emerged essentially in its present shape. It had grown from small beginnings, by cautious but steady progress into a national organisation of nearly 4,000 members. Further, it had added to the traditional trade union activities in the field of wages and working conditions, the comprehensive services of a

K

provident society. In contrast, the second fifty years represent a period of consolidation and growing strength, rather than one of any fundamental change in nature or structure.

This is not to say that the Association merely marked time or rested on its laurels, nor was there any slackening of the missionary effort and extension. A few names were added to the list of independent Branches from time to time, mainly of small towns. In this way Branches were added at Bathgate in 1904, Alloa in 1906, Wick in 1907, Dingwall in 1912, Berwick in 1915 and Haddington in 1917. The outcome of the additions, subtractions and amalgamations of the period is a present total of 32 Branches, embracing a membership of 5,573. But the scope for extension by the creation of new Branches was obviously limited, and in the main, missionary efforts took a different form. In fact, three main lines of action can be distinguished. Firstly, efforts were made to extend the membership of existing Branches and to bring into the fold non-union offices. Complete organisation in union offices was assisted by the adoption, in 1907, of a resolution to the effect that members should not be permitted to work beside non-union men. This rule, however, has been criticised on several occasions, on the grounds that it was a handicap to the organisation of non-union offices, since all eligible employees had to become members of the Association before an office could be recognised as a union one. Proposals to relax or amend this rule have been made from time to time, but without success; the rule is still adhered to.

The second approach to the question of organisation concerned the outlying areas surrounding the main Branches. The need to organise these areas became obvious early in the period, improved transport bringing them into direct competition with the larger centres. At first the officials of the larger Branches were responsible for this task. In 1907, for example, Dundee reported on its organising efforts in Cupar, St Andrews, Leven, Alyth and Kirriemuir, members in these areas being attached to the

Dundee Branch. Later Aberdeen similarly became responsible for a larger and more widely scattered area, including
Orkney and Shetland. In 1908 Dundee suggested that the
task was too great for the Branch officials, and that the
time had come for the Association to follow the example
of England and appoint an official organiser. In 1911 this
suggestion was approved by a Delegate Meeting and the
post of Organiser and Assistant Secretary created. Two
years later the post was abolished and the General Secretary became responsible for organisation, a Financial
Secretary being appointed to assist him. Steady progress
has since been achieved in the organisation of the outlying
areas, the larger Branches continuing to play an important
part in this task.

The third phase of organisation occurred in the inter-
war period and culminated in the formation of the Auxiliary Section. Changes in production methods and increased
mechanisation brought into the printing office a number
of semi-skilled workers, many of them women, and it was
to the organisation of these workers that the Association
next turned its attention. In 1918 the following declaration
of its organising aims was issued—'Membership of the
Scottish Typographical Association is open to all workers
in printing offices in Scotland who are employed in opera-
tions directly connected with the production of printed
matter; that is to say, compositors, readers, assistant readers, composing-machine operators, composing-machine
casters, composing-machine mechanics and assistants,
pressmen, printing-machine minders, assistants, feeders
and flyers, male and female.' Until this, membership had
been confined to compositors (hand and machine operators), readers and pressmen. The following year a number
of Branches reported the formation of an Auxiliary Section
for the semi-skilled workers. This action, however, immediately brought protests from the National Union of
Printing, Bookbinding, Machine Ruling and Paper
Workers and from the National Federation of Printing
and Kindred Trades, of which both the Association and
the Paper Workers were members. A Delegate Meeting

decided that further action in the development of an Auxiliary Section must have the approval of the Federation, and during the next few years conferences were held with the Federation, the Paper Workers and the National Society of Operative Printers and Assistants. No satisfactory agreement could be reached, however, and in 1924 the Delegate Meeting decided that the Auxiliary Section be developed without further delay. As a consequence the Association was expelled from the Federation, and in the following years charges of poaching were brought against it by the Paper Workers. The matter was brought before the T.U.C. and the Scottish T.U.C., while the Scottish Alliance of Employers also attempted to secure reconciliation. Not until 1928, however, was an agreement reached and the question of demarcation settled. Thereafter the organisation of the Auxiliary Section progressed steadily, and it now embraces twenty-six Branches with a total membership of 1,670, of whom 1,260 are women. Auxiliary members do not enjoy full membership of the Association, but the Section now has its own Delegate Meeting, held prior to the Association Delegate Meeting, which must ratify its decisions. It has its own schemes on similar lines to those of the parent body. It is now represented on the Executive Council of the Association, and also on most of the organisations with which the Association is affiliated. The question of merging the Association and the Auxiliary Section was examined in 1946 but was rejected, chiefly on the grounds that such an amalgamation would change the Association from a craft to a general union.

While women predominated in the Auxiliary Section, the number of female compositors remained small and these were confined to a few areas, of which Edinburgh was the principal one. The policy of the Association remained one of opposition to the employment of cheap female labour in this skilled section, but at the same time recognition was granted to those already in the industry. In 1911 the formation of an Edinburgh Female Compositors' Society was approved, and the following year reported a membership of over two hundred. In 1918 a female Section of the Aberdeen Branch was formed.

The organisation of non-union offices has received some attention in recent years. In 1949 a Delegate Meeting resolved: 'That this Conference considers the time opportune for an all-out campaign to recruit the remaining non-Society offices in Scotland, and remits the question to the E.C. for consideration and report.' As a result a detailed survey was made and a report submitted in 1950. The position may be summed up by the following conclusions of this report:

(1) The majority of the non-recognised offices are one-man businesses and not likely to expand.

(2) Our weakest area is in the south-west of Scotland. This we understand is true of Trade Unionism generally, largely because of its remoteness and its purely rural character.

(3) On the daily newspaper side, however, we are still confronted with the position in Dundee and Edinburgh. The newspaper position in these two cities remains our largest black spot, both in numbers and importance.

The statistics collected for this report showed that the gross total of unorganised workers was approximately 550 or just over seven per cent of all known letterpress workers. Of these, non-union daily newspaper offices in Dundee and Edinburgh accounted for 323.

Early in the period the breach created in the ranks of the Association by the secession of the Edinburgh Press and Machinemen was closed. Negotiations for amalgamation were opened in 1904, and an agreement was finally approved by the Delegate Meeting of 1907. A major point of disagreement and cause of delay was the Association's ruling that there should be only one Branch in any one town. The Machinemen were afraid of being swallowed up by the Edinburgh Society. Finally, it was agreed to relax the rule in this case and a separate Edinburgh Machine Branch of the Association was established. The question of organisation was taken up by the new Branch and by 1910 it was reported that the machine section of the Edinburgh trade was 98 per cent organised.

While liable to some fluctuations, the financial strength

of the Association increased considerably during the period. The major calls on the funds came during the several prolonged spells of unemployment. Again, the two world wars brought periods of considerably reduced income, special arrangements being made to relieve those on service from contributions, while at the same time claims on the Funeral Scheme by dependants of those killed on active service were heavy. The only other major claim on resources occurred in 1926, when the General Strike was responsible for the payment of over £48,000 in strike allowances. As a result of such special circumstances, some of the schemes were from time to time in deficit, but this was never allowed to continue for long. In such cases special levies were usually imposed, and, if necessary, contributions increased, until each separate scheme was again on a sound financial basis. At the same time, a strong Protective Fund was built up. By 1924 the total at the credit of the Association had exceeded £100,000, by 1939 it was nearly £200,000, and at present approximates £300,000. Of this total some £170,000 stands to the credit of the Provident Schemes, while the Protective Fund amounts to £86,000, the Administrative Fund taking up the remainder.

The affairs of the Association continued to be managed by an Executive Council elected by a vote of the members. The composition of the Council, however, has been altered from time to time, in an effort to make it as widely representative as was consistent with efficient management. As a result of the 1903 Delegate Meeting the Branches were arranged into seven groups, each appointing one member of the E.C., with the exception of Glasgow and Edinburgh who each appointed three members. A reorganisation of the groups by the 1913 Delegate Meeting reduced the elected representatives to seven, in the interests of economy and efficient management. This followed a period when administrative matters had been allowed to get rather out of hand, and when the financial position of the various schemes had been allowed to deteriorate. Further small changes in the grouping of Branches and the composition of the E.C. have since occurred, but the principle of election has remained the same. Representatives have also been added from the Female Compositors' Section and the Newspaper Section, as well as from the Auxiliary Section. The E.C. at present consists of fifteen members—President, General Secretary, Financial Secretary, and twelve group representatives. If the General Secretary is a compositor, the Financial Secretary must be a machineman. Also, where a group has the right to elect two representatives, one must be a compositor and one a machineman.

A number of additions to the Rules have been designed to secure closer co-operation between the E.C. and the Branches. Thus the Delegate Meeting of 1928 approved a resolution to the effect that 'the E.C. members shall confer with the Branch Committees or Committees of Branches by whom they were elected, on any important business'. The same Meeting resolved that two Branch representatives be present at E.C. meetings when a question submitted by a Branch was being considered. In addition, the increasing complexity of the affairs of the Association, and the increasing specialisation within the industry, have resulted in the appointment of a number of committees to safeguard the interests of particular sections and advise the E.C. on special matters. Thus, it was decided in 1928 to appoint a National Machinemen's Committee; a National Compositors' Committee was approved in 1936, but abolished by the Delegate Meeting of 1946; finally, a Newsmen's Advisory Committee was appointed in 1946.

The E.C. continued to be located in Glasgow. Until 1911 the location was decided by a vote of the members, but a Delegate Meeting of that year resolved that the headquarters of the Association be permanently located in Glasgow, the permanency being qualified by the fact that future Delegate Meetings could decide otherwise. No attempt to change this decision has been made, and in 1923 the present Head Office building was purchased.

The Rules and policy of the Association continued to be determined by periodic Delegate Meetings, with special meetings when the occasion or the wish of the members demanded. In the inter-war period annual conferences of Branch secretaries and officials were held, and since the war there has been some attempt to establish annual Delegate Meetings with a restricted field of business. Both of these, however, are now in abeyance, and Delegate Meetings of each Section are held only once every three years.

During the period there has grown up fairly elaborate machinery governing relations with other kindred unions and with employers. There has been a growing tendency towards negotiation of wages and working conditions on a national level. Some progress has also been made on the lines of joint consultation; and, as a member of the Printing and Kindred Trades Federation, the Association also enjoys membership of the Joint Industrial Council for Printing. Although a member of the Federation, however, the Association has retained a certain amount of autonomy and reserved the right to negotiate independently conditions and agreements with the Scottish Alliance of employers. One important consequence of these developments, however, is that wages and hours, since 1918, have been the subject of national negotiation and agreement, not of local movements. The question of reducing the disparities and securing greater uniformity among the Branches has been similarly dealt with by means of agreed grading schemes.

As before, particular aspects of the Association's affairs and problems will be considered in more detail in the succeeding chapters. Here it may simply be recorded that, in addition to the negotiation of wages and working conditions, the Association was concerned, during a considerable part of the period, with the problem of unemployment. As a consequence of this and of increasing mechanisation, with a renewed threat of cheap labour, apprentice restriction and training became important issues. Finally, towards the end of the period, the Association was faced with a new situation and new problems, created by full employment.

CHAPTER THIRTEEN

WAGES, HOURS AND WORKING CONDITIONS

I. A General Survey

Of the many factors affecting wage rates and their negotiation during this period, some have tended to simplify the task of surveying general progress, others to complicate it. The replacement of local advance movements by national negotiation, for instance, makes it easier to summarise the over-all changes from 1918 onwards. Similarly, the grouping of Branches into a number of grades has reduced and regularised the differences in rates prevailing throughout the Association. During this period, also, Edinburgh succeeded in abolishing the pernicious mixed system of payment, which had so long been a source of grievance. Finally, a resolution was passed in 1920 abolishing piece-work, and thereafter the gradual adoption of time rates throughout the Association has further simplified the task of the recorder. On the other hand, changes in production methods, increased mechanisation, and the extension of the Association to include auxiliary workers, have replaced the single 'stab rate with a series of rates within each grade or district. A similar, but slightly different series of rates occurs in the Newspaper Section, in which rates in general have remained higher than those for book and jobbing.

As a result of the change from local to national negotiation, the period obviously falls into two broad divisions, that prior to 1918, when the old method of wage negotiation applied, and that after 1918 when movements were on a national scale. Of these two, several sub-divisions are possible. The first period falls into two parts—the pre-war years up to 1914, and the war years. The second period similarly divides into three—the inter-war period, the war years 1939 to 1945, and the post-war period. While some of these periods include a number of movements, which might suggest further subdivision, an attempt will be made here to summarise progress within these five periods.

(i) 1903–1914

At the end of the first fifty years it was reported that, in the matter of wages, the Association was tending to fall behind in a period of rising prices. The period from 1903 to 1914 was one of slow upward progress in wages and some reduction in hours—characterised, however, by an astonishing diversity in the success with which the Association's efforts were attended in different areas. The last general advance movement had occurred in the early 1890's. The first movement came from the Glasgow Branch, who applied in 1903 for an increase of 3/6 per week. The claim was put to arbitration, but was rejected. The chief reason for rejection was that in Edinburgh the rates were already some 2/– lower for a longer working week. A further rise in Glasgow would result in the loss of work to Edinburgh, including some of Glasgow's share in the London book trade. Edinburgh's competitive position was further improved by the fact that a considerable number of female compositors were employed there, while there was a complete ban on them in Glasgow. The Glasgow Branch renewed its appeal for an increase of 3/6 in 1907, and after protracted negotiations, during which notices were tendered, finally accepted an increase of 1/6, with a further 6d the following year. This was the first increase that had been granted since 1891. Overtime rates were agreed at time and half, with a minimum of 1/1 per hour. In 1911 a claim for a further increase of 4/– and reduction of hours to 48 per week was proposed, but received insufficient support within the Branch. This claim was renewed in 1913, and early in 1914, prior to the outbreak of war, an advance of 2/– on the 'stab rate was granted. In addition to these general advances, during this period the Glasgow Branch was also concerned with the question of rates for the various machines introduced. In 1904 an attempt was made to secure a wage of £2 for Monotype operators, and this was finally achieved, after some friction, in 1905. In 1906 the scale for rotary machines came into operation, and a scale for mechanical composition in book and jobbing was approved. As part of the general advance of 1907 the rate for mechanical composition was increased by 2/–, while a further increase of 3/– was granted in 1914. The newspaper scale was also revised during this period. Negotiations, which proved lengthy, were opened in 1906, and the case went to arbitration in 1907, when five of the six points in dispute were decided in favour of the Branch. A movement for an increase in the 'stab wage in this section was stopped by the outbreak of war in 1914.

The outcome of the movements in Glasgow during this ten-year period was a 'stab wage for book and jobbing of 38/– for a 50-hour week, an increase of 4/– over the period, with no reduction in hours; for composing machines the rates were 45/–, and 43/– for Monotype. In the Newspaper Section, the 'stab wage was 44/6 for a 48-hour week of day work, and 47/6 for a 45-hour week of night work; for mechanical composition the rates in this section were 45/– for a 46-hour week of day work, and 52/6 for a 42-hour week of night work.

During this period Edinburgh continued to lag behind Glasgow. Two movements occurred. In 1908 hours were reduced to 50 per week, and an increase of ½d granted on time rates only. A similar reduction of hours was achieved by the Machine Branch in 1909. In 1910, as a result of an agreement with employers about female labour, the Branch agreed to a moratorium on advance movements for three years. In 1911 and 1912 attempts were made to secure the abolition of piece-work, but these were unsuccessful. Another attempt early in 1914 met a similar fate, but a general advance in rates was then secured. The 'stab wage became 35/– for a 50-hour week, with 38/6 for mechanical composition. There was no Newspaper Section of this Branch, the main Edinburgh newspaper offices remaining non-union.

Throughout the rest of the Association advances of varying amounts were achieved during this period, although there were no marked or concerted general movements. As a result of a decision of the 1903 Delegate Meeting a circular was sent to the Branches urging them to take steps to secure greater uniformity in wages and hours. Each year thereafter brought reports from some Branches of increases in wages and, in some cases, reductions in hours. At the end of the period the lowest 'stab rate was 27/6, the rate of the Dingwall Branch, while Buchan, Cupar (Fife), Stranraer and Wick all had 28/–; Greenock and Paisley had both obtained the Glasgow rate of 38/–. In the matter of hours, the lowest was 48 per week, enjoyed by the Dingwall Branch, thus partly off-setting the low wage rate, and the highest $52\frac{1}{2}$ per week in the Dumbarton Branch. Most Branches, however, worked a 50-hour week. For this reason the Association did not become signatories to the 1911 National Federation agreement with employers for the gradual reduction of hours everywhere to 51.

During the early part of this period the question of overtime working received some attention. In years of fairly heavy unemployment protests were made at the considerable amount of overtime worked by the men. Attempts were made to limit such extra working by members to 12 hours per week, but repeated violations of this rule were reported, particularly by Glasgow, and fines were imposed. The 1911 Delegate Meeting reduced the overtime permitted to 9 hours per week, and in 1913 a tax of 1d per hour was imposed on all working overtime, the revenue going to the Out-of-Work Fund. The question lost its urgency, however, with the general improvement in trade. Also allied to the problem of unemployment was that of short-time working, which was at this time permitted by the Association. Abuse of this resulted in the 1911 decision that one week's notice must be given by the employers before introducing short-time.

(ii) 1914–1918

The immediate effect of the outbreak of war was to bring to a standstill a number of wage movements throughout the Association. Through time, however, the claims of the fighting forces and war industries eliminated the unemployment problem and produced a labour shortage. Agreement was reached regarding the dilution of labour, and rules were to some extent relaxed. At the same time, rapidly rising prices produced numerous demands for higher wages. The years from 1915 to 1918 were marked by repeated wage increases throughout the Association, although it was claimed that these were hampered by the excessive amount of overtime working and the consequent high level of earnings. The first step towards national wage negotiation occurred in 1918, when two advances received by Edinburgh, Glasgow, Aberdeen, Dundee and Perth were the result of federated effort and applied to printing and allied trades in these towns.

In all, during this period, the increases in wages obtained ranged from 16/– in Forfar to 32/– in Dundee. In Glasgow the increases in the book and jobbing sector totalled 30/–, giving a 'stab rate of 68/–, with 73/– and 75/– for mechanical composition. In the Newspaper Section, the rates became 70/– for day work and 77/– for night work, the increases here being less than 30/–, while for morning newspapers the rates for mechanical composition became 83/– and 85/–, a rather higher increase. In Edinburgh the 'stab rate increased by 31/– to 66/–, the rate for mechanical composition becoming 68/6, an increase of 30/–. In the provinces, Greenock and Paisley had secured the Glasgow 'stab rate of 68/–, while the lowest rates prevailed in Forfar with 46/–, and Banff and Hawick each with 47/6.

The war years also brought to the Glasgow area the first Sunday newspaper, for which wages and working conditions were negotiated.

(iii) 1919–1939

Since 1919 local wage movements have been replaced by national negotiation. The first step towards national negotiation in Scotland was taken by the employers, who, in this matter, anticipated the Whitley Report. At their instigation a conference was held in Edinburgh in 1917 with representatives of the unions in the printing and kindred trades, Sir George Askwith acting as independent chairman. The purpose of the meeting was to consider the possibility of national wage negotiation for the Scottish printing and kindred trades and the establishment of a Scottish Wages Board. Progress towards this was slow and there followed about a year of negotiation and conferences. One hindrance to progress was the fact that the Bookbinders' Union was not in the National Federation of Printing and Kindred Trades. By the end of 1918, however, the Board was finally established. It consisted of eleven members from each side of the industry, and three of the workers' representatives were appointed by the Association. Many Branches voiced warnings and complaints about the loss of autonomy involved in this method of wage negotiation, and some friction at first arose. It was agreed, however, that any claim from one union be submitted to the Workers' Panel of the Board, who would consult other sections of the industry so that a common claim might be put forward to the Board. On the whole, this method worked smoothly, and the Association remained a staunch supporter of the Board until its demise in 1924; by this date only one other union remained a member. The principle of national negotiation, however, did not die with the Board; all wage matters continued to be settled for the entire Association by direct negotiation with the Scottish Alliance of Master Printers.

During the first two years of this period four increases were obtained throughout the Association, giving a total increase in the general trade of 29/6 in all Branches. The post-war boom was short-lived, however, and the following years of depression forced on the Association, for the first and only time in its history, a number of wage reductions. Between 1921 and 1923 flat-rate reductions totalling £1 were imposed on all Branches. No other flat-rate increases or decreases occurred during this inter-war period; an attempt to secure a general increase of 2/6 in 1924 was unsuccessful, and again in 1939 after the outbreak of war a claim for an all-round increase of 15/6 was rejected; attempts to impose further reductions in the depressed years of the early 1930's, however, were successfully opposed.

But this is not to say that there were no further wage movements during the period; many Branches in fact received considerable advances. The abandonment of local wage negotiation soon brought demands for the reduction of the wide disparity in rates prevailing throughout the Association; flat-rate wage movements threatened to perpetuate differences which were to some extent fortuitous. With the object of securing greater uniformity in rates a scheme for the grouping of Branches into a number of grades was presented to the employers through the medium of the Wages Board in 1921. In 1922, after protracted negotiations, proposals and counter-proposals, a Grading Scheme was approved and signed. The Branches of the Association were arranged in five grades, the difference between the rates agreed for Grades I and V being 12/–; the rates for Linotype and Monotype operators exceeded the 'stab rates by 8/6 in the first grade and 6/6 in the fifth grade. The scheme was to operate for one year without revision. Further, a condition of the wage decreases agreed in 1922 and 1923 was that no wage alterations should take place before January 1924. In the interval, complaints from the Branches regarding the scheme mounted up; many claimed that they should have been placed in a higher grade; Edinburgh, for example, had not been included in Grade I, but had been given a rate 2/– below that of Glasgow;[1] also by the beginning of 1924 proposals from Branches for a flat-rate increase ranged from 12/6 to 5/–.

In 1924 the Association presented a new Grading Scheme to the Wages Board for the approval of the employers, the proposals incorporating a flat-rate increase of

[1] A similar discrepancy had, in fact, long existed between the two Branches.

2/6. No agreement was reached, however, and the matter was submitted to the Scottish Joint Industrial Council. Further negotiations with the employers followed and finally, by the end of the year, a new Grading Scheme was approved, but with no flat-rate increase. Under the new scheme the number of grades was reduced to four, thus reducing the discrepancy between the highest and lowest to 9/–; Edinburgh was included in Grade I; sixteen Branches obtained an increase of 3/– and one an increase of 6/–.

This scheme remained in operation for the rest of the period, no alteration occurring in the rates of any Branch. The question of revising the scheme was raised in 1936, when a Delegate Meeting decided that there should be only one grade in Scotland. Action was postponed until the completion of an hours' movement then in progress, and the question was not taken up until 1938. Then it was found that the achievement of one grade was impossible, but a proposal for two grades with a difference of only 3/– was presented to the employers. It was argued that since the present rates were fixed in 1924, changes had occurred which not only gave rise to anomalies, but tended to reduce differences in the cost of living in various parts of the country. In support of this, figures of average expenditure on certain essential items were collected from various Branches. The employers, however, opposed any radical alteration, and would only agree to consider anomalies. This attitude, it was felt, was the result of a similar reply given by the employers in England to Federation efforts to secure re-grading there. In England there were then six grades in addition to the London one; the difference between the highest grade and the lowest was 15/–; while the difference between the London rate and the lowest grade was 26/6; the lowest English rate was 10/6 less than the lowest Scottish rate. Meantime improved means of transport and communication were widening the areas of competition. By the end of 1939, however, no revision of rates had occurred. The Grade I rate of 77/6 applied to Glasgow, Edinburgh, Airdrie, Dumbarton, Dundee,

Greenock, Hamilton and Paisley. Aberdeen, with a wage of 75/6 was in Grade IA. The rates in Grades II, III and IV were 74/6, 71/6 and 68/6 respectively. In each case the rates for mechanical composition were 7/6 above the 'stab rate. Membership of the Newspaper Section still suffered from the effects of the General Strike, but rates in Glasgow union offices were 102/– for day work, 109/– for night work; the corresponding rates for mechanical composition were 108/3 and 116/3.

During this period also, national agreements were made regarding rates for apprentices and female compositors. In 1920 a scale of apprentice rates, rising from 14/6 in the first year to 49/6 in the seventh year was approved, and it was agreed that thereafter the rates be adjusted proportionately with the journeymen's rates. The wages of female compositors in Aberdeen and Edinburgh were fixed at seventy per cent of the male rate. An agreement was also concluded with the employers regarding rates and conditions of work for the Auxiliary Section.

During this period the Association participated in the hours and holidays movements of the National Federation. In 1919 an agreement was reached which granted a 48-hour week, one full week's holiday in the summer, and six general holidays throughout the year. At this time the Association was endeavouring to secure a 40-hour week, and only accepted the Federation agreement after this proved impossible. The years 1934 to 1937 witnessed another short hours' movement which culminated in the 45-hour week, with an 11-day fortnight for the Newspaper Section. It was then agreed that no major concession be asked for three years. Again the Association sought a 40-hour week and at first opposed the Federation's agreement, but a majority of the Federation's members were in favour of its acceptance.

A major problem during this period was unemployment, and this influenced policy and decisions regarding working conditions. As well as being the main reason for the Association's advocacy of the 40-hour week, it affected issues concerning overtime, short-time working and double shifts. The increase of unemployment in 1920 again switched attention to the excessive amount of overtime worked; in Glasgow a special committee was set up, with representatives from the Branch and local employers, to secure the limitation of overtime working as much as possible. The question again became urgent in the depression years of the early 1930's, and in 1933 a conference was held with the employers. Then it was agreed that where cases of unreasonable overtime working were reported, the Secretary of the Alliance and the Association Secretary should investigate these and, if necessary, submit them to the National Conciliation Committee. Records of the amount of overtime worked were kept and these compared with the amount of unemployment. In the first four months of 1937, for instance, £6,340 was paid in overtime rates, while for the same period the Association paid £4,277 in unemployment benefit. The matter was again taken up with the Alliance, who agreed to circularise their members asking them to reduce overtime as much as possible. In the meantime, a number of Branches, including Dundee and Edinburgh, started the operation of a double shift as an alternative to overtime. An agreement on this was reached with the employers in 1939. The same year an agreement was signed with the employers regarding the limitation of overtime while men were on notice through lack of work. This agreement also contained a new principle, which, it has been claimed, made it unique in Trade Union history—no worker could be compelled to work overtime.

Abuse of short-time working resulted in a decision by the Delegate Meeting of 1924 to abolish it. The following year this was incorporated in an agreement with the employers, under which short-time working and suspension were forbidden. An attempt was made by the Alliance to remove this ban in 1931, when, they argued, the rule was causing hardship to both sides. Conditions for short-time working were drawn up, but these were rejected by a vote of the membership.

Finally, it must be recorded that early in the period

there ended a long-standing grievance of the Edinburgh Branch, namely the mixed system. Towards this end, several unsuccessful attempts had been made to abolish piece-work, and in 1921 Edinburgh reported that this had been achieved.

(iv) 1939–1945

As in other trades, this was a period when wages were rising in an attempt to offset the rising cost of living. On the rejection by the Alliance of the Association's wage claim in 1939, a vote of the membership was taken to decide whether the claim was to be further pressed or the alternative of joining the National Federation's movement for a war bonus accepted. The vote was in favour of the latter. This was the first time that the Scottish Association had asked the Federation to negotiate for them in the matter of wages, but all subsequent general wage increases during this period were the result of Federation movements. The Federation's claim was for an increase of 10/– for men and women on men's work, 7/6 for other women, and 4/– for juveniles. The claim was rejected and the matter eventually went to National Arbitration. The Tribunal awarded increases of 5/–, 2/6 and 1/6 respectively to these specified grades. In 1941 a further increase of 5/–, 3/6 and 2/– respectively was approved.

While joining with the Federation in the negotiation of general increases, the Association also secured further advances for some of its members by a revision of the Grading Scheme. The ultimate aim of the Association here was one grade for Scotland, and in 1942, having failed to instigate a further general claim because the Federation was negotiating on regrading in England, a proposal for two grades in Scotland was presented to the Alliance. The Alliance in turn proposed three grades. Negotiations, however, reached a stalemate and the question was submitted to the Scottish Joint Industrial Council. As a result of the award, three grades were eventually established, applying to both Association and Auxiliary members. For the allocation of towns to these grades, however, appeal had to be made to the Conciliation Committee the following year.

With the completion of the re-grading movement, pressure for a general increase was renewed, and in 1943 the Federation presented a claim for a 20/– increase for men and women, with 75 per cent of the increase for juveniles. The claim was refused and, the machinery of the Joint Industrial Council being unable to overcome the stalemate, was submitted to National Arbitration. The Award rejected the claim as applied to men, women on men's work, and juveniles, but granted a 4/– increase to other women. The award produced consternation in the Federation, and the Unions were left free to take what action they could. The Association took up their claim with the Alliance, and on its being rejected, took a vote of its members on a proposal to ban all overtime until the claim was settled. The vote was in favour and the ban imposed. The Alliance's protest that this was a new wage claim and should therefore have been submitted through the various negotiating channels before such drastic action was taken, was upheld. Negotiations were reopened, however, between the Federation and the employers, and finally a National Wage and Stabilisation Agreement was signed. This granted an increase of 7/6 to men and women on men's work, 2/6 to other women, and 3/– to juveniles. The stabilisation clause bound the Federation to seek no further increase during the war or for twelve months thereafter, unless as a result of a rise in the cost of living. While subject to this agreement, the Association negotiated a separate agreement with the Alliance concerning rates for apprentices. These were fixed as percentages of the Grade I rate, rising from 20 per cent in the first year to 60 per cent in the seventh year.

In 1945 the Federation sought a revision of the 1943 Agreement, on the grounds of the rise in the cost of living, particularly after the end of hostilities. After proposals and counter-proposals, a new agreement was signed and came into operation in January 1946. This granted an increase of 8/6 for men and women on men's work, 7/6 for other women, 4/– for juveniles, and an appropriate percentage increase for apprentices. Under the stabilisation clause no further claim was to be made before 30th June, 1947 provided the cost of living remained at approximately the same level; this did not preclude Federation action on hours and holidays, however.

The outcome of these movements was a general increase of 26/–, making the 'stab rate for book, jobbing and weeklies in Grade I 103/6, in Grade II 100/6, and in Grade III 97/6. In each grade the rate for Linotype operators was 7/– above the 'stab rate, and that for readers and Monotype operators 5/– above it. In the Daily Newspaper Section, the Glasgow rates were—compositors and machinemen 128/– for day work, 135/– for night work; readers 130/6 for day work, 137/6 for night work; Linotype operators 134/3 for day and 142/3 for night work; upmakers 133/– for day and 140/– for night work. The newspaper rates in Aberdeen, Greenock and Paisley were 3/6 less than the Glasgow rates. In the Auxiliary Section, the Grade I rate for males was 86/–, Grade II 84/–, and Grade III 82/6; for females, the corresponding rates were 55/–, 53/6 and 52/–.

No reduction in hours occurred during this period, it being agreed at the outset that the time was inopportune. Hours therefore remained at 45 per week, with 44 for day work in the Newspaper Section, and 41¼ for night work. Early in the period, when unemployment had been increased by the immediate effects of the war, the question of short-time working was raised. An agreement permitting this was in force from 1939 to 1940, when it was cancelled by the Association because the employers would not agree to a minimum of 40 hours per week. It was again permitted in 1945, following a compulsory Government Order for the reduction of fuel consumption, the employers on that occasion agreeing to pay the full rate of wages for half of the hours deducted.

Some further relaxation of rules was conceded to meet the needs of war conditions. Agreements were made concerning the transfer of workers from one Branch to another, the employment of a member by more than one employer, the employment of superannuated members, and the introduction of non-union labour. The Association, however, successfully opposed dilution of labour, in spite of the attempts of the employers to overcome the shortage of labour in this way, particularly by the introduction of females. Of the agreements on working conditions made by the National Federation, the Association adopted only one—that governing procedure during air raids. This provided at first for the suspension of work during raids and part payment of the time lost, but later was altered to permit of work continuing, provided certain safeguards were available.

(v) 1946–1952

During this period the upward movement in the cost of living and in wages continued, and was accompanied by some improvement in hours and holidays. At the beginning of the period an unsolicited all-round advance of 10/– was obtained through the Federation, as part of an Hours and Holidays Agreement. At the same time an advance of 8/– for men and 7/6 for women was granted to the Auxiliary Section. Thereafter the autonomy of the Association in wage matters was restored, and although several attempts were made to create a national wages structure, negotiated through the Federation, wage movements in Scotland have continued to be negotiated by the Association and the Scottish Alliance.

Early in 1947 the Association lodged a claim for an advance, the claim being for the same rate as the highest paid to any other kindred union. This, in effect, meant an increase of 9/–, to give the rate then paid to stereotypers. There was some delay before the claim was considered, and by that time advances were being sought by several kindred unions, including that of the stereotypers, because of the rise in the cost of living. In view of this, the employers sought the co-operation of the Federation in the creation of a united and co-ordinated wage policy for the industry. No progress was made towards this end, however, the Federation deciding it did not have a mandate from its members to negotiate a wages structure. Meantime, the Alliance had intimated to the Association a decision to negotiate only through the Federation, and in protest, a ban had been placed on overtime working after a vote of the members. The Scottish Joint Industrial Council had condemned this action of the Association as a violation of the established conciliation provisions, but the Association had refused to grant the request to remove the overtime ban. On the breakdown of the national movement, however, the Alliance reopened negotiations with the Association, and early in 1948, on the grounds of the rise in the cost of living, an increase of 9/- was granted, with 7/6 to men and 5/6 to women in the Auxiliary Section.

Another attempt to negotiate a wages structure was started in England at the beginning of 1948, and concrete proposals were put forward by the unions. On the appearance of the Government White Paper on Wages and Incomes, in February of that year, however, the employers declined to continue negotiations. Subsequently, claims by individual unions were renewed, and in June the Association submitted a claim to the Alliance for an increase of 9/-. The basis of this claim was to secure parity with the stereotypers, following the example of the English Typographical Association. Again the employers pointed out that such parities could not be established by piecemeal negotiation, but only by the creation of a national wages structure. As a result of a parallel movement in England, the Federation took up the question of a wages structure once more, the majority of its members being in favour of this. There followed many conferences on the subject and a genuine attempt to co-operate. The difficulty, however, was the machinery required for such a policy and the loss of autonomy required from the unions concerned. Finally, failure had to be admitted, and in 1949 the unions returned to their former policy. The Association was pledged, by a Delegate Meeting decision, to work with the Federation in this wage movement, and for a time was one of four affiliated unions who endeavoured to pursue a joint policy. This also proved unsuccessful, however, and eventually direct negotiation with the Alliance was resumed. By November 1949 an agreement had been signed granting an increase of 8/6. At the same time it was agreed that both sides co-operate to increase efficiency, and where possible, incentive schemes were to be introduced. On the question of manpower, the term of apprenticeship was reduced to six years, and a bonus ration of 85 apprentices approved.

In 1951, as a result of an award to the London Society of Compositors, a new move was started for a national wage agreement between the Federation and the employers. The agreement sought by the employers covered wage increases, regrading, stabilisation, cost of living, sliding scale, incentives and manpower. Although opposed to many of the employers' proposals, the Association for a time joined in the Federation movement, but eventually withdrew and reverted to its former policy. A claim for an increase in wages, to meet the rise in cost of living, was lodged with the Alliance, and in May 1951 a Wages and Stabilisation Agreement was signed. In addition to granting an increase of 12/6, the Agreement attached the basic minimum rates to the official Index of Retail Prices at September 1950, when the Index, based on June 1947, was 114, and provided for a six-monthly review and cost of living bonus, calculated on movements of the Index. For each point rise or fall in the range above the Index figure of 114 the bonus was to be increased or decreased by 1/– for men and 9d for women per week. The agreement to co-operate to increase production, if necessary by incentive schemes, was reaffirmed, and a further extra ration of 80 apprentices agreed. The whole Agreement is to remain in force for five years from November 1950, and thereafter until six months' notice to terminate is given by either party.

In 1951 also, a claim was lodged for revision of the Grading Scheme. Again the aim of the Association was one grade for all members, but to this the employers would not agree. Finally, in March 1952, an Agreement was signed, dividing the Branches into two grades, with a wage differential of 3/–. Grade I now includes the following towns: Aberdeen, Airdrie, Alexandria, Alva, Ardrossan, Ayr, Barrhead, Beith, Bellshill, Clydebank, Coatbridge, Dalkeith, Dumbarton, Dumfries, Dundee, Dunfermline, Edinburgh, Falkirk, Glasgow, Greenock, Hamilton, Helensburgh, Johnstone, Kilmarnock, Kilsyth, Kirkcaldy, Kirkintilloch, Motherwell, Paisley, Perth, Port Glasgow, Renfrew, Rutherglen, Stirling and Wishaw.

In the Daily Newspaper Section also four wage increases have been received. In 1946 the Section shared in the unsolicited increase of 10/– awarded by the Federation movement. Following the granting of an increase to the general trade in 1948, a claim was lodged with the Scottish Daily Newspaper Society for an increase of 9/– for day workers and 20/3 for night workers. The claim for night workers was made up of 9/– plus 25 per cent of all increases since 1939, the Association having recently restored to the general trade the pre-war differential of 25 per cent over the day rate for night shifts. The claim went to arbitration, and the award granted the 9/– increase to day workers and 12/– to night workers. The Arbiter rejected the claim for a 25 per cent differential as applied in the general trade, on the grounds that the relevant differential was between day and night work within the Newspaper Section, and this his award would restore to the pre-war level. The rate for the Saturday shift in the production of Sunday newspapers, which had been $2\frac{1}{2}$ times the night rate, under this award received an increase of 15/–, or $2\frac{1}{2}$ times half of the increase granted to night workers. Further, this rate in future was not to vary automatically with variations of normal night rates. The arbiter stated that this rate at present was the highest in any part of the country for the production of Sunday papers, which was his reason for including only half of the present increase in the formula.

In 1949, again following the completion of an advance movement in the general trade, a claim was submitted for an increase of 10/– for day workers and 12/6 for night workers on daily newspapers. This, it was claimed, was necessary to preserve the traditional differential between the two sections of the trade. The employers refused the claim, on the grounds that there was no specific traditional differential. Pending a settlement, the Association imposed certain restrictions on the working of members in this section, an action which the employers claimed was a violation of the agreement on working conditions, concluded in 1948, under which certain conciliation machinery was provided. This the Association denied, and refused to consider the removal of the sanctions imposed. Finally, the employers threatened to close all offices unless sanctions were removed within 48 hours and repeated an earlier offer to submit the claim to national arbitration. To this the Association agreed, and the arbiter awarded an increase of 6/9 to night workers, and 5/– to day workers. He rejected the claim for an automatic adjustment to preserve the differential with the general trade, but admitted that the rate in the Newspaper Section had always been higher. The recent advance in the general trade reversed this relationship for the night worker, hence the increase of 6/9 which made the night rates equal in both sections. The increase to day workers was necessary to preserve the internal differential between night and day work.

Finally, in 1951, a claim was submitted for an increase similar to that obtained by the general trade, on the grounds of the rise in the cost of living. An agreement was reached, after submission to the Conciliation Committee, which granted a 12/6 increase, with a sliding-scale cost-of-living bonus of 1/– per point of the official Index of Retail Prices above 114. The Agreement included the same stabilisation clause as that agreed for the general trade.

The Auxiliary Section also shared in all the wage advances of this period. Male workers received increases totalling 32/6 and females 23/–. The Association re-grading scheme also applied to this Section.

The present wage position in the various sections of the Association may, therefore, be summarised as follows: Grade I—compositors and machinemen 143/–; Monotype operators and readers 148/6; Linotype operators 151/–. Grade II—3/– less in each case. Newspaper Section —Grade I, Day work—compositors and minders 164/6; readers and upmakers 169/6; operators 170/9; night work —176/3, 181/3 and 183/6. Grade II—3/6 less in each case, except that of operators on day work for whom the differential is only 2/6. Auxiliary Section, Grade I—males 118/6; females 78/–, with 85/6 after five years' experience as adult workers. Grade II—2/– less for men and 1/6 less for women. Apprentices receive 36/– in their first year, rising to 86/– in their sixth year. For female learners (Auxiliary Section) the starting wage in Grade I varies from 35/– to 43/–, according to age, rising to 78/– at the end of four years' training; in Grade II the corresponding rates are 33/6 to 41/6, rising to 75/–. In all cases these are the standard minimum rates awarded by the 1951 Agreements, and determined on the basis of the Index of Retail Prices at September 1950; to them must be added the present[1] cost of living bonus of 21/– for men, and 15/9 for women.

In addition to these wage movements, an Hours and Holidays Agreement was concluded, through the National Federation, during this period. In 1946 a claim was lodged for a 40-hour week, with a fortnight's holidays in the summer. Negotiations were protracted, the case was submitted to the Joint Industrial Council, strike action was threatened, twice the Ministry of Labour intervened, and a Court of Inquiry was set up. Finally an Agreement was signed granting a fortnight's holidays with pay, a 43½-hour week, with the promise of a reduction to 42½ hours when the labour situation permitted, and a five-day week, subject to variation due to local circumstances. A similar Agreement applied to the Newspaper Section.

II. THE COMPARATIVE POSITION

At the outset some attempt must be made to sum up and simplify the detailed movements described in the previous

[1] i.e. that obtaining during the second half of 1952, based on the Index at May 1952.

section. In the general trade, taking the Glasgow rate as the equivalent of the Grade I rate throughout, and for the moment, considering only the 'stab rate, there has been an increase during the second fifty years of 130/–, while hours have been reduced from 50 to 43½ per week. In the Newspaper Section, the 'stab rate for day work has increased by 150/–, that for night work by 157/3; hours for day work have been reduced from 48 per week to 40 per week, and for night work, from 42 to 37½ per week. At the beginning of the period composing machines were just starting to invade book and jobbing houses, while in the newspaper offices they were largely paid by piece rates. Since 1914, however, the rates for mechanical composition in the general trade have increased by 127/–; in newspaper offices the increases have been 146/9 for day work, 152/– for night work, while hours have been reduced to 37½ hours per week for day work and 35 hours for night work, piece-work having disappeared. For the Auxiliary Section, which was not organised until the inter-war period, the increases since 1939 have totalled 79/6 for men and 58/9 for women, with an extra 7/6 for women with five years' experience as adult workers.

The period has also witnessed the virtual elimination of piece-working, with the adoption of a time wage for mechanical composition, the ending of the mixed system in the Edinburgh book houses, and the gradual adoption of a time wage in practically all other offices. A resolution in favour of its abolition was passed at the Delegate Meeting of 1920, and at present it survives only in two small offices, where it has been agreed that it shall continue for those individuals concerned. The present Rules contain a clause to the effect that there shall be no further introduction of piece-work without agreement between the Association and the Alliance.

In reviewing the fifty-year period as a whole, some attempt must be made to assess the relative value of the advances obtained, to compare them with advances in other industries and with changes in the cost of living. For this purpose the following table has been drawn up, which summarises the movements in the main sections of the industry during the five periods already considered, the rates being expressed as percentages of the 1914 rate, and compares them with changes in the cost of living as measured by official and other Index Numbers. The rates throughout are those of the Glasgow Branch, which is equivalent to the Grade I rate. As a result of the various Grading Schemes and the narrowing of local differentials, the percentage increases in many other Branches were, however, greater.

| Year | BOOK, JOBBING, ETC. | | NEWSPAPERS | | | | Cost of Living[2] |
| | | | DAY WORK | | NIGHT WORK | | |
	'Stab	Mechanical Composition[1]	'Stab	Mechanical Composition[1]	'Stab	Mechanical Composition[1]	
	(1)	(2)	(3)	(4)	(5)	(6)	(7)
1903	89·5	–	76·4	–	84·2	–	91
1914	100·0	100·0	100·0	100·0	100·0	100·0	100
1918	178·9	166·7	157·3	–[3]	162·1	161·9	203
1920	256·6	231·1	240·4	232·2	240·0	239·0	249
1923	203·9	188·9	229·2	240·6	229·5	221·4	174
1933	203·9	188·9	229·2	240·6	229·5	221·4	140
1939	203·9	188·9	229·2	240·6	229·5	221·4	159
1946[4]	272·4	245·6	287·6	298·3	284·2	271·0	236
1950	344·7	307·8	341·6	351·7	344·7	325·7	289
1952[5]	431·5	382·2	416·8	426·2	415·3	389·5	340[6]

[1] The rate chosen here is that for Linotype operators; Monotype operators receive 2/6 less.

[2] 1903–1914—from A. L. Bowley, *Wages and Income in the United Kingdom since* 1860. 1914–1938—Ministry of Labour Retail Price Index. 1938–1952—London and Cambridge Economic Service Index, calculated by R. G. D. Allen, linked to the old index based on 1914.

[3] No rate given.

[4] Rates paid from beginning of January 1946 as a result of an advance negotiated in 1945.

[5] Rates paid during the second half of 1952, including bonus calculated on the Official Interim Index of Retail Prices at May 1952.

[6] Average of the first six months.

The history of wages in the Association during this period shows that the members have been able, on the whole, to compare their pay packets favourably with those of other trades. There has, however, been a fairly general tendency for the differences between different types of workers to close in.

A number of comments may be made regarding the general trends revealed. Firstly, the relatively small increase between 1914 and 1918 was typical of the period, and is a reflection of the fact that during that period earnings were more important than rates. The considerable amount of overtime worked, for example, has already been noted as a factor unfavourable to wage increases. Again, the reductions of the period 1921 to 1923 were universal. The stability of rates throughout the Association for the remainder of the inter-war period, however, suggests two comments. Firstly, as during the first fifty years, the Association's ability to retain wage rates during a depression reasserted itself in the early 1930's, when many trades suffered reductions. Secondly, while some other trades secured increases during the last few years of this period, from 1936 onwards, rates in the Association remained the same until after the outbreak of war. The fact that the Association did not share in the reduction of the early 1930's may help to explain this. Also, 1937 saw the completion of a shorter hours movement, in which the Association participated. Turning to a more recent period, the increases obtained between 1946 and 1950 were high compared with other skilled trades, although this must be modified by the fact that in some other trades earnings advanced more rapidly than rates. In the matter of hours the Association appears to have fared better than many other trades, securing a reduction to 48 as early as 1919, and to 45 in 1937. Holidays with pay were also secured unusually early, one week being granted in 1919 and two weeks in 1946. In fact, holidays with pay were, for many trades, an issue of the period from 1945, when there was a tendency to regard them as an alternative to wage increases.

The internal wage structure of the Association has not

remained unaffected by these general movements, as a
comparison of the changes in the first six columns of the
table reveals. Comparing columns (1) and (2), the percentage increase received by mechanical compositors is
much smaller than that of the 'stab rate, revealing a narrowing of the differential between the two in the Book and
Jobbing Section. In fact, the money difference has remained practically unchanged throughout—7/– in 1914
and 8/– in 1952. The corresponding differential for day
work in the Newspaper Section has increased, as is shown
by columns (3) and (4). Here, however, it must be noted
that in 1914 the rate for mechanical composition was only
6d more than the 'stab rate, while in 1920 it was actually
2/6 less; in 1921, it became 6/3 above the 'stab rate, and
this money difference has remained unaltered, so that since
1921 this differential has also been narrowing. Columns
(5) and (6) show the differential between the two rates for
night work in the Newspaper Section to have been approximately maintained until 1920, and to have been narrowing thereafter. Here the money difference has remained at
7/3 since 1921. Comparing night work and day work in
the Newspaper Section, the differential between the 'stab
rates has been only slightly reduced, but that between the
rates for mechanical composition has been considerably
reduced, largely because of the relatively low day rate for
mechanical composition in 1914. Comparing the Book
and Jobbing Section with the Newspaper Section, columns
(1), (3) and (5) show that for the 'stab rates the differential
has been maintained and slightly increased. Columns (2),
(4) and (6) show that for mechanical composition the differential has been increased, particularly for day work; in
fact, the 1914 rates were the same for day work in the
Newspaper Section and in the Book and Jobbing Section,
while at present the former is 19/9 above the latter.

Summing up, mechanical composition in all sections re-
ceives more than the 'stab rate, but, with the exception of
day work in the Newspaper Section, the differential has
narrowed; rates in general are higher in the Newspaper
Section than in the Book and Jobbing Section, being

highest for night work in the former Section, and here the differentials have been maintained and increased, relative to 1914. A comparison of 1939 and 1952, however, shows that the Association has shared in the general tendency for differentials to narrow, largely as a consequence of flat-rate increases granted to meet the rising cost of living during the war. The cost-of-living bonus incorporated in the present wage agreements will further accentuate this.

A narrowing of the differential between the rates for skilled and unskilled jobs, again common to industry in general, is revealed by the trend of rates in the Auxiliary Section. Since this Section was only formed during the inter-war years, no comparison over the longer period is possible. Comparing 1939 with 1952, however, the rate for male Auxiliary workers rose from 77·4 per cent of the Grade I 'stab rate to 85·1 per cent. This represents a rather smaller differential than the general average between skilled and unskilled rates.

The rates for female workers show a similar trend, again conforming to the general movement. The majority of women in the Association are Auxiliary workers, the majority of the latter being women. Expressing their rates as percentages of the rates for male Auxiliary Workers, there has been an increase from 58·3 per cent in 1939 to 67·2 per cent in 1952, rising to 72·6 per cent after five years' experience as adult workers. The position of the female compositors attached to the Aberdeen and Edinburgh Branches has similarly improved. The wage agreements of the inter-war period fixed their rates at 70 per cent of the male rate for the Branch, but their relative position has since been improved by granting them the same increases as the skilled men. They now receive 84 per cent of the full 'stab rate.

A comparison of the Association rates with those of England shows that, London excepted, Scotland has fared relatively well throughout most of the period. In the matter of grading, Scotland, until recently, was ahead of England, both in respect of the number of grades and of the difference between the highest and the lowest rates;

the latter advantage in fact still holds. The present position is one in which there are only two grades in both England and Scotland. The Federation Agreement, secured for England in 1951, fixed the basic minimum rate for Grade I at 143/6, compared with 143/– in Scotland, and for Grade II at 138/–, compared with 140/6 in Scotland. The same cost-of-living bonus agreement applies in each case. Thus, the position in Scotland is still the more favourable, particularly in view of the fact that towns in England are graded according to an index number based on size of population and number of journeymen members, a basis on which only Edinburgh and Glasgow would qualify for the Grade I rate.

The wage advances of the first fifty years were compared with those of two other skilled trades—engineering fitters and masons. Here this comparison may be continued, but bricklayers shall be substituted for masons, the small number of masons now remaining receiving the same rate as the bricklayers. Again the Glasgow rates only are compared. At the end of 1902 the relative positions of the three crafts were—compositors 38/–, fitters 36/– and masons 42/6. By the end of 1951 the wage rate of fitters had risen to 118/1½, bricklayers to 137/6, and compositors to 143/– plus cost-of-living bonus of 15/–. The Association has therefore gained a relative advantage, particularly in comparison with the fitters; the discrepancy here, however, is somewhat modified by the fact that earnings are more important to the latter than rates, although in the Book and Jobbing Section of the Association also, a large percentage at present receive merit money in addition to the minimum rates. In both cases, however, the hours are longer than those of the Association, while the bricklayers' rate is that for summer hours.

Finally, a comparison may be made of the changes in relation to changes in the cost of living as measured in column (7). From this it is evident that during the first world war rates fell behind the cost of living, but the discrepancy was not so great as these figures suggest because of high earnings. The increases obtained during the years

M   S.T.A.

immediately following 1918, however, more than closed the gap, while the reductions of 1921 to 1923 were less than the fall in the cost of living. The ability of the Association to maintain its rates during the depression of the early 1930's meant a rise in real wages for those remaining in employment, the cost of living falling during this period to 140 in 1933. In more recent years, the increases in wages have more than kept pace with the rise in the cost of living. While allowance must be made for the deficiencies of an Index measure of the cost of living, and particularly one linking up the old with the new basis, the conclusion that the Association members have improved their position in real terms remains valid. In the matter of wages and conditions the history of the Association is one of success.

CHAPTER FOURTEEN

PROVIDENT SCHEMES

By the end of the first fifty years the Association had already assumed the responsibilities of a full-scale friendly society and the provident schemes had already taken shape. Although finally, towards the end of the period, modified in the light of the Government's National Insurance policy, the original schemes have been retained and, in general, improved during the second fifty years. Both the schemes and the financing of them, however, have had to be adjusted to meet the problems and changing circumstances of the twentieth century. In particular, unemployment has been an outstanding and recurrent problem, which has made heavy calls on the funds of the Association. The two world wars, also, brought special problems, affecting both the income and expenditure of the schemes. Finally, growing State responsibility for social welfare has been an important feature of the period, and legislation towards this end has called for adjustments in the Association's schemes.

I. Out-of-Work Scheme

The problem of unemployment reappeared early in the period, and in 1905 a deficit on the Out-of-Work Fund was reported for the first time since 1894. In the years 1908 to 1910 the problem was severe, particularly in the Glasgow area, but thereafter the position improved until the outbreak of war in 1914. During this period the rate of benefit granted by the Association was increased. A Delegate Meeting in 1907 increased the allowance from 6/- to 8/- per week, payable for six weeks in each quarter, while the earnings of those in part-time employment were made up to 14/– per week, as far as the 8/– allowance would permit. The subscription to the scheme was 2d per week, while the revenue was further augmented by the tax of 1d per hour on overtime introduced in 1913.

During the worst years of this period, however, some of the Branches took special steps to supplement Association benefit. In 1908, the members of the Glasgow Branch levied themselves 3d per week in order to pay an allowance of 5/– per week to members for the seven remaining weeks in each quarter after Association benefit had been exhausted. The following year this supplementary allowance was increased to 11/– per week and the Branch paid £1,239 to its members, in addition to £1,417 paid by the Association.

The outbreak of war in 1914 brought an increase in unemployment and heavy calls on the Fund. Under the National Insurance Act of 1911 the Association qualified for a rebate on its Out-of-Work payments, and in 1915 an attempt was made to secure an emergency grant from the Board of Trade on the grounds that abnormal unemployment existed in the trade. The verdict, however, was 'not proven', and the claim was rejected. From 1916 until the end of the war a labour shortage existed, and the reserves of the scheme were consequently strengthened.

At first the members returning from the forces were fairly well absorbed in most areas. A Delegate Meeting in 1920 abolished the overtime tax, increased the subscription to the Fund to 4d per week and the benefit to 16/–, still payable for six weeks in each quarter. The post-war boom was short-lived, however, and from 1920 the number of unemployed steadily increased. A conference was held with the employers and some restrictions were imposed. A special committee was appointed by a Delegate Meeting to consider the problem, and as a result, the allowance was made up to £2 per week during the first half of 1921; to meet this a special levy of 1/4 per week was imposed. Thereafter this special allowance and levy ended for purely financial reasons—expenditure had exceeded income during the six months by £15,000—and the former rates were resumed. A special Delegate Meeting later in the year increased the subscription to the scheme from 4d to 2/–; the rate of benefit remained at 16/–, but was to be continuous instead of only for six weeks per quarter. The Glasgow Branch, however, retained the special levy and paid 30/– per week in benefit. By 1925 the position had improved sufficiently to permit a reduction in the subscription to 1/2, while in 1928 it was reduced to 6d.

During this period the Association also administered the scheme of State unemployment benefit, under the Unemployment Insurance Act of 1920; the call-book was signed and both State and Association benefit paid weekly at Branch offices. New regulations introduced in 1928, however, resulted in a decision to discontinue administration of the scheme; the chief difficulty was the requirement that Association benefit be paid to all recipients of State benefit, which would have necessitated important changes in the Association rules governing eligibility for benefit. The Association re-adopted the scheme in 1930, when this condition had been removed from the regulations.

The next challenge to the scheme came with the depression of the early 1930's, particularly 1931 to 1933, when conditions were serious, although printing did not suffer so badly as many other trades. In 1932 a special levy of 8d per week was imposed, while a Delegate Meeting of that year increased the subscription to the Fund from 6d to 1/– and the rate of benefit to £1 per week. Before these new rates came into operation, however, the increasing seriousness of the problem was the subject of a Special Delegate Meeting. As a result, the subscription was further increased to 2/10 and benefit fixed at 16/– per week. A further meeting in 1933 introduced the principle of graded benefit, the rates being fixed at 16/– per week for 26 weeks and 10/– per week thereafter; the contribution was reduced to 2/8. Some improvement occurred in the following years, although unemployment remained about seven per cent. The reduced rate of benefit lasted until 1935, when continuous benefit of 16/– per week was restored. By 1936 the position had improved sufficiently to permit a reduction of the subscription to 1/8. Trade was good during the closing years of the inter-war period, and in 1939 the subscription was reduced to 1/6 and the allowance increased to 18/–.

The war brought some immediate increase in unemployment, which unfortunately coincided with the introduction of higher benefits and lower subscriptions, with the result that expenditure exceeded income by over £8,000 in 1940. The unemployment was, however, short-lived and the balance remaining to the credit of the scheme substantial. Until 1941 benefit was paid from the Fund to members who had become trainees for other industries under the Ministry of Labour scheme, ceasing when the Government grant to trainees was increased. During this period the financial position of the scheme was sound and its strength was further increased by the full employment subsequently experienced. The subscription to this Fund was reduced twice during the war years, in 1941 and 1943, the amount deducted being reallocated, on the first occasion to the Administrative Fund and on the second to the Superannuation Fund.

The position of all the Association's provident schemes was affected by the advent of the new National Insurance Scheme in 1946, and a Special Delegate Meeting was held to consider them in the light of this. The outcome was the merging of the Out-of-Work, Sick and Superannuation Funds into a single Provident Fund, and the equalisation of benefits at 10/–, at which rate it remained until the end of 1952. A Delegate Meeting of that year increased the uniform rate of benefit to 15/– as from January 1953.

II. SICK SCHEME

The history of the Association's Sick Scheme during this period is one of remarkably little change, particularly in the rates of allowance. Two important factors here, of course, were the entry of the State to this sphere early in the period and the subsequent formation of the Scottish Typographical Insurance Society.

At the beginning of the period three grades of benefit were paid from the Association Fund—10/-, 7/6 and 5/-. In 1911 it was agreed that those in receipt of third-grade benefit should be exempt from contributions to the schemes. In 1928 the third-grade benefit was abolished, and in 1936 exemption from contributions was extended to all in receipt of sick benefit. In 1939 benefit was increased by 2/-, and finally in 1946 the scheme was merged into the Provident Fund, benefit becoming 10/-.

By this date, the maximum sum granted to the permanently disabled was £75, while the recent Delegate Meeting decided that it be increased to £100 in 1953, when sick allowance would also be increased to 15/-.

In 1914 the scheme became the Sick and Funeral Scheme, the latter allowance being transferred to it from the Protective Fund. As a consequence, the finances of the scheme suffered a considerable drain during the period of the first world war, when numerous claims were made for funeral allowance, following the death of members on active service; 270 members lost their lives during that period, compared with 96 during the second world war. In 1920 the funeral allowance was increased to £20.

The beginning of the period found the Executive Council repeatedly warning members that the financial position of the Sick Fund was unsound. In 1906 a levy of 1d per week was imposed, and in 1907 the subscription was increased to 2½d. Further increases followed in 1913, 1916 and 1920, when the subscription had reached 6d. In 1928 it was increased to 9d, at which it remained until the merger of 1946.

The Scottish Typographical Insurance Society was formed as a result of the 1911 National Health Insurance Act. Then, by a vote of the members, it was agreed to carry on the Association Sick Scheme in addition to the State one, and also, to form an Approved Society to operate the State Scheme; further, this Society was to be open to all qualified persons employed in or about a printing

office. By 1913 the membership of the Society was reported to be over 6,000. In 1920 it was decided to transfer
the Society to the Association, and from 1921 it became
the National Health Insurance Section. The following
years brought a steady increase in the additional benefits,
cash and non-cash, provided. In 1922 legal aid was provided to members of the Section in claiming compensation
for injuries received at work; this service was extended to
all members of the Association in 1928. Dental services
were added to the benefits in 1927 and optical in 1931. By
1937 the membership had increased to about 8,000 and
the benefits granted were nearly 200 per cent higher than
in 1921. The Association's services as an Approved Society ended with the passing of the National Insurance Act
in 1946, and in November 1947 the Section ceased to
exist.

III. Superannuation Scheme

At the beginning of the period three grades of superannuation benefit were paid, 6/–, 8/– and 10/–, according
to length of service, the minimum age being 55. In 1918 a
2/– increase was granted on these rates, in view of the rise
in the cost of living, while in 1920 the rates were further
increased to 10/–, 12/– and 15/–. These rates prevailed
until 1946 when superannuation payments were made
from the Provident Fund at the uniform rate of 10/–; this
rate is also increased to 15/– as from January 1953.

In this case also, Association allowances were, for much
of the period, additional to State benefits, and some adjustments were made in the Association's scheme to accom-
modate those also in receipt of State pensions. For a time
the income limitation on the State pension induced some
members voluntarily to forego part of their Association
allowance in order to qualify for a full State pension. When
the increase of 2/– was granted in 1918, an appeal was
made that this should not be deducted from the State
pension. When this was refused, a system was introduced
which permitted recipients of State benefit to receive the

full Association increase in the form of a voucher, representing payment for 'Goods'. In later years adjustments
were made in Association allowances to permit members
to receive the State pension in full.

The financial side of this scheme has never been satisfactory. While a fund had been allowed to accumulate in
the first instance before any payments were made, the
beginning of this period saw this amount steadily dwindling,
as the number of recipients increased with the general age-
ing of population. With improved working conditions and
health services, the death rate declined and compared
favourably with that of other trades. Further, increased
mechanisation and unemployment added to the number of
older members claiming from the Fund. The income
could not meet the expenditure and the steadily declining
Fund had to be bolstered up by levies and increased subscriptions. In 1903 the subscription was increased from
1d to 2d and in 1906 a levy of 1d per week was imposed.
In 1907 the subscription was further increased to $2\frac{1}{2}$d. By
1920 it had been increased to 7d and an almost uninterrupted upward movement continued until 1936, when it
reached the sum of 2/–, at which it remained until 1943,
when there was a further increase from the subscription to
the Out-of-Work Fund.

In recent years the Superannuation Scheme has been
the subject of some controversy. Its financial position has
been almost continuously unsound, and the steadily rising
subscription has made it the most expensive of all the
Association's schemes. The main difficulty derives from
the fact that the scheme is not a superannuation one in
the usual sense of the word; there is no insurance coverage
or guarantee of a definite return for the sum contributed
by a member during his working life. It is, in fact, simply an
allowance granted to those who have retired and subscribed
by those who are still working members of the Association. Further, it can be altered upwards or downwards, or
even abolished, at any time by a Delegate Meeting, in
whose deliberations superannuated members have no voice
or vote. This was demonstrated by the 1946 decision to

form a Provident Fund and equalise all benefits at 10/–. The new rate applied to all recipients, including those previously receiving allowances of 12/– and 15/–. Some have argued that this allowance should be scrapped entirely, on grounds of its expense and in view of the extension of National Insurance. The majority, however, have been emphatically in favour of continuing some payment to retired members, thus retaining the scheme of which the members of an earlier period were justly proud. Others have protested that the 1946 decision was most unfair to those beneficiaries already in receipt of a higher allowance, for which they have paid contributions. This, however, is based on a misconception of the nature and finance of the scheme; a reduced total subscription was considered desirable, in view of the increased compulsory contribution to National Insurance, and a reduced subscription from the working members must be accompanied by reduced benefits to the retired members.

IV. Summing Up

The three main schemes reviewed above give some indication of the extent to which the Association has been concerned, during this period, with the welfare of its members; in addition to these main schemes, removal grants and emigration allowances have also been continued and increased. In all, the Association has paid out over £1,120,000 under these schemes, of which over £1 million was spent during the last fifty years.[1] In keeping with the rise in the cost of living and the fall in the purchasing power of the pound, the underlying long-term trend in allowances and subscriptions, throughout most of the period, has been upwards. Superimposed on this, however, have been short-term fluctuations, chiefly reflecting fluctuations in trade and employment. Thus, during the depression of the early 1930's the subscription increased sharply, as a result of the heavy calls on the Out-of-Work Fund, and benefits

[1] The details of expenditure under the various schemes are given in Appendix III.

from the latter had to be reduced; as trade improved, however, subscriptions were reduced and allowances restored.

In the matter of expenditure the most fluctuating item has been that on Out-of-Work benefit, the most stable that under the Sick Scheme, while the most consistently increasing item of expenditure has been that on superannuation allowances. Financial policy has aimed in the main, with short-term lapses, at solvency for each individual scheme, with the exception of the superannuation one. In an emergency, or between Delegate Meetings, an excessive increase in expenditure or alarming drain on any one fund has been met by a levy. This has usually been subsequently reinforced by an increase in the subscription. The policy of meeting a deficit on one scheme by re-allocating part of the subscription to another was resorted to only rarely, as, for example, during the second world war, when the total subscription to the Association remained unaltered; in contrast, during the first world war the subscription was increased by 1/6. These trends are reflected in the course of the total subscription. At the outset it was 8d per week; by 1913 it had risen to 1/- and by 1921 to 3/9; by 1928 it had fallen to 2/7, but in the following depression rose to a peak of 5/4 in 1932; in 1939 it was reduced to 4/7, at which it remained until 1946; at the end of the period it was 3/-, of which 2/6 went to the Provident Fund, 4d to the Administrative and 2d to the Protective. The Delegate Meeting of June 1952, however, increased the rate of benefit from the schemes to 15/-, as from the beginning of 1953, and in consequence, the contribution became 3/6.

The amalgamation of these schemes into one Provident Fund with uniform rates of benefit is, in a sense, a culmination and tidying up of the Association's development on friendly society lines; such a scheme was, in fact, proposed at a Delegate Meeting by the Dundee Branch in 1936, but found no seconder. It is also, however, a solution to the situation presented by the introduction of an all-embracing Government Scheme of National Insurance. In this sense it is a compromise; the need to provide such allowances is no longer so urgent as in the period when the Association schemes were founded, yet there is scope to augment the minimum benefits of National Insurance and so retain the schemes which have become such an important and fundamental part of the Association's functions.

In spite of the financial preponderance of the provident schemes, however, the Association is very far from becoming merely a glorified friendly society. The provision of these schemes has been in addition to, and not at the expense of, its traditional and fundamental functions as a trade union. The fact that less than £100,000 has been spent during the century on strike and victimisation allowances, compared with over £1 million on provident schemes, is a tribute to and a reflection of its strength as a trade union. The Protective Fund has been preserved and strengthened throughout. This aim was aided by the formation, in 1913, of an Administrative Fund to relieve it of certain charges and reserve it as a fighting fund. The subscription to the Protective Fund has varied little, remaining at 6d. per week from 1916 to 1939, when it was reduced to 3d.; since then it has been further reduced to 2d. The biggest drain on the Fund occurred during the General Strike of 1926, but a special levy was imposed until the loss had been made good. Apart from this, the amount at the credit of the Fund has steadily increased; in 1913 the immediate aim was declared to be £6,000, in 1932 £60,000, while by 1946 the actual total was just under £100,000. In 1947, with the formation of the Provident Fund, £10,000 was transferred to it from this Fund, and £5,000 to the Administrative Fund; in spite of this, the present figure is again approximately £90,000.

CHAPTER FIFTEEN

APPRENTICES

Throughout most of the first fifty years the records
revealed repeated references to the apprentice
problem and the need to restrict the number of
entrants; the regulation limiting apprentices to one to
every three journeymen was more honoured in the breach
than the observance, until the closing years of the period
and the arrival of the composing machine. By contrast the
second fifty years has been a period of definite and effective apprentice restriction; with a few exceptions, there has
been little difficulty or dispute over the ratios permitted by
the Association's rules and these generally have been effective. But this is not to say that there have been no problems connected with the apprentice question, or that it has
ceased to be a topic of debate and decision. The period has
witnessed considerable changes in the conditions and requirements of the industry, with consequent repercussions
on the apprentice question. Firstly, mechanisation of the
industry has advanced considerably and rapidly, in comparison with the earlier period; secondly, the twentieth
century has been a period of less general and rapid industrial expansion; finally, and not unconnected with these
two, there have been several prolonged spells of heavy
unemployment. In consequence, the number of skilled
craftsmen required by the industry has not been markedly
expanding—indeed, in the inter-war period it was declining—and the Association has pursued a more rigid
policy of restriction. The other main aspect of the period
has been the growing emphasis placed on the training of
apprentices, with the object of improving the skill of the
craft and adapting its members to the technical changes in
the industry. While the emphasis, during most of the

period, has been on restriction and training, the closing years have brought a new problem. The recent post-war period has been characterised by a shortage of skilled labour and agitation from the employers for a relaxation of the Association's apprentice rules. Some concessions have, in consequence, been granted, but these have been accompanied by expressions of caution regarding the prospects of continuing full employment and the possible trend of technical changes.

I. THE LIMITATION OF ENTRY

During the early years of the period the general rule of one apprentice to three journeymen prevailed, while the maximum allowed to one establishment was ten. A few references to the numbers exceeding this rule appeared during this period—e.g. from Aberdeen in 1908, and Dundee in 1909—but in general the restriction was effective. The Delegate Meeting of 1911 introduced the first variation of the rule, as it affected large establishments; according to this, when the number of apprentices, determined by the ratio, had reached ten, thereafter apprentices could be taken on in the ratio of one to five. This, and subsequent modifications on similar lines, might be taken as an indication of the growing size of a few establishments, a tendency aided by mechanisation, although the small business remains numerically the greater in Scotland.[1]

During the first world war steps were taken to prevent the exceptional conditions resulting in a large influx of boys, and in 1915 an agreement was reached with the employers. According to this agreement, the number permitted to a firm was to be that permitted in August 1914; apprentices on active service were to be regarded as still in the employment of the firm for purposes of determining the ratio; replacement of apprentices on service was permitted only where the apprentice had served not more than one year of his apprenticeship, or had been within one year

[1] At present some fifty per cent of the recognised union offices consist of one-man departments.

of its completion before joining the forces. In spite of the agreement, however, it was reported that in several areas apprentices were taken on considerably in excess of the number permitted. At the end of the war an agreement, described as 'fair and generous', concerning the reinstatement, pay, and training of apprentices returned from the forces, was signed with the Alliance. Some increase in the number of apprentices, however, inevitably followed from the practice of the war years.

In the early inter-war period, when conditions elsewhere were fairly good, Edinburgh experienced considerable unemployment, chiefly due to a contraction of the book trade there. In 1920 an agreement was reached with the Alliance which put a complete moratorium on new apprentices in Edinburgh; in 1921 the Alliance reported that it had been compelled to permit some of its members to start new apprentices, but the restriction at this time was considerable.

In 1920, by a decision of a Delegate Meeting, a table of apprentice ratios was approved for the first time; this permitted one apprentice to an establishment with only one or two journeymen and thereafter the ratio declined as the number of journeymen increased. Some alterations occurred in the scale of ratios during the remainder of the inter-war period, chiefly extending it and making provision for larger establishments. In 1936 a Delegate Meeting resolved that an apprentice should only be permitted where three journeymen were employed. This, however, was not successfully carried into the mutual rules, although the wartime agreement of 1942 prohibited apprentices in one-man establishments. Throughout most of the inter-war period, taking the total of apprentices admitted to the total journeymen membership, the effective ratio was one in five.

During the second world war, the position of apprentices was to some extent determined by the Military Training Act, at least in such matters as the allowance of the period on service towards the apprenticeship period, and reinstatement. The Association, however, was concerned to ensure that the entry of new apprentices was more effectively controlled than it had been between 1914 and 1918. In 1941 a Delegate Meeting passed a resolution in favour of a complete moratorium on apprentices for the duration. This the employers refused, and the case went to the Conciliation Committee of the Scottish Joint Industrial Council. The decision was against a complete ban on apprentices, and the two sides of the industry were instructed to confer and formulate an agreement. As a result a wartime agreement was signed in 1942. The agreement covered the training and reinstatement of apprentices after the end of hostilities, as well as the admission of apprentices during the war years. A new scale of ratios was approved as follows—1 apprentice to 2 journeymen, 2 to 5, 3 to 10, 4 to 15 thereafter rising by 1 apprentice and 5 journeymen, up to a total of 10 apprentices to 45 journeymen, 1 additional apprentice being permitted for every 10 journeymen above 45. Apprentices on active service were counted as part of the permitted ratio, and replacements could be made only if an apprentice died on active service, or intimated in writing that he would not return to the trade; if, however, five years of the apprenticeship had been completed before enlistment, then a new apprentice could be started at the time when this apprenticeship would normally have expired. As a result of this agreement, the restriction on the entry of apprentices was more severe and effective than during the first world war. Some idea of its extent may be gathered from the fact that between 1940 and 1944 the six largest branches started 158 apprentices, compared with 575 in a pre-war five-year period.

At the end of the war a new agreement was reached and the ban on new apprentices to replace those on service, whose time would normally have expired, was lifted. A new scale of ratios was agreed, which retained the war-time innovation of a ban on apprentices in one-man departments. In 1946, also, a revised agreement was signed concerning the reinstatement and pay of those whose apprenticeship had been interrupted during the war. Under this agreement, apprentices returning after their time would normally have been completed were to receive the full journeyman's wage, part of this being in the form of a State allowance.

The wage agreement of 1949 included clauses concerning production and manpower; following the raising of the school leaving age to 15, the period of apprenticeship was reduced from 7 to 6 years, including compulsory National Service occurring during the apprenticeship, provided at least 5 years of actual craft training was completed. The same agreement provided for the admission of a special extra ration of apprentices—60 compositors and 25 machinemen. In 1950 negotiations were opened by the employers for a further increase in manpower; it was maintained that trade was being lost to the industry here, and British orders were being sent abroad, because of the shortage of labour; further, there had been an increase in the labour force of the printing industry in the main overseas countries compared with 1939, whereas in the United Kingdom there had been a decrease. No further concessions, however, were immediately granted, but the wage agreement of 1951 granted another special extra ration of apprentices—60 compositors and 20 machinemen. Permission has thus been given for the admission of 165 apprentices in addition to the normal quota which is at present fixed in the ratios of 1 apprentice to 2 journeymen, 2 to 5, and 1 additional apprentice for every 5 additional journeymen up to a total of 75 for which 16 apprentices are permitted; thereafter the rule allows for 1 additional apprentice for every 10 journeymen.

A rigid policy of restriction has been adhered to throughout the period, being demonstrated in its most extreme form by the 1942 wartime agreement. The conditions of the industry in the inter-war period—the increased mechanisation and the persistent unemployment—would appear to have justified the policy adopted, and while the scarcity of skilled labour felt in the recent post-war period might be regarded as a consequence of pre-war policy, its most immediate cause is rather the extreme restriction of the war years. Here the Association's policy was justified

N

in view of the experiences of the first world war and the years immediately following it; then the apprentice agreement was not fully observed; also, the post-war boom was short-lived and increasing unemployment quickly suggested a surplus labour force. The apprentice agreement of the second world war, however, was effectively carried into practice; also, full employment has prevailed in the industry for the seven years since the end of the war; in the light of this, the bonus rations of apprentices were necessary and justified. Of the future requirements of the industry little can be said; they will depend on the fate of full employment policy, and on the trend of mechanical development.

II. Training

While attention in the early years of the Association's life was almost exclusively concentrated on the number of apprentices admitted, the need for better training of apprentices was beginning to be recognised by the end of the first fifty years. The chief factor in this was the increased mechanisation of the industry and the consequent need for technical training. Soon, in the larger Branches at least, steps were taken to assist in the provision of such training and to encourage the attendance of apprentices, at first at evening classes. In 1903 the Glasgow Branch accepted an invitation to be represented on the Committee of the Glasgow and West of Scotland Technical College.[1] The Branch made an annual grant of £2 2/– to the College, and in subsequent years it was reported that full advantage was taken by the members of the classes provided. About this time the suggestion was made that there should be examinations for apprentices, but these were not introduced until a much later date. Meantime, steps were taken to provide, via the Technical College, the facilities for training in mechanical composition. In Edinburgh, also, the question of improved training was considered. Here, in 1912, discussions were held with the employers,

[1] Now The Royal Technical College.

the Merchant Company and the School Board being interested parties, on the possibility of devising a scheme for the attendance of technical classes during the day.

It was not until the inter-war period, however, that substantial progress was made with apprentice training schemes, the pioneer being the Edinburgh Branch. While the 1919 Apprentice Agreement provided for the reinstatement of all ex-service apprentices, with a guarantee of facilities for efficient training, nevertheless the unemployment of the early 1920's, which was particularly severe in Edinburgh, affected considerable numbers of the young members. Further, it was found that many of those who had started their apprenticeships during the war years had been badly trained. The Edinburgh Branch, with the co-operation of the Ministry of Labour, instigated a scheme of training for unemployed compositors, day-classes being provided at the Heriot-Watt College; training was given in both hand and mechanical composition. The success of this venture led to the formation in 1923 of a Joint Apprentice Training Committee, composed of three representatives from the Branch and three from the employers. The duties of the Committee included the supervision of the selection of apprentices and the provision of adequate training facilities in the form of both day and evening classes. Considerable success was reported for the scheme during the following years. The need for further improvement, however, in the method of selecting apprentices led to the introduction of a new scheme in 1928, under which applicants had to undergo an entrance examination. The scheme was worked out with the co-operation of the Governors of Heriot-Watt College, the University of Edinburgh and the Medical Officer of Health. Applicants were submitted to a test of medical, educational and vocational fitness, and the scheme was operated by an independent Examining Board, set up by the Heriot-Watt College. In addition to raising the standard of craftsmanship, the selection and training scheme was used to good purpose by the Edinburgh Branch in the 1930's to offset the effects of increased mechanisation and to mitigate unemployment.

The policy adopted was one of anticipating changes in the industry and providing the training necessary for the increased specialisation occurring. Special courses were provided from time to time for composing-machine operators, readers, monotype casters and the like, and the Branch aimed at being able to fill any local vacancy from the ranks of its membership.

In the 1920's and the 1930's increased facilities for technical training were gradually provided throughout the rest of the Association, the lead being taken by the larger Branches—Glasgow, Dundee, Aberdeen and Ayr. In 1935 a general scheme for the selection and training of apprentices, on the lines of the Edinburgh scheme, was sponsored by the Joint Industrial Council, and accepted by many Branches; provisions for day classes, however, have been made only in Edinburgh and Glasgow, the latter at the Stow College of Printing.

In the recent post-war years attention has been given to the training of those whose apprenticeship was interrupted by war service. For this purpose the Association, through the National Federation, became a party to the scheme prepared by the Joint Industrial Council and approved by the Government in 1945. In addition, provisions were made in the larger Branches for refresher courses to journeymen returning from war service.

As a result of these developments the provision of adequate training has become an integral part of apprentice regulation. It is on the grounds of inadequate training facilities, for example, that the ban on apprentices in one-man departments, recently secured, has been justified. Further, the apprentice ratio granted by the rules is conditional on the provision of efficient training, and it has been agreed by both sides of the industry that even where a firm is entitled, under the ratio, to an additional apprentice, permission to start one may be withheld if the opportunities for adequate training are lacking. Such provisions would appear to provide the Association with a valuable line of defence against unfavourable repercussions from future technical developments, not by opposing these developments, as some trade unions did in the early days of mechanisation, but by adapting its members to meet the changed requirements.

CHAPTER SIXTEEN

CHANGES IN THE LABOUR FORCE

Some reference has already been made in the foregoing chapters to the changes in technique which have affected the industry during this period, and to some of the repercussions of these changes on the labour force required. These changes can be summed up as increased mechanisation, and it is chiefly the effects of this that will be considered in this chapter. No attempt will be made to discuss the technical details of the many new machines introduced; this is not the place for such a discussion, nor is the writer competent to undertake it. Consideration will be given only to the broad trends, to their effect on the labour force, and to the reaction of the Association to the changes which have occurred. Finally, special consideration will be given to the part played by female labour; while this is mainly relevant to the effects of mechanisation, it forms a topic in itself by reason of its history, and of the fact that separate Female Sections of the Association have been formed.

I. MECHANISATION AND ITS EFFECT ON MANPOWER

While this period has not been marked by any clear-cut changes, such as that from hand to mechanical composition, nevertheless it has witnessed a considerable improvement in and expansion of mechanisation, particularly in the press or machine section, and a consequent multiplication of the types of machines. In the composing section both the Linotype and Monotype machines had appeared before the end of the first fifty years; the later period, however, has witnessed considerable development of and improvements on these machines, in addition to their more widespread use. In the press section new methods and machines have been introduced more or less steadily throughout the period; the general trend has been towards larger and speedier machines, and towards the mechanisation of those parts of the process formerly performed by hand. Thus, while at the beginning of the period the latest invention in this section was that of the rotary printing press, the following years saw the development of this principle, and its incorporation in larger and larger machines, and by the 1930's it had been further improved by the addition of automatic feeding.

Considering first of all the over-all effect of this increased mechanisation, the immediate effect of new and more efficient machines was, naturally, some displacement of labour. Such was reported with the more widespread use of composing machines during the first decade of the period. At the same time the press section was becoming more highly mechanised and there was an evident consciousness of an increased tempo in the industry and the introduction of a more impersonal element; competition was becoming keener, and the men most often displaced appear to have been the older members, who were compelled to retire. Looking back at the period up to the first world war, however, and excluding the years of general depression, when mechanisation undoubtedly added to the number of unemployed, there was no net displacement; certainly the conclusion made at the end of the first fifty years, that the effects of the composing machine were not so bad as feared, still largely applied. During the inter-war period, however, the position deteriorated, particularly from the mid 1920's to the mid 1930's. For much of this period, of course, general depression prevailed, caused by a variety of factors, but the evidence suggests that the position in printing was aggravated by increased mechanisation. Some rough indication of the over-all effect on manpower may be gathered from changes in the total membership of the Association, although such figures must be used with extreme caution, since they also reflect changes in the number of recognised union offices. In 1913 the total journeyman membership was 4,679; in the early 20's it increased to a peak of 4,905 in 1925; by 1938 it was 4,222, and at the end of 1951, 4,554. The main factor qualifying this picture concerns the General Strike of 1926, after which the Scottish newspaper offices became non-union. Except in Edinburgh and Dundee, this lost ground has been mainly recovered, and the inclusion of the Aberdeen Press in 1941 and the Outram Press, Glasgow, in 1942 account for much of the increase between 1938 and 1951. After allowing for this factor, however, the figures suggest a slight decline in the total journeyman membership; this conclusion is reinforced by the fact that the membership continued to decline after the initial impact of the 1926 strike. The total change is very small, however, and almost suggests a stable labour force. Within these totals, however, a more marked change has occurred in the proportion of compositors to machinemen; in 1925 there were 3,356 compositors and 1,549 machinemen, while in 1951 the corresponding figures were 2,986 and 1,568. The other major change not revealed by the totals concerns the Edinburgh Branch, of which the membership has definitely declined. This trend, in fact, became evident at the beginning of the inter-war period, and continued throughout most of the 1930's; the number of compositors has fallen from 1,040 in 1913 to 607 in 1951, and that of machinemen from 628 to 447. The chief factor here appears to be the changes in the book-trade, which was a staple feature of the Edinburgh industry.

Mechanisation has also affected the composition of the labour force required. Here two main changes have occurred. In the first place, the operation of the new machines has required a new type of skill, and the labour force has become more specialised, the operation of each machine requiring some special training. Secondly, the extension of mechanisation has created new jobs, some requiring a degree of skill, some unskilled, and in consequence, a new labour force has been brought into the industry, consisting of machine feeders, assistants, and the like.

These changes in the labour force have necessitated changes in the attitude and organisation of the Association, particularly since 1918. It has already been noted that the Association was, in the main, successful in securing the operation of composing machines at the outset for their own members. During the early part of this period constant vigilance was necessary to maintain this position, but the Association has been successful in preventing the employment of cheap labour on these machines. While they reserved the keyboards and operation of the composing machines for their members, nevertheless some attendant labour was recruited from outside; such labour, however, was eventually brought into the Association, as, for example, in 1918, when it was agreed that Monotype casters be included. In the press section, attention was given during the early years to securing agreement regarding the manning of and working conditions for some of the new machines introduced, chiefly through the medium of the branches. Some of the machines, however, were manned by labour outwith the Association, the most notable example being rotary press machines in newspaper offices. In the inter-war period greater attention was given to the problems of increased mechanisation in this section, where the problem of unemployment appears to have been more acute. Special Machine Committees were appointed from time to time to investigate new machines and draw up rules for their working, while in 1929 a National Machinemen's Committee was formed, which thereafter dealt with all matters concerning this section. In 1929, also, an agreement was reached with the National Society of Operative Printers, as a result of which newspaper rotary pressmen were transferred to the Association.[1] Attempts were made by this Committee at the beginning of the 1930's to secure an embargo on machine apprentices in Scotland because of the unemployment prevailing, but without success. The solution then adopted, on the recommendation of the employers, was to train the men for the specialised work created by the machines. This policy, in

[1] See Chapter 17.

which the Edinburgh Branch took the lead, met with considerable success. Thus the new machines were manned from within the Association, and its membership adapted to the new requirements and specialisation. Finally, the semi-skilled and unskilled labour force introduced by mechanisation was incorporated in the Association with the creation of the Auxiliary Section in the 1920's. Full membership, however, has not been granted to this Section. The Association has remained a craft union, providing the most highly-skilled labour required from its own ranks, but it has recognised and taken under its wing the attendant labour necessary to the machines.

II. The Association and Female Labour

The statement that the Association succeeded in reserving composing machines for its own members must be qualified. In a few areas attempts were made to operate the machines with cheap female labour; the principal offender here was Edinburgh, which already had a large number of female compositors prior to the introduction of machines —a legacy of the strike of 1872. Aberdeen had a similar problem, although on a smaller scale, while the early years of the period witnessed some use or attempts to use underpaid female labour in Dundee, Perth and various smaller Branches. The main problem, however, was that of Edinburgh, for long recognised as a special case and an exception to the general rule prevailing regarding the use of underpaid female labour on skilled work. By the beginning of this period there were between 700 and 800 women compositors employed in Edinburgh, more and more of whom were being transferred from hand composition to the ever-growing number of composing machines in use; indeed, they had almost secured a monopoly of the Monotype machine. The rate of wages paid to the women was rather less than half of the recognised rate for men.

The problem acquired a new urgency after the arbiter's decision on the Glasgow wage claim of 1903, when one of the main reasons for rejection was the presence of female compositors in Edinburgh, which adversely affected the Glasgow industry's ability to compete. In consequence, a special Delegate Meeting was held in 1905, at the instigation of the Glasgow Branch, to consider the employment of women in both sections of the printing office. Those Branches where women had already secured a footing wanted some recognition of women workers by the Association, to enable them to tackle their problems by organisation. The Branches where women had been excluded, led by Glasgow, opposed any form of recognition, fearing that this would lead to a more widespread introduction of female labour. All resolutions for recognition were defeated, and the Delegate Meeting, in fact, contributed nothing to the solution of the problem. A resolution was passed forbidding any further introduction of women into any department of any Branch from that date, but it was left to the Branches concerned to take the initiative, as opportunity presented itself, to deal with the existing problem. The subject was also raised with the Printing and Kindred Trades Federation and a special conference held, but no action was taken.

In 1906 both Aberdeen and Edinburgh opened negotiations with the employers for a solution to their local problems. In the following year Aberdeen successfully concluded an agreement, under which there was to be no further introduction of women to skilled jobs, but only after a strike of fifteen weeks and the loss of one office. In the same year, Dundee reported that the number of women compositors had been reduced to two, while in 1909 Perth reported the end of underpaid female labour in that area.

The Edinburgh movement had meantime been suspended until the completion of the fifty-hour movement, but in 1909 the question was taken up again. The policy originally adopted had aimed at not more than fifty per cent of females in any office, but the terms of the memorial presented to the employers in 1909 were 'That from 1st January 1910 there shall be no further introduction of females into our trade in Edinburgh, nor any importation of female compositors from other centres, and that in future machine composition be solely undertaken by male union labour'. There followed a lengthy dispute which was not settled until September 1910, after strike notices had been tendered by all members of printing and kindred unions in Edinburgh. The main difficulty concerned the manning of composing machines, the employers expressing their readiness to reduce the ratio of women employed on hand composition. The rapid increase in the number of composing machines, however, made a contraction in the number of women employed on hand composition inevitable in any case, and underlined the importance of securing agreement on the operation of the machines. In March 1910 the matter was handed over to the Executive Council and the National Federation, local action having been exhausted. Protracted negotiations, proposals and counter-proposals followed, but no settlement was reached. On the 30th August a mass meeting of kindred unions was held in Edinburgh and attended by over 2,000, who resolved to support the Branch in the dispute; and notices were accordingly tendered at the beginning of September. New proposals and counter-proposals followed, and an agreement was eventually signed at the end of the month. According to this, the women then in the composing department were to remain, but no new recruits were to be taken on up to 30th June 1916. All new keyboards of composing machines were to be operated by male union labour, and fifty per cent of upmaking and corrections were to be done by males. As a condition of the agreement, the Branch was to maintain peace on all questions of hours and wages for the next three years. Although the ban imposed on female apprentices was originally for a period of six years, in fact it has become a permanent one. The female compositors at present in the Edinburgh trade were all apprenticed before this agreement and therefore represent a dying section of the trade.

As a result of the support given by the women themselves during this struggle, it was felt that the Association in turn should assume responsibility for their organisation, and in 1911 a Delegate Meeting approved of the formation of the Edinburgh Female Compositors' Society. By 1918 it was reported that the Edinburgh women compositors were now fully organised, and in the same year they were granted a vote on Association affairs. In 1920 they were granted the right to be represented on the Executive Council and at Delegate Meetings, and in 1922 the Society became amalgamated with the Edinburgh Branch, of which it has since formed a Section. A similar Section of the Aberdeen Branch was formed in 1918.

In the organisation and progress of the Edinburgh female compositors, considerable inspiration and encouragement was given by one 'Juvenus', apparently of their number. From March 1914 until April 1922, with a short gap during the war years, 'Juvenus' contributed to the *Journal* a weekly column, addressed to the female compositors, reporting and commenting on events relevant to their position. These articles contained praise for progress achieved, scolding and exhortation to both members and non-members, comment on and criticism of events in particular offices and of actions by employers, nicely interspersed with nostalgic references to the writer's native glen or to the awe-inspiring authority of 'her' old dominie. The articles were written in a chatty, feminine style, but although the inside knowledge they revealed led some to question the gender of 'Juvenus'—thereby calling down on themselves the scorn of the dominie for their poor Latin scholarship—few discovered the author's real identity. This 'jewel to Edinburgh printers' as the *South African Typographical Journal* described 'Juvenus', was indeed a gentleman, an active member of the Association.

Recognition of the female compositors led to a gradual improvement in their position and a reduction of the disparity between the male and female rates of pay. Indeed, women taken on to replace male compositors during the first world war secured the male rate, although this was considerably more than that paid to those in Edinburgh and Aberdeen. The numbers taken on, however, were small, and early in the inter-war period those receiving the full male rate had all retired or been replaced. Women compositors continued only in the Aberdeen and Edinburgh Branches, as at present, and under the national wage agreements of the inter-war period were paid seventy per cent of the male rate; they could only accept employment outside these areas, however, if given the full male rate. The wage increases granted since 1939 have been equal for men and women on men's work, thus further narrowing the gap between the two rates. During the second world war the Association refused the request of the Alliance and the Ministry of Labour to replace males at the keyboard of composing machines with women.

While the female compositors represent a dying section of the Association, and the operation of machines in both departments of the printing office has been reserved for male craft members, there are nevertheless a considerable number of women employed in the printing office on a variety of tasks necessary to the machines. These are the women who were brought into the Association in the inter-war period with the creation of the Auxiliary Section, of which they form the major part. It is customary to regard the Auxiliary Section as the organisation for semi-skilled and unskilled labour, in contrast to the craft labour making up the membership of the Association itself. The distinction applies more accurately in the case of the male labour involved, however, as many of the women in the Auxiliary Section are employed on tasks requiring some degree of skill, and for which they have to serve four years as learners.

CHAPTER SEVENTEEN

RELATIONS WITH KINDRED UNIONS

While the development of the Printing and Kindred Trades Federation has helped to secure greater co-operation among the unions in the printing industry, the changes in the labour force of the industry during this period and the extension of organisation have brought the unions into closer contact and sometimes conflict. The question of demarcation between the unions has in consequence been an important subject of negotiation. Similarly, the introduction of a new machine has often been followed by rival claims for the right to operate it. In consequence, relations between the unions have become more formalised and the subject of specific agreements. At the same time, several attempts have been made to secure closer amalgamation of the unions in the Federation, although without success. Some limited progress has been made, however, in the operation of reciprocity schemes between some of the member unions. These main aspects of the relations of the Association with the kindred unions will be considered in more detail in the following sections of this chapter.

I. DEMARCATION

On the question of demarcation, the Association found itself most in conflict with the National Society of Operative Printers and Assistants, or Natsopa as it is generally called, and the National Union of Printing, Bookbinding, Machine Ruling and Paper Workers. The first question to be raised with Natsopa concerned rotary pressmen in newspaper offices. These machines had been manned by engineers and labourers, who had been organised within

Natsopa. At first the Association had made no attempt either to secure the machines for its own members or to admit the labour manning them. In 1914, however, negotiations were opened to secure the transfer of those in charge of the machines to the Association, evidently the first step towards the widening of the basis of membership. In 1915 an agreement to this effect was signed, but many of the men concerned refused to transfer to the Association, and in 1917 Natsopa declared itself unable to implement the agreement. In 1919 the matter was submitted to the Federation, but no decision was given, because by this time both unions had become involved in the wider issues raised by the Association's proposal to form an Auxiliary Section.

The Association's original declaration in 1918 of the workers it proposed to organise met with some opposition from the Federation, in view of the possible threat to the position of other affiliated unions. The two other unions chiefly concerned in this were Natsopa and the Paper Workers Union, and in 1920 the Association met representatives of these unions and of the Federation to try to formulate a common policy. The conference proved unsatisfactory, but finally agreed to the Association's proposal that a settlement might be achieved by allocating the chief towns in Scotland to the other two unions, and the rest of Scotland to the Association for purposes of organisation. The Association subsequently proposed that Aberdeen, Edinburgh, Glasgow and Dundee be regarded as the sphere of operation of the other two unions. This the Paper Workers rejected, while Natsopa made acceptance conditional on the transfer to its ranks of newspaper assistants in Aberdeen, who were already members of the Association. Negotiations continued, after some delay due to the Federation's preoccupation with wage reductions, and in 1922 the unions concerned agreed to submit the matter to the Federation for decision. The Federation again advised the Association not to continue its proposed organisation policy, but, in the interests of fuller organisation, particularly in small areas, urged the unions to co-operate on a joint policy. Later the same year a conference of the three unions produced a draft agreement to the effect that each would concentrate on the organisation of the workers for whom it had hitherto catered, but in small areas one union might act for the others. The proposed agreement, however, was rejected by a vote of the Association's membership. There the matter rested until the Delegate Meeting of 1924, when it was decided to proceed with the formation of an Auxiliary Section. The consequence of this was the expulsion of the Association from the Federation.

Following the Association's decision to form an Auxiliary Section and its expulsion from the Federation, the Paper Workers Union in 1925 lodged complaints against it to the Disputes Committees of the Trades Union Congress and the Scottish Trades Union Congress. To the former a specific charge of poaching was submitted, but after investigation, the T.U.C. decided the charge had not been established. The Scottish T.U.C. considered the general question at issue, no specific case having been submitted, and decided in favour of the Association provided certain guarantees were given regarding the enrolment of former members of the other union. These the Association gave, reaffirming its decision that the Auxiliary Section was for unorganised workers. During the following two years further complaints on this question were made to both T.U.C.s, and in 1926 an attempt was made by the Alliance to assist in achieving a settlement. The deadlock continued, however, until late 1927, when the Paper Workers Union took the initiative in proposing a conference. Subsequently, in 1928, an agreement was signed whereby the Association was given the right to organise all eligible workers in printing offices outside Aberdeen, Dundee, Edinburgh and Glasgow. In the four cities membership of the Auxiliary Section was limited to those wholly employed as assistants to Association members in the case and machine rooms. With the ending of this dispute, the Association once more became affiliated to the National Federation.

In 1929 the question of rotary pressmen was again raised and an agreement reached with Natsopa, under the terms of which all machine minders were to become members of the Association. Vacancies in this section were to be filled alternately by members of Natsopa and the Association, but when a member of Natsopa was promoted to the position of machine minder he had to transfer to the Association. In return, the Association had given to Natsopa the position of copyholders. The next two years saw some difficulties in the interpretation of the promotion clause of this agreement, but these were finally settled in 1931 by the Arbitration Board of the National Federation. Thereafter the agreement appears to have worked satisfactorily until 1942, when the Outram Press office in Glasgow, which had been non-union from the time of the General Strike, again became a union office. A number of machine minders, who had been readmitted to Natsopa, refused to transfer to the Association, as was required by the 1929 agreement. In 1944 Natsopa expelled the men concerned, but they in turn contested at law the union's right to do so. It transpired that the men had not been informed of the need to transfer to the Association when they were readmitted, and in consequence, Natsopa had no grounds for expulsion; the men were accordingly reinstated. Following this decision, Natsopa in 1945 informed the Association that the 1929 agreement was no longer enforceable or acceptable to its membership, and also alleged that it had, in any case, been nullified by infringement of its terms by the Association. There followed a lengthy dispute which was not settled until 1948. Failing to reach an agreement by direct negotiation, the Association submitted the dispute to the Federation in 1945. Two conferences held later that year under the auspices of the Federation proved fruitless, and in 1946 the dispute was submitted to the Federation Arbitration Board. The award granted, in effect, reiterated the 1929 agreement; all machine minders were to be members of the Association; vacancies were to be filled in rotation by members of the two unions, subject to the condition that a

Natsopa candidate must agree to transfer to the Association; the existing machinemen employed in Outram's were, however, regarded as outwith the terms of the award. This did not end the dispute as Natsopa subsequently refused to accept the terms of the award, and appeal had to be made once more to the Federation. In 1947 Natsopa agreed to accept the terms of the award, but later the same year intimated a desire to cancel the agreement on which the award was based. By the end of the year, however, the two unions had met and drawn up a new agreement, which was to be submitted to their members. Still the dispute remained unsettled, as in 1948 the Natsopa membership rejected the proposed agreement. The threatened tendering of strike notices by the Association members employed in the Outram office brought intervention from the Ministry of Labour and a Committee of Investigation was set up. The findings reiterated the basic principles of the previous award, but once more Natsopa refused to accept them. The dispute was referred back to the Federation, and finally, towards the end of the year, an agreement was reached by a conference of the two unions and the Federation. The existing position of machine minders in Outram's was accepted, and subsequent vacancies were to be filled in accordance with the terms of the former agreement between the unions. Natsopa, however, had repudiated the 1929 agreement and refused to re-endorse it, so that the position which emerged from the settlement, accepted by both sides, was one in which Natsopa agreed to observe the principles of the agreement in the matter of manning the machines, although not accepting the agreement itself. Nevertheless, the settlement has proved satisfactory in practice.

In other cases amicable agreements have been reached with kindred unions on questions of the right to particular machines, and in general, relations are good. This state of affairs, although in recent years no doubt assisted by the prevalence of full employment, has also been fostered by the unions' joint membership of the National Federation and increasing experience of federated action.

II. Amalgamation

On a number of occasions throughout the fifty years the question of amalgamation of all or some of the unions in the Federation has been the subject of conferences and negotiation. The question was first raised in 1908, when the Association was invited by the London Society of Compositors to attend a conference in Manchester, along with the English Typographical Association and the London Machine Managers' Society, as a preliminary to the amalgamation of these unions. The Association approved of the principle, provided a satisfactory scheme could be devised. Preliminary proposals were submitted to a vote of the membership in 1909, when a majority were in favour, although only a small number voted. In 1910, however, negotiations reached a deadlock over the question of autonomy and the scheme was abandoned.

In 1912 a conference was held by the National Federation at which it was agreed to draft proposals for the amalgamation of the unions represented. Negotiations continued into 1913, but no concrete scheme was evolved, the feeling being that the unions were not yet ready for national amalgamation.

The next attempt at amalgamation, again at the instigation of the Federation, occurred in 1920, when a conference on the subject was held in London. It was reported that sixteen unions in the Federation were in favour of amalgamation, but the proposals put forward were rejected on the grounds that they simply implied an extension of the federation principle. On this occasion the Association proposed that all members of the Federation be amalgamated into one union, the whole country to be divided into geographical areas, each with its own Executive Council, and national affairs to be managed by a National Executive Council. This proposal, however, was defeated, and it was decided to let the question drop in the meantime.

In 1924 the question was taken up again by the English

Typographical Association, and the Scottish Association sent representatives to a conference in Manchester. The conference concluded that amalgamation of the two Associations was both possible and desirable. Later the same year a third union was admitted to the negotiations, when a conference was held with Natsopa. Again the conclusions were favourable to the proposed amalgamation of the three unions, and details of a scheme were prepared. After lengthy negotiations and the completion of a detailed draft of the proposed constitution and rules, the Association broke off negotiations because of disagreement about the status of female compositors in Scotland. The Association requested that the women be granted the right to take posts outside their present area, provided they received the male rate, but the English Association insisted that they must be confined to their present area. An attempt was made by Natsopa to resume negotiations in 1927, but without success, as the attitude of both Typographical Associations remained unaltered. In 1928 the T.U.C. invited the Association to attend a conference with a view to the amalgamation of unions in the printing industry, but the invitation was declined when it was learned that the English Typographical Association was not taking part.

The subject was not raised again until 1943, when the Paper Workers Union proposed to the Federation's Annual Conference that all the unions in the Federation be amalgamated into one common unit. On this occasion the proposal was opposed strongly by the craft unions, particularly by the London Society of Compositors and the Scottish Association. After a lengthy discussion, the resolution was defeated, and there has been no subsequent attempt to revive the question of amalgamation.

III. Reciprocity Schemes

The reciprocity scheme between the Association, the English Association and the London Society of Compositors for the payment of unemployment and strike benefit, which had been instigated by the Scottish Association, was

the subject of a conference at Manchester in 1904. The
rules of the scheme were revised in the light of the difficulties which had so far been experienced in its operation.
The scheme remained a difficult one to operate, however,
and by 1912 the London Society of Compositors had withdrawn from it.

In 1913, under the auspices of the Federation, a new
and broader scheme was drawn up to be operated by the
English Typographical Association, the London Society
of Compositors, the Scottish Association, the Printing
Machine Managers Trade Society, the Dublin Typographical Provident Society, and the Association of Correctors of the Press. The scheme provided as before for the
payment of strike or unemployment benefit to a member,
eligible for such benefit, who had moved into the area of
one of the other unions operating the scheme. While
continuing his membership of and subscriptions to his
original union, the member could be admitted to associate
membership of the local union, on payment of a nominal
2d per week, in return for which he was entitled to all the
privileges of membership. It was further agreed that a full
member of two or more societies be entitled to draw benefits from both at the same time.

Since then the scheme has continued more or less successfully, although the number of unions operating it has
declined, chiefly due to the administrative difficulties involved. In 1937 it was proposed to the annual conference
of the National Federation that the scheme be extended to
other federated unions. The proposal was rejected, but the
Federation was instructed to investigate the subject and
report. No further action on expansion was taken, however, and by 1944 it was reported that the scheme was then
operated by three unions—the Printing Machine Managers Trade Society, the English Typographical Association and the Scottish Association—and that it was working with complete satisfaction.

CHAPTER EIGHTEEN

DISPUTES

The fifty years have again been mainly peaceful ones, the number of disputes involving strike action being few and generally of short duration. Indeed, the major dispute of the period, and the most costly, was the General Strike of 1926, which had serious repercussions for the Association. Apart from this, the three main struggles of the period were the dispute in Aberdeen and Edinburgh over the female question in 1909 and 1910, a lock-out in Edinburgh and Glasgow over the 1912 rules, and a similar lock-out in 1916 over a wage claim from a small section of the National Society of Operative Printers and Assistants. Details of the dispute over the female question have already been given in an earlier chapter;[1] here the Edinburgh and Glasgow lock-outs and the General Strike will be further considered.

I. THE EDINBURGH AND GLASGOW LOCK-OUTS

A number of alterations were made to the rules of the Association by the 1911 Delegate Meeting, including a reduction of the overtime permitted from twelve to nine hours per week, the abolition of suspension and the introduction of a rule requiring employers to give one week's notice before introducing short-time working. In 1912, according to custom, the Branches embarked on the task of revising their local rules to conform to these decisions. Several Branches, however, reported similar opposition to the new rules from the employers, who had evidently agreed to act in concert; about this time the Scottish Alliance of employers was formed. Attention centred on the

[1] See Chapter 16.

Glasgow case, where disagreement over the rules had been the subject of protracted negotiation, and where the Branch had succeeded in putting into practice the new overtime limit, although the rules had not been signed by the local employers' organisation. At the end of the year the Alliance stepped in and announced that failing the withdrawal by the Association of the new rules, or a joint conference on them, lock-out notices would be posted in Glasgow and Edinburgh. A conference was held in January 1913, when an attempt was made to get some modification of the new rules, particularly that on overtime. The Association reported back to its membership a request by the employers for the suspension of the 1912 rules until the end of 1913, or until a mutual agreement was reached. This the members rejected, and at the end of January lock-out notices were posted. Further conferences were held in February under the auspices of the National Federation, when it was finally accepted that all rules in future must be the subject of mutual agreement; also, the 1912 rules were to be the subject of a joint conference, and no new rules were to be introduced before the end of 1913, unless by mutual agreement; lock-out notices were to be withdrawn, pending a settlement of the rules in dispute. As a result of conferences held in April, the mutually approved rules were, for the first time, embodied in a national agreement. Although a Delegate Meeting later in the year rejected the particular agreement proposed, the principle was accepted and a modified national agreement was signed in January 1914. Thereafter, all resolutions passed by Delegate Meetings amending the rules relating to working conditions became the subject of joint negotiation and only if mutually approved were they incorporated in a national agreement. This principle was the real issue of the dispute, although objections to specific rules had been the original pretext.

While the 1913 dispute concerned a fundamental principle of importance to the entire Association, the lock-out in 1916 resulted from an Edinburgh wage dispute concerning a small section of the National Society of Opera-

tive Printers and Assistants. In 1915 a claim for a wage of
29/– per week for stone and plate preparers had been submitted to the employers, and in the course of the movement strike notices had been handed in. As a result some
eleven men lost their jobs and the employers refused to
consider their reinstatement. The lithographers refused to
handle work prepared by the non-union labour replacing
these men, and the dispute was submitted to the Federation. A conference between the Federation and the Alliance failed to produce a settlement and lock-out notices
were posted affecting the Edinburgh and Glasgow members of unions affiliated to the Federation. The Board of
Trade intervened and after two conferences a settlement
was achieved; lock-out notices were withdrawn, and the
eleven men reinstated at a wage of 28/–, rising to 29/–
later in the year. The Edinburgh federated unions had
supported the eleven victims of the dispute, but Glasgow
had not been in any way involved until lock-out notices
were posted. While about half of the employers in each
city took no part in the dispute, nevertheless in both some
700 journeymen members of the Association were locked
out.

II. The General Strike

After a lengthy discussion, the Executive of the Association agreed to obey the instructions of the Trades
Union Congress, received on 3rd May 1926, that all
members should cease work on the following day in support of the miners. The difficulty facing the Association
arose from the fact that their agreements with the employers required them to give fourteen days' notice of strike
action; indeed, just prior to the receipt of the T.U.C.'s instruction, the Association had agreed that its members
should tender such notices, in the event of a General Strike
being called. The decision to break the national agreements with the employers was supported on the grounds
that it would have been difficult to persuade the members
to work for a fortnight, after the workers in other industries had come out, and to ask them to do so would be to

ask them to act as 'blacklegs'. After nine days the Strike was called off by the T.U.C. as suddenly as it had been ordered, and the workers were left with the dissatisfied feeling that little, if anything, had been gained. Further disillusionment followed when it became evident that no attempt was to be made by the T.U.C. to ensure that the workers who had come out at its behest were taken back into employment.

In addition to facing the task of securing the return to work of its members, in the knowledge that their action in support of the T.U.C. had cut across the agreements with the employers, the Association had to tackle the problem raised by the fact that the employers in the Scottish Daily Newspaper Society had decided against the employment of trade unionists in future. To the credit of the Alliance of employers, they approached the Association and suggested a conference, as a result of which the members were taken back into employment on the old terms. In return, the Association had to agree not to victimise any employee who had remained at work or returned during the strike. In addition, the Alliance sought a pledge that the Association would not take part in any lightning strike in future. While membership of the T.U.C. prevented the Association from giving this pledge, they agreed that in all disputes of a trade nature they would act strictly in accordance with the national agreements with the employers. This issue was subsequently put to a vote of the members, when an overwhelming majority voted in favour of adhering to these national agreements at all times and in all cases.

At first the Association hoped to arrange for all who had come out to return to work at the same time, but failure to reach agreement with the proprietors of the daily newspapers made a partial restart inevitable, and the agreement with the Alliance was put into operation immediately. Meantime, the proprietors of the daily press in Aberdeen, Dundee, Edinburgh and Glasgow, with the exception of the Glasgow *Daily Record* and *Evening News*, had refused to reinstate their employees unless they gave up their membership of the Association. As an incentive to the members thus victimised to remain loyal to the Association, it was agreed that, as from the end of the second week of the General Strike, they would be paid the minimum weekly wage of their branch, instead of the £2 per week strike allowance. The majority of the newspaper members, however, did not respond to the incentive, and many agreed to the employers' terms. The Association then embarked on a policy of boycott, in co-operation with the other printing unions affected. Over a million copies were distributed of a leaflet containing a list of the publications now produced in non-union offices, with an appeal not to purchase them. Meetings, processions and demonstrations also formed part of the boycott campaign, although it is doubtful if much was achieved. Part of the campaign, however, was directed at a new weekly publication which appeared in Glasgow, soon after the General Strike, called the *Scots Observer*. Attempts had been made by the Association to secure the printing of this for a union office, but without success. Accordingly, widespread publicity was given to the fact that it was produced by non-union labour, and since the paper was primarily intended for sale to church members, a letter was sent to every minister in Scotland. Whether as a result of the campaign, or for other reasons, the printing of the paper was given soon afterwards to a union office in Hamilton. Thereafter, the Association publicised the fact that it was now produced by union labour and urged support for it.

While continuing the boycott campaign, several attempts were made by the Association in 1927 to secure interviews with the proprietors of the non-union press, but all without success. The details of these attempts were issued in circular form to the citizens of Aberdeen, Dundee, Edinburgh and Glasgow, and some 500,000 copies were distributed in these cities. Finally, at the end of 1927, the T.U.C. appealed to the Scottish Daily Newspaper Society to meet the Association, and offered its services as mediator. The offer was refused by the proprietors, who intimated that their staffs were entirely satisfied with the present arrangement, and asked that the Association now accept this decision as final. At this time the T.U.C. were conferring with employers' representatives on the subject of 'Peace in Industry', and it was resolved to bring up the case of the Scottish daily press at the next joint meeting.

In spite of these efforts, the majority of the Scottish newspapers remained non-union, and it was not until the early years of the second world war that any substantial newspaper section of the Association could be rebuilt, although repeated attempts were made to secure this in the intervening years. In 1941 the Aberdeen press again became union, thus bringing in some 64 new members, and in the following year success was at last achieved with the Outram office in Glasgow, as a result of which over 150 were added to the Association's ranks. In 1946 a Newsmen's Advisory Committee of the Association was formed, and thereafter the Association became responsible for all negotiations and agreements for this section. The newspapers of Dundee and Edinburgh, however, still remain non-union; the former case, a legacy of the General Strike, is at present the subject of national dispute; the latter case, however, is of much earlier origin, the *Scotsman* having been non-union since 1872 and the *News* since 1877.

While the financial position at the outset of this dispute was sound the events of 1926 virtually exhausted the Association's Protective Fund. In 1926 a total of £48,298 was paid on strike and victimisation allowances and other expenses arising from the dispute, while a further £2,734 was paid in 1927. At the beginning of 1926 the Fund had a total balance of £41,892, and in August of that year a special levy of 1/- per week per member towards the Fund was imposed. This levy was continued until the end of 1928, by which time the Fund had been restored to £33,548. In August 1926 the Executive decided, because of the heavy financial drain, to discontinue payment of victimisation allowance to those who had not been reinstated and to replace this with the smaller strike allowance. As a result of strong protests from Aberdeen, Dundee and Glasgow, however, victimisation allowance was continued until the end of September. As the same Branches still opposed the reduction, the members were asked to vote on a proposal to increase the existing strike allowance, for which an additional levy of 1/– per member per week would be necessary. The members rejected the increase, and thereafter strike allowance was paid. The financial burden of the dispute was particularly heavy on the Association because of the repercussions. The General Strike lasted for only nine days, but the action of the majority of the daily newspaper proprietors prevented the reinstatement of many Association members.

CHAPTER NINETEEN

RELATIONS WITH EMPLOYERS AND OTHER ITEMS

In this chapter shorter mention will be made of a number of other items of interest and importance to the story of the second fifty years. The first and most important of these concerns the Association's relations with the employers, viewed from its position as an independent trade union and as a member of the Printing and Kindred Trades Federation. Secondly, there is the story of its attitude during this period to national politics and the question of affiliation to the Labour Party. Finally, a brief account will be given of the *Journal*, which, early in the period, became the official organ of the Association.

I. Relations with the Employers

In the early days of trade union organisation, negotiations were carried on between local Branches and individual employers or local bodies of employers, but this period has witnessed the emergence and development of negotiation at a national level. While the Association has been a member of the Printing and Kindred Trades Federation since its inauguration, with the exception of some five years in the 1920's, and consequently some of the agreements governing relations in the industry are national in the wider sense of the word, nevertheless it has retained a considerable degree of autonomy as the negotiating body for Scotland with the Scottish Alliance of employers.

National negotiation, in the sense of negotiation applying to Scotland as a whole, dates from 1913, two years after the formation of the Alliance, when the 1912 rules of the Association were the subject of dispute.[1] Prior to this,

[1] See Chapter 18.

rules passed by Delegate Meetings had been incorporated in local Branch rules and these locally negotiated with the employers. After 1913, however, the decision of Delegate Meetings became the subject of negotiation between the Association and the Alliance, and the rules approved were incorporated in national agreements. To consider difficulties arising out of these mutually agreed rules, a National Conciliation Committee was established by the Association and the Alliance in 1921, and since then it has performed a useful service in obviating many open disputes; the occasions on which a dispute concerning the mutual rules has had to be submitted to the arbitration of the Joint Industrial Council have been few.

National negotiation of working rules was followed by national negotiation of wages. The Alliance first suggested this possibility at a conference in 1917, and the suggestion was eventually put into practice with the establishment of a Wages Board for the printing and allied trades in Scotland at the end of 1918.[1] Although the Board only survived until 1924, the national negotiation of wages between the Association and the Alliance has continued up to the present time, with the exception of the period of the second world war, when Scotland shared in the wage movements of the Federation. Since the end of the war the Association has re-established its autonomy in wage negotiation for Scotland. In the matter of hours and holidays, however, conditions in the Association are now determined by Federation agreements, although at an earlier stage the Association did not join in the Federation movements for shorter hours, chiefly because the working week in Scotland was then generally shorter than in England.

The Association's relations with the employers are affected in other ways by the fact of its membership of the National Federation. As a member of the Federation, the Association is also a member of the Joint Industrial Council and the Scottish Joint Industrial Council for the printing industry. Through these Councils facilities are afforded for the joint discussion of current problems and of all

[1] See Chapter 13.

matters of common concern as affecting the future of the industry. Thus, to the Scottish Joint Industrial Council were referred at the end of the war questions relating to the rehabilitation of ex-service members, apprentices and technical training. The Councils also provide the conciliation machinery to which disputes in the industry may be submitted, when local action fails to produce a settlement.

Finally, the link between the Association and the Federation as bodies negotiating with the employers, has been strengthened in recent years by the formation in 1943 of a Scottish Advisory Committee of the Federation, whose functions are 'to consider matters entirely or predominantly concerning Scottish interests, or questions of federal policy which have an application in Scotland in anywise different from other areas'. The position of this Committee was strengthened in 1945, when the Association was given authority to call emergency meetings of the Committee when matters demanding immediate decisions arose.

II. NATIONAL POLITICS

In 1903 the question of Labour Representation in Parliament was again put to a vote of the Association members. The result showed a majority in favour of this, but the total vote was too small to justify any action. In 1905, however, a sufficient majority voted in favour of affiliation, and the Delegate Meeting of 1907 approved a resolution to establish a Parliamentary Representation Fund, towards which the Association was to pay 1/6 per member per year. Because of recent law court decisions it was decided to take legal opinion on the position of the Association before taking further action. The opinion given was that the Association was outside the scope of the 'Osborne' decision, since it was not a registered society, and accordingly, in 1908, a Parliamentary Representation Fund was inaugurated.

In 1910, however, a Glasgow compositor member, Thomas Wilson, was granted an interim interdict against the Association to prevent it from using any part of its funds for the promotion of representation in Parliament. The same member raised a further action in the Court of Session to have the rules of the Association relevant to this declared illegal and reduced. In this he was successful, an interlocutor being given against the Association in January 1911. In spite of the legal opinion formerly obtained by the Association, the basis of this decision was the 'Osborne' judgment. The Association appealed against the decision, but the appeal was rejected in February 1912. While the Association funds could no longer be used for political purposes, it was reported that as a result of an appeal to the Branches, contributions had in many cases been made to the Special Fighting Fund of the Labour Party.

The position was changed by the Trade Union Act of 1913 and the Delegate Meeting of 1913 approved a decision to take a vote of the members on the question of adopting this Act and so becoming affiliated to the Labour Party. The war intervened, but the decision was reaffirmed by a Delegate Meeting in 1920 and the vote then taken; the result was a substantial majority against adoption of the Act. Subsequent Delegate Meetings have similarly decided for a vote of the members on this question, but the result has always shown a majority against. In all, a vote on this question has been taken four times since 1920—in 1928, 1932, 1937 and 1947.

III. The 'Journal'

The *Scottish Typographical Circular*, founded and conducted by the Edinburgh Branch, was taken over by the Association early in the period and has appeared as its official organ since January 1909 under the title of the *Scottish Typographical Journal*. Prior to this an annual grant had been made towards the cost of the *Circular*, but financial difficulties and a growing desire for a more elaborate publication which could be regarded as the official mouthpiece of the Association, led to the decision of the 1907 Delegate Meeting that the *Circular* be taken over by the

Executive Council. As a result of the transfer the sum of £100 was paid to the Edinburgh Branch.

From the outset it was intended that the *Journal* should provide a link between the Executive and the general membership; the first editor was a member of the Executive and a former editor of the *Circular*. At the same time a *Journal* Committee of three Executive members was appointed to co-operate with the editor in an advisory capacity. The size and scope of the *Journal* were immediately expanded; the amount of reading matter contained in the first volume was about double that of the *Circular*; reports and contributions were received from a larger number of Branches, and official news was provided by the 'Notes from Headquarters'; a good number of special articles on topics of interest to the industry also appeared. The first issue of the new *Journal* was a free one, some 7,000 copies being distributed. Thereafter the *Journal* was sold at its former price of 1d, the Branches acting as agencies. By the end of two years the circulation was about 4,500 per month, compared with the 2,700 copies of the *Circular* formerly issued. In addition special issues were occasionally made gratis, chiefly for propaganda purposes. For example, over 10,000 extra copies were so distributed of the number containing the details of the Edinburgh movement against underpaid female labour; some of these were issued to kindred unions in recognition of the support they had given to the movement.

This expansion in size and circulation, combined with the use of better quality paper, inevitably meant higher costs of production. To meet this the charge of 1d per copy was quite inadequate and at the outset a deficit of over £100 was recorded. The choice of policy here appeared to be either to regard the *Journal* as one of the services provided from the funds and issue it free to members, or to attempt to put it on a paying basis by increasing its price; in fact, the policy followed was somewhere between these two, the former charge of 1d per copy being continued and the deficit met from the Protective Fund. During the years prior to the first world war, however, the deficit declined and there seemed to be hopes of making it a paying proposition without any increase in price. The war crushed these hopes; costs rose steadily, while revenue from both advertisements and sales declined. The deficit consequently increased and by 1919 had reached the level of some £450 per annum. In the following years the position improved as a result of increased income from both sales and advertisements, and also some administrative changes designed to reduce costs. In consequence the deficit was reduced, but it was never eliminated. No attempt was made to increase the price of the *Journal*, which was fixed by rule and could only be altered by a Delegate Meeting.

During the second world war difficulties similar to those of 1914 to 1918 again affected the financial position of the *Journal*, although special measures to keep down costs modified the increase in the deficit. Since the end of the war, however, the steady increase in printing costs has more than doubled the deficit. By 1949 it amounted to some £660, and in that year the Delegate Meeting approved of an increase in price to 2d per copy. At first a slight decrease in the deficit followed this but since then rising costs have more than offset the increase in income; the deficit at the end of 1951 was over £700.

Whatever future changes may be made in the finance of the *Journal*, however, it is generally recognised that its assistance in the educative and protective work of the Association entitles it to some call on the funds. Through its 'Association Jottings' it now provides an official report of the monthly proceedings of the Executive Council; details of disputes, negotiations and national agreements help to keep informed the scattered membership; by reports and special articles their interest is kept alive in matters concerning trade unionism in general, and their own craft in particular.

EPILOGUE

To have completed a century of continuous existence, particularly in a period of social and industrial changes as great as those experienced, is in itself an achievement which only a few trade unions can claim. Further, in spite of the many changes incorporated, the Scottish Typographical Association of 1953 is essentially the same as that which came into being in 1853. Although an Auxiliary Section has been added, the Association itself is still a craft union, representing the skilled workers in the two main sections of the printing industry—composing and press; no amalgamation with other unions has occurred.

At the outset the Association was primarily concerned with improving wages and working conditions, and this is still its major function, although far-reaching changes have occurred in the machinery by which this is achieved. In the early years of its life, the Association performed the function of guiding and co-ordinating the efforts of individual Branches towards this end. These individual efforts were strengthened by the support and backing of the Association, which also provided financial assistance to members victimised. In the last resort, however, wages and conditions were determined locally and there were wide variations. In contrast to this, wages and conditions are now the subject of direct negotiation between the Association and the Alliance of employers. As a result of this, greater uniformity has been achieved in the increases granted. Further, by means of the Grading Schemes secured by the Association, the initial differences have been considerably narrowed and a high degree of uniformity now prevails. While this development conforms to the general trend towards the national negotiation of wages and conditions, the Association can claim to have been a party to it at an early stage, a Wages Board for the industry being established in 1918.

Another object of the original Association, directly connected with the improvement of the position of its members, concerned the control of entry and limitation of apprentices. This, too, has remained an important function of the Association and one which in recent years has been carried out with a degree of success beyond the hopes of the founder members. Indeed, in this matter the carping critic might say the Association has been too successful, the consequence being a shortage of certain types of skilled labour in the industry. From the Association's point of view, however, the experiences of the inter-war period provided ample justification for limitation, and while the post-war situation demanded some concessions, which were given in the form of bonus rations of apprentices, the development of the industry, particularly in the matter of technical innovations, is too uncertain to justify any drastic sweeping aside of barriers to entry.

The other major function of the Association concerns the comprehensive range of benefits of a provident nature provided to its members. This represents the greatest change in and development of the Association since its inauguration. The rules of the 1853 Association made provision for financial assistance to Branches for the relief of tramps when the burden on the Branches was particularly heavy, but this constituted the sole provident scheme of the Association. The growth of the Association as a friendly society has been described in detail in the preceding chapters; while a comprehensive National Insurance Scheme has now been made available to all by the State, similar benefits were provided much earlier by the Association for its members in the fields of unemployment relief, health insurance and superannuation. In addition to its pioneering work in these fields prior to the advent of the State schemes, the Association has in more recent years adapted its provident schemes to the new conditions and continued its activities as a friendly society, thus providing a welcome addition to State benefit.

In spite of this development as a friendly society, however, and in spite of the present financial preponderance of
provident expenditure, the Association is still primarily a
trade union, and above all a craft union, performing the
functions appropriate to such a union. Nor has it merely
survived as such; it has also grown in strength and position. The number of Branches is now thirty-two compared with the original five, while the total membership
has grown from some 600 to over 7,000, including
Auxiliary members. Its financial position has been
similarly strengthened.

Of the many and diverse factors contributing to the
progress of the Association during the past century, two
in particular are suggested by the story of the preceding
chapters. Firstly, the keynote of its history is one of peaceful growth. Its present position and strength have been
achieved gradually and largely by peaceful means. There
have been disputes, of course, but relatively few of these
have been of a major character. The Association's relations
with the employers are good and a considerable degree of
joint co-operation exists on matters of common interest.
Secondly, while retaining its identity as a craft union, the
Association has shown sufficient adaptability to changing
conditions to make its survival possible. The greatest
changes have occurred in the technique of the industry as
a result of mechanisation. By not opposing mechanisation
but adapting its membership to the new conditions, and
continuing to represent the interests of the skilled men of
the industry the Association secured survival and continuity. The creation of the Auxiliary Section is further
evidence of this adaptability, and has enabled the Association to retain its identity as a craft union and, at the same
time, bring into its ranks the semi-skilled labour required
by the machines.

The future of the Association naturally depends on the
future of the industry, and here no long-term forecasts are
possible. There is certainly little prospect of any decline in
the demand for the industry's products, but the methods
of production are constantly changing and little can be

said about the nature of future technical developments or their repercussions on the labour force required. But changes there almost certainly will be, and the future of of the Association will depend largely on its ability to adapt itself to the new conditions and continue to represent the skilled men who will surely be required by the industry whatever its future form. Fortunately, here the outlook is bright; it is, in fact, in the matter of adaptability that the example of the past is most important and most hopeful. Remembering this the Association can enter its second century with confidence, and with the knowledge that it has behind it a hundred years of progress.

APPENDIXES

APPENDIX I

Rules of the General Typographical Association of Scotland, 1841

1. That all journeymen and apprentices, members of a Typographical Society in Scotland, be eligible to become members of this Association.

2. That the quarterly subscription of journeymen be one shilling; and the contributions of apprentices be regulated by the Society to which they may belong. Should any extraordinary expenditure become necessary, the members of the Association to be assessed as the Central Board may deem requisite.

3. That the purposes to which the funds of the Association shall be appropriated are the following: To afford pecuniary assistance to those members who may resign their situation in consequence of refusing to submit to a reduction of wages, the taking of a disproportionate number of apprentices, or other proceedings affecting the interests of the profession, and to defray the incidental expenses of the Association.

4. That in the cities of Edinburgh and Glasgow, the established wages of journeymen compositors be not lower than 25s per week, and in the provinces not less than 20s per week; and that the established wages of journeymen pressmen in the cities of Edinburgh and Glasgow be not lower than 25s per week, and in the provinces not less than 20s per week.

5. That the rates now paid for piece-work in Edinburgh and Glasgow be continued, and that $4\frac{1}{2}$d per thousand be the minimum rate of prices for compositors in the provinces for book-work, 5d per thousand for newspapers and pamphlets, and $5\frac{1}{2}$d per thousand for jobs. Non-pareil type to take an advance of $\frac{1}{2}$d per thousand, and pearl type 1d per thousand, on the above rates. The piece-work prices for pressmen in the provinces to be regulated by the Edinburgh and Glasgow Scale, as may be agreed on.

6. That when journeymen employed on established wages are required to change to piece-work prices, a fortnight's notice to that effect be given by the employer, previous to such change taking place.

7. That journeymen called on to assist in any office, shall not be paid less than half-a-day's wages.

8. That it be remitted to the Local Societies in connection with this Association, to use every legal means to suppress the number of apprentices introduced to the profession, to frame rules to carry this object into effect, and submit the same to the Central Board.

9. That in the case of newspapers which may come into existence after the passing of this resolution, not more than one compositor apprentice and one press apprentice for a once-a-week newspaper—two compositor apprentices and one press apprentice for a twice-a-week newspaper—three compositor apprentices and one press apprentice for a thrice-a-week newspaper—be allowed for the first year; one additional compositor apprentice for the second year, and thereafter the office to be regulated by the rules of the Society in the town in which it may be established.

10. That a Register of the names of all apprentices throughout Scotland, with the date of the commencement of their servitude, be kept by the Secretary of the Association; and that it be the duty of the office-bearers of the Branches of the Association to use their endeavours to induce the employers to indenture apprentices.

11. That in the case of an apprentice leaving his employer without a reason which shall appear substantial to the Local Society, he shall be expelled, and reported as an individual whose conduct is inimical to the interests of the profession.

12. That whenever a dispute may arise between the employer and employed, in any town where the Society is in connection with this Association, respecting the introduction of apprentices, the reduction of wages, or any other matter involving the interests of the profession, the Secretary of such Society shall transmit to the Secretary of the Association a correct, clear and full statement of the dispute—which statement shall be immediately submitted to the board, and instructions forwarded as to the line of conduct to be pursued.

13. That when a dispute of any description shall have terminated, the Secretary of the Society where it existed shall immediately communicate the same to the General Secretary, whose duty it shall be to make it known to the various Branches of the Association.

14. That when a member of a Society in connection with this Association shall be under the necessity of leaving his situation, in consequence of supporting the principles on which the Association is instituted, he shall be allowed the sum of £3 10s from the general

fund, to be paid by instalments of 10s per week; but should there appear to be no chance of the dispute being settled at the expiry of two weeks, and the member be desirous of leaving the town, the remaining sum to be given at once. Persons travelling in search of employment, under such circumstances, will be furnished with a COLOURED CARD, signed by the President and Secretary of the Association, on presenting which to any of the Societies in connection, he shall be entitled to double the sum allowed to persons travelling under different circumstances.

15. That backed cards of all recognised Unions be relieved in the same manner as those of this Association.

16. That the date of the members entry into the Society be marked on the back of his card.

17. That Secretaries of Local Societies correspond with the Secretary of the Association, at least every three months, forwarding the quarterly subscriptions, with a list of those members refusing or neglecting to pay their contributions, together with any matters which may affect the interests of the profession; and in the month of July, each year, such Secretaries shall give in a report of their proceedings for the past year, with a list of dishonourables, and journeymen refusing to join the Society.

18. That the names of the members three quarters in arrears be published.

19. That Subscriptions be forwarded by Bank or Post-Office orders, in the names of the Treasurer and Secretary of the Association.

20. That a meeting of Delegates be held at least once in two years, in the city or town in which the Central Board is located; to be composed of one Delegate from each Branch of less than 100 members, two Delegates from each Branch of more than 100 members, together with (at least) the President, Treasurer, and Secretary, from the Central Board; and in order to secure as full a representation of the Branches as possible, the travelling charges of Delegates shall be discharged from the General fund.

21. That the Central Board of the Association shall consist of a President, Vice-President, Treasurer, Secretary, and nine members of Committee, to be chosen from the Society of such city or town as the Delegate meeting may fix on for the sitting of the Central Board.

22. That the President be empowered to call meetings of the Central Board whenever occasion may require—the expenses of which to be defrayed from the general fund.

23. That the Treasurer receive all the money belonging to the Association, which shall be lodged in a Bank, in the names of the President and Treasurer, with the exception of £10 which he shall retain in his hands to answer any immediate demands which may be made on the funds. He shall also submit his accounts, quarterly, to the Central Board; and that, annually, two auditors be chosen by the Central Board, to examine his accounts, and prepare an abstract statement of the receipts and disbursements to be appended to the annual report.

24. That the Secretary of the Association shall take minutes of the proceedings of the Central Board, at all meetings, together with copies of resolutions on different subjects submitted to it, and the names of those by whom they were proposed and seconded, which shall be inserted in the minute book, read at the next meeting and signed by the President. The Secretary shall also write all letters on behalf of the Association; insert copies of the same in a book kept for that purpose; file all letters received by him, after having been first submitted to the President and a meeting of the Board; besides publishing circulars when required, and drawing out the annual report of the Association. For those duties the Secretary shall receive £10 per annum.

25. That should the Secretary of the Association remove from the town where the Board is located, or from any cause whatever, resign his situation during the year, the board shall appoint a proper person to fill the situation till a new election takes place.

26. That, after the passing of this resolution, in all cases where persons are required to pay an extra entry money in consequence of having acted contrary to the interests of the profession, one half of the sum received shall go to the Association Fund.

27. That in the event of an unfair person applying for admission into any Society, his case is not decided upon until reference has been made to the Secretary of the Society against whose interest he first offended.

28. That branches of less than twelve Members, being heavily burdened by tramps, forward to the Central Board, on the 1st of January and July, each year, a return of the number of tramps relieved for the preceeding six months with the sum paid to each— the distance from the nearest towns on the routes generally taken —the numbers of members composing the Branch, and the sum paid monthly for the relief of tramps alone—when the Board shall grant such reimbursement as the case may warrant.

29. That persons in possession of cards, on entering any Branch in connection with this Association, shall lodge the same in the hands of the Secretary.

30. That it is desirable that all foremen become members of the Association, that they may lend their influence in forwarding the interests of the profession.

31. That in the case of offices which are exclusively composed of apprentices, no journeyman be permitted to assist as a jobber, in any pressure of work, till such offices be placed on a fair footing.

32. That all members in search of employment are required, before applying for work in any town where there is a Society, to call on the Secretary.

33. That the Central Board be empowered to decide in any case not provided for in these resolutions.

34. That the preceding Resolutions be printed, and every member of the Association furnished with a copy.

APPENDIX II

The General Secretaries

Any record of the Association's progress would be incomplete without some mention being made of the many who have served it in an official capacity. The achievements of the hundred years are a tribute to those who, by their leadership and service on the Executive Council and in the Branches, have helped to raise the Association to its present position and strength. The list is a lengthy one and the task of the recorder is difficult. Time and space do not permit of any detailed biographical research, and the dangers of omissions or unequal distribution of praise are great. Here it is proposed simply to record the names of those who have held the increasingly onerous office of General Secretary. In all cases these men had served the Association in other capacities, in the Branches and on the Executive Council, before succeeding to the Secretaryship. During the hundred years thirteen have held this office, including the present General Secretary.

The first Secretary was Mr John Baird who held the office until his death in 1858. Mr Baird had taken a leading part in the old Scottish General Typographical Association and, in the words of the records, 'to his exertions we may be said to owe the formation of the present Association'. He died in harness, one of his last actions being to attend an Association meeting. The following year a tablet, subscribed for throughout the membership, was erected over his grave in the Necropolis.

Mr William Govan succeeded Mr Baird, and he held the office for twelve years. Prior to this, Mr Govan had been an active member of the Glasgow Society and had also occupied the position of Association President. He was evidently an outstanding figure in the trade union movement, and was noted for his lively interest in the social and political questions of his time, as well as being a religious teacher of some repute. It is recorded that one of his most treasured possessions was a letter from Garibaldi, received as a result of his interest in and championship of the cause of freedom for Italy.

Following the retiral of Mr Govan in 1871, the duties of Secretary were performed by Mr George Craig and Mr Simon Martin for periods of one and two years respectively. Both were active members of the Glasgow Society.

In 1874 Mr John Battersby became Secretary and he continued in office until 1887. During this period the organisation and functions of the Association underwent major changes, and Mr Battersby played an active and important part in the shaping of the new Association.

Mr Battersby in turn was succeeded by Mr Robert Johnstone who ably performed the duties for six years, resigning in 1893 when he was appointed secretary of the *Glasgow Echo* Newspaper Company, formed by the Glasgow Society on the occasion of the *Citizen* lock-out.

Mr John Templeton then became Secretary and held the office until 1911, when he accepted a post outside the Association. It was during his tenure that the post became a full-time one at a salary of £120. Mr Templeton's name is closely associated with the part played by Scotland in the formation of the National Printing and Kindred Trades Federation, of which he became Vice-President.

In 1911 Mr John White became General Secretary. A member of the Glasgow Branch, Mr White had already served for a lengthy period as Treasurer of the Association. Two years later he was succeeded by Mr James Brown who held office until 1917. Mr Brown had formerly been Secretary of the Dundee Society, and in 1911 became the first Organiser of the Association.

Mr John Watt was General Secretary from 1917 to 1921. Mr Watt came from the Glasgow Branch, and had previously served on the Glasgow Town Council as a Labour member. He died in office.

Mr Watt was succeeded by Mr Robert Watson who held the position for twenty years, dying two days after his resignation in 1942. Mr Watson was a native of Kilmarnock and for some time Secretary of the Kilmarnock Branch. In 1918 he became Financial Secretary to the Association. During his long tenure considerable changes occurred in the industry and the Association, and much of the credit for the close-knit organisation of the present must go to him. He was for many years also an active member of the Executive of the National Federation.

Mr Watson was succeeded by Mr Robert Lean, whose death the Association so recently mourned. Mr Lean's connection with and work for the Association, in the Glasgow Branch, as Association President, Financial Secretary and finally General Secretary, is well known to present members.

The present General Secretary, Mr Harry Girdwood, came from the Edinburgh Machine Branch to the Executive Council, and held the position of Financial Secretary from 1942.

APPENDIX III

BENEFITS PAID BY THE ASSOCIATION, 1853–1952

Year	Strike, Lock-out and Victimisation Allowance			Out-of-Work Allowance			Sick Allowance			Funeral Allowance			Removal Grants		
	£	s	d	£	s	d	£	s	d	£	s	d	£	s	d
1853–54	2	0	0												
1855	4	2	0												
1856	12	10	0												
1857	—														
1858	—														
1859	5	0	0												
1860	5	0	0												
1861	9	0	0												
1862	19	9	8												
	57	**1**	**8**												
1863	16	0	0												
1864	57	10	0												
1865	45	19	5												
1866	32	12	3												
1867	16	0	0												
1868	43	1	11												
1869	20	0	0												
1870	80	6	7												
1871	194	18	6												
1872–3	6135	7	4½												
	6641	**16**	**0½**												
1873	126	11	8												
1874	82	1	3												
1875	89	10	1												
1876	109	17	0												
1877	581	19	4												
1878	97	11	2							30	0	0	28	6	0
1879	31	5	6							23	0	0	73	7	8
1880	25	6	0							48	0	0	113	12	0
1881	66	5	8							62	0	0	61	0	0
1882	20	0	0	153	9	4	215	10	10	87	0	0	75	4	0
	1230	**7**	**8**	**153**	**9**	**4**	**215**	**10**	**10**	**250**	**0**	**0**	**351**	**9**	**8**

Emigration Grants	Superannuation Allowance	Grants to other Trades	Trades Union Congresses	Scottish Typographical Journal	National Printing Trades Federation
£ s d	£ s d	£ s d	£ s d	£ s d	£ s d
				—	
				—	
				—	
				—	
				10 0 0	
				10 0 0	
				7 10 0	
				15 0 0	
				13 10 0	
				56 0 0	
				12 0 0	
				12 0 0	
				12 0 0	
				12 0 0	
				12 0 0	
				12 0 0	
				12 0 0	
				12 0 0	
				12 0 0	
				12 0 0	
				120 0 0	
				12 0 0	
				12 0 0	
				12 0 0	
				—	
				12 0 0	
		10 0 0	3 3 0	12 0 0	
		7 2 0	4 4 0	12 0 0	
		—	3 3 0	12 0 0	
		8 0 0	3 3 0	12 0 0	
		5 5 0	3 3 0	12 0 0	
		30 7 0	**16 16 0**	**108 0 0**	

Year	Strike, Lock-out and Victimisation Allowance			Out-of-Work Allowance			Sick Allowance			Funeral Allowance			Removal Grants		
	£	s	d	£	s	d	£	s	d	£	s	d	£	s	d
1883	6	15	4	333	4	9	478	5	3	90	0	0	67	16	0
1884	16	5	7	532	10	10	575	7	3	119	0	0	89	4	0
1885	70	10	0	598	10	4	585	18	$11\frac{1}{2}$	168	0	0	95	12	0
1886	45	17	11	740	13	$3\frac{1}{2}$	709	0	11	174	0	0	123	2	0
1887	189	10	$9\frac{1}{2}$	614	12	6	830	19	7	127	0	0	134	14	0
1888	115	14	3	936	16	5	753	7	0	167	0	0	116	4	0
1889	48	15	10	1031	17	$0\frac{1}{2}$	860	15	11	206	0	0	124	10	0
1890	1150	4	$10\frac{1}{2}$	765	9	7	1104	13	6	212	0	0	142	12	0
1891	371	13	$7\frac{1}{2}$	917	13	$1\frac{1}{2}$	1225	2	2	163	0	0	120	2	0
1892	32	6	10	740	6	10	1125	8	$10\frac{1}{2}$	272	0	0	109	6	0
	2047	15	$0\frac{1}{2}$	7211	14	$8\frac{1}{2}$	8248	19	5	1698	0	0	1123	2	0
1893	1425	5	5	1225	12	5	1048	13	2	303	0	0	106	9	6
1894	6	14	0	1661	10	8	1243	16	3	216	0	0	127	16	0
1895	88	10	6	1417	13	$6\frac{1}{2}$	1263	12	2	325	0	0	118	1	0
1896	12	4	0	1138	6	11	1574	5	10	295	10	0	128	4	0
1897	88	0	6	1213	12	$9\frac{1}{2}$	1492	7	7	438	0	0	126	8	0
1898		—		1169	18	6	1509	10	8	369	0	0	142	0	0
1899	20	6	1	1113	3	7	1590	1	2	339	10	0	159	16	0
1900	1056	4	0	1478	14	$7\frac{1}{2}$	1815	18	8	378	19	0	154	0	0
1901	108	2	10	1018	0	10	1560	8	4	383	10	0	182	8	0
1902	9	4	8	926	11	2	1627	14	9	453	12	1	140	18	0
	2814	12	0	12,363	5	$0\frac{1}{2}$	14,726	8	7	3502	1	1	1386	0	6
1903		—		719	15	10	1672	10	5	440	0	0	100	0	0
1904	34	15	8	1124	8	3	1768	0	6	454	0	0	119	8	0
1905	27	8	10	1566	12	2	1612	14	8	473	0	0	129	4	0
1906	36	2	9	1482	16	5	1585	18	2	378	0	0	143	18	0
1907	832	17	5	1187	16	0	1900	11	1	518	16	0	145	8	0
1908	273	8	6	2675	10	3	2109	12	0	511	0	0	171	16	0
1909	96	15	10	3228	18	8	2006	17	9	576	0	0	145	8	0
1910	505	6	1	2749	0	4	2244	9	10	564	0	0	160	10	0
1911	275	15	8	2287	19	11	2288	9	3	851	0	0	137	16	0
1912	894	15	10	2654	11	4	2209	0	4	512	16	0	155	0	0
	2977	6	7	19,677	9	2	19,398	4	0	5278	12	0	1408	8	0

Emigration Grants			Superannuation Allowance			Grants to other Trades			Trades Union Congresses			Scottish Typographical Journal			National Printing Trades Federation		
£	s	d	£	s	d	£	s	d	£	s	d	£	s	d	£	s	d
						19	9	0	3	3	0	12	0	0			
						16	8	0	3	3	0	12	0	0			
						15	0	0	3	3	0	12	0	0			
						18	8	0	3	3	0	12	0	0			
						7	4	0	3	3	0	12	0	0			
						15	0	0	3	3	0	12	0	0			
						14	4	0	3	3	0	12	0	0			
44	4	0				3	3	0	3	3	0	12	0	0			
28	16	0				115	0	0	3	3	0	12	0	0			
32	16	0				41	9	0	3	3	0	12	0	0			
105	**16**	**0**				**265**	**5**	**0**	**31**	**10**	**0**	**120**	**0**	**0**			
73	0	0	133	11	0	—			3	3	0	12	0	0			
13	8	0	225	12	0	—			4	4	0	12	0	0			
42	14	0	236	12	0	—			4	4	0	12	0	0			
41	4	0	605	14	8	6	3	0	4	4	0	12	0	0			
30	0	0	676	13	0	10	2	0	6	6	0	12	0	0			
26	0	0	722	14	0	26	18	0	48	13	2	12	0	0			
37	4	0	790	2	3	6	16	0	69	6	1	12	0	0			
24	8	0	1004	12	0	18	3	0	30	17	11	12	0	0			
58	4	0	1173	12	8	7	3	0	47	6	6	12	0	0			
104	16	0	1329	16	8	8	6	0	40	2	6½	12	0	0	190	1	5
450	**18**	**0**	**6899**	**0**	**3**	**83**	**11**	**0**	**258**	**7**	**2½**	**120**	**0**	**0**	**190**	**1**	**5**
130	8	0	1457	7	3	6	6	0	39	17	6	12	0	0	183	18	0
71	12	0	1612	12	8	34	19	0	37	18	10	12	0	0	186	15	8
75	16	0	1799	8	8	29	1	10	47	16	7	12	0	0	190	10	0
114	12	0	1922	9	8	1	1	0	36	1	4	12	0	0	190	5	0
171	12	0	2019	3	4	19	8	0	45	3	9	12	0	0	185	17	2
57	14	0	2270	18	0	13	13	0	46	3	1	12	0	0	199	11	2
102	4	0	2491	15	4	6	4	0	43	11	8	—			191	13	0
334	6	0	2731	11	0	18	14	6	29	6	0	—			209	3	0
318	8	0	2930	6	5	11	5	0	—			127	14	9	202	16	0
249	18	0	3010	4	11	4	4	0	52	15	0	280	17	3	202	16	0
1626	**10**	**0**	**22,245**	**17**	**3**	**144**	**16**	**4**	**378**	**13**	**9**	**480**	**12**	**0**	**1943**	**5**	**0**

Year	Strike, Lock-out and Victimisation Allowance			Out-of-Work Allowance			Sick Allowance			Funeral Allowance			Removal Grants		
	£	s	d	£	s	d	£	s	d	£	s	d	£	s	d
1913	1131	0	2	1752	10	11	2771	10	9	559	0	0	175	2	0
1914	44	1	3	2117	5	3	2908	0	11	734	0	0	143	18	0
1915	302	9	10	1618	5	3	2728	8	7	859	0	0	154	16	0
1916	4404	7	1	705	14	7	2550	2	7	923	0	0	111	14	0
1917	8	12	11	167	6	5	2123	13	7	1326	0	0	92	12	0
1918	4	10	0	117	1	10	2244	18	9	1423	10	0	78	14	0
1919	31	12	0	1520	19	3	2447	19	6	750	0	0	106	11	0
1920	66	6	6	2753	3	11	2712	9	6	689	0	0	135	6	0
1921	14	17	6	29,712	15	3	4004	17	5	1145	4	0	177	18	0
1922	150	9	0	16,821	16	0	4337	6	3	1299	0	0	213	6	0
	6158	**6**	**3**	**57,286**	**18**	**8**	**28,829**	**7**	**10**	**9707**	**14**	**0**	**1389**	**17**	**0**
1923	9	0	0	11,246	13	6	4078	11	5	1149	0	0	280	8	0
1924	72	13	0	7416	3	10	4496	0	3	1112	0	0	295	12	0
1925	99	6	7	5747	17	5	4591	17	6	1376	0	0	334	0	0
1926	48,298	2	9	7872	9	11	5049	4	6	1271	0	0	344	18	0
1927	2734	2	3	11,356	15	10	4726	13	9	1473	0	0	390	0	0
1928	175	2	6	9743	8	2	4617	4	7	1602	0	0	329	8	0
1929	108	9	6	5364	16	4	6105	11	8	1220	10	0	280	4	0
1930	209	9	6	6692	10	8	5850	12	10	1622	10	0	238	12	0
1931	250	15	8	16,199	1	5	5586	16	10	1383	10	0	125	12	0
1932	101	12	6	25,029	14	8	6553	15	0	1687	10	0	188	12	0
	52,058	**14**	**3**	**106,669**	**11**	**9**	**51,656**	**8**	**4**	**13,897**	**0**	**0**	**2807**	**6**	**0**
1933	81	7	6	24,389	12	4	6157	7	10	1489	10	0	220	4	0
1934	7	13	4	17,094	8	6	5719	14	2	1898	0	0	283	4	0
1935	11	12	6	13,181	9	0	5859	9	6	1508	0	0	254	8	0
1936	34	17	6	12,427	10	6	6013	1	8	1606	0	0	242	8	0
1937	—			7350	7	8	6721	0	4	2498	10	0	320	4	0
1938	286	13	4	5198	14	10	5700	7	8	1577	0	0	249	12	0
1939	431	6	1	11,608	14	5	5457	13	4	1816	0	0	192	4	0
1940	89	17	0	20,455	9	2	6948	11	8	2304	0	0	132	0	0
1941	39	17	5	2472	6	0	5957	16	2	2120	0	0	218	12	0
1942	—			324	14	6	5778	3	4	1619	0	0	69	0	0
	983	**4**	**8**	**114,503**	**6**	**11**	**60,313**	**5**	**8**	**18,436**	**0**	**0**	**2181**	**16**	**0**

Emigration Grants			Superannuation Allowance			Grants to other Trades			Trades Union Congresses			Scottish Typographical Journal			National Printing Trades Federation		
£	s	d	£	s	d	£	s	d	£	s	d	£	s	d	£	s	d
241	12	0	3012	14	4	23	8	0	50	7	10	341	6	7	209	1	0
54	2	0	3225	14	0	4	2	0	33	10	0	76	16	1	209	1	0
13	8	0	3241	10	0	—			42	10	1	107	11	5	218	1	0
27	10	0	3263	5	0	—			57	17	5	143	1	4	164	13	3
—			3162	12	0	—			50	0	5	205	2	11	347	11	11
6	6	0	2988	8	8	—			71	6	3	315	11	7	285	11	4
16	0	0	3689	14	0	—			63	12	4	457	9	11	298	10	0
155	8	0	4319	4	6	—			128	4	4	748	16	1	304	2	4
232	12	0	5256	0	0	—			111	19	9	471	9	9	361	2	10
167	8	0	5466	2	6	—			141	6	10	169	19	3	373	2	4
914	**6**	**0**	**37,625**	**5**	**0**	**27**	**10**	**0**	**750**	**15**	**3**	**3037**	**4**	**11**	**2770**	**17**	**0**
456	16	0	5826	3	0	—			155	2	6	175	19	4	383	7	4
179	2	0	6624	3	0	—			163	2	8	132	13	4	413	8	0
93	0	0	7155	12	0	—			171	13	0	161	16	9	—		
308	8	0	7410	4	6	—			197	4	4	32	8	2	—		
206	8	0	8403	11	0	—			199	17	6	186	0	4	—		
100	8	0	9225	6	0	—			178	3	2	121	11	1	—		
108	4	0	10,402	12	0	—			188	5	4	171	18	11	176	5	0
50	8	0	11,182	4	6	—			181	13	11	144	5	6	361	15	0
16	4	0	11,725	12	6	10	0	0	156	15	3	153	18	6	304	3	9
6	8	0	12,834	4	6	50	0	0	154	9	8	102	17	6	309	0	0
1525	**6**	**0**	**90,789**	**3**	**0**	**60**	**0**	**0**	**1746**	**7**	**4**	**1383**	**9**	**5**	**1947**	**19**	**1**
—			13,992	17	0	—			162	19	10	105	13	11	301	13	6
—			15,790	12	0	51	18	0	157	19	6	86	2	6	307	13	6
0	16	0	17,321	9	0	31	18	0	196	4	3	121	11	2	288	13	0
14	0	0	18,377	5	0	50	0	0	177	16	6	100	17	0	301	18	6
51	0	0	18,310	3	0	—			205	9	1	119	7	1	305	9	0
36	0	0	19,217	0	0	—			239	11	2	175	15	4	334	0	8
14	8	0	19,190	0	0	215	0	0	248	13	7	173	19	7	300	3	2
—			19,714	4	0	—			183	19	4	156	8	5	342	4	0
—			19,428	18	0	—			176	10	7	235	2	10	301	5	4
—			18,514	11	6	—			192	9	9	206	16	2	340	11	7
116	**4**	**0**	**179,856**	**19**	**6**	**348**	**16**	**0**	**1941**	**13**	**7**	**1481**	**14**	**0**	**3123**	**12**	**3**

Year	Strike, Lock-out and Victimisation Allowance			Out-of-Work Allowance			Sick Allowance			Funeral Allowance			Removal Grants		
	£	s	d	£	s	d	£	s	d	£	s	d	£	s	d
1943	32	15	0	298	12	10	6317	19	10	1888	10	0	57	0	0
1944	2	0	0	146	2	0	6069	18	0	1959	10	0	86	12	0
1945	14	5	0	85	8	4	6132	12	2	1706	0	0	173	8	0
1946	54	15	0	297	16	0	6642	9	6	2348	14	0	383	4	0
1947	55	8	0	139	12	4	4458	0	10	2203	10	0	415	16	0
1948	91	7	6	140	0	1	4327	13	4	2126	0	0	364	8	0
1949	11	19	0	77	6	1	5082	3	3	1777	0	0	406	14	0
1950	8	4	0	45	10	0	5025	13	4	1702	0	0	254	14	0
1951	22	2	0	56	11	8	5147	17	8	2456	0	0	292	12	0
1952	750	0	0	218	16	8	4931	16	8	1904	10	0	170	8	6
TOTAL	1042	15	6	1505	16	0	54,136	4	7	20,071	14	0	2604	16	6

SUMMARY OF

Years	Strike, Lock-out and Victimisation Allowance			Out-of-Work Allowance			Sick Allowance			Funeral Allowance			Removal Grants		
	£	s	d	£	s	d	£	s	d	£	s	d	£	s	d
1853/54–1862	57	1	8												
1863–1872/73	6641	16	0½												
1873–1882	1230	7	8	153	9	4	215	10	10	250	0	0	351	9	8
1883–1892	2047	15	0½	7211	14	8½	8248	19	5	1698	0	0	1123	2	0
1893–1902	2814	12	0	12,363	5	0½	14,726	8	7	3502	1	1	1386	0	6
1903–1912	2977	6	7	19,677	9	2	19,398	4	0	5278	12	0	1408	8	0
1913–1922	6158	6	3	57,286	18	8	28,829	7	10	9707	14	0	1389	17	0
1923–1932	52,058	14	3	106,669	11	9	51,656	8	4	13,897	0	0	2807	6	0
1933–1942	983	4	8	114,503	6	11	60,313	5	8	18,436	0	0	2181	16	0
1943–1952	1042	15	6	1505	16	0	54,136	4	7	20,071	14	0	2604	16	6
TOTAL	76,011	19	8	319,371	11	7	237,524	9	3	72,841	1	1	13,252	15	8

Emigration Grants			Superannuation Allowance			Grants to Other Trades			Trades Union Congresses			Scottish Typographical Journal			National Printing Trades Federation		
£	s	d	£	s	d	£	s	d	£	s	d	£	s	d	£	s	d
—			18,580	19	0	—			175	1	7	256	11	8	269	1	11
—			18,493	14	0	—			178	0	9	131	5	11	306	17	0
13	12	0	18,508	18	8	—			181	5	9	387	6	10	242	1	4
168	4	0	20,365	15	0	—			203	9	9	441	6	1	288	2	4
689	18	0	14,545	10	0	23	9	0	286	11	4	530	7	11	278	12	8
527	10	0	13,873	0	0	4	4	0	280	16	11	563	12	5	276	11	0
240	4	0	13,968	10	0	12	2	0	399	7	3	667	13	8	338	4	6
158	0	0	13,812	10	0	12	2	0	528	5	7	507	0	6	314	4	6
417	18	0	13,527	10	0	15	4	0	736	5	9	759	10	0	344	16	4
309	0	0	12,965	10	0	48	0	0	617	9	5	807	17	10	341	4	11
2524	**6**	**0**	**158,641**	**16**	**8**	**115**	**1**	**0**	**3586**	**14**	**1**	**5052**	**12**	**10**	**2999**	**16**	**6**

TEN-YEAR TOTALS

Emigration Grants			Superannuation Allowance			Grants to Other Trades			Trades Union Congresses			Scottish Typographical Journal			National Printing Trades Federation		
£	s	d	£	s	d	£	s	d	£	s	d	£	s	d	£	s	d
												56	0	0			
												120	0	0			
						30	7	0	16	16	0	108	0	0			
105	16	0				265	5	0	31	10	0	120	0	0			
450	18	0	6899	0	3	83	11	0	258	7	2½	120	0	0	190	1	5
1626	10	0	22,245	17	3	144	16	4	378	13	9	480	12	0	1943	5	0
914	6	0	37,625	5	0	27	10	0	750	15	3	3037	4	11	2770	17	0
1525	6	0	90,789	3	0	60	0	0	1746	7	4	1383	9	5	1947	19	1
116	4	0	179,856	19	6	348	16	0	1941	13	7	1481	14	0	3123	12	3
2524	6	0	158,641	16	8	115	1	0	3586	14	1	5052	12	10	2999	16	6
7263	6	0	496,058	1	8	1075	6	4	8710	17	2½	11,959	13	2	12,975	11	3

INDEX